AF560747

CENTRES OF POWER

'Bureaucrats by definition are trained to observe, listen, remember, record and recall. Kautilya listed them as intelligent, persevering, dexterous, eloquent, energetic, bold and firm in loyalty. Modern-day diplomats are a species of this genre and Ambassador Gharekhan would be counted amidst them. His recollection of time spent with Prime Ministers Indira Gandhi and Rajiv Gandhi is an invaluable record of happenings in those eventful times. This was displayed by the time spent by him in the United Nations in various positions.'

—M. Hamid Ansari
Former Vice President of India

'Chinmaya Gharekan's book is so good that it is ensured a very large readership.'

—K. Natwar Singh
Former External Affairs Minister of India

'My path crossed with Amb. Chinmaya Gharekhan when I was serving as the Deputy US Ambassador to the United Nations Security Council (UNSC) and he was Secretary General Boutros Boutrous-Ghali's representative to the UNSC. In that capacity, he had the unenviable task of crossing swords with P-5 occasionally. He calmly defended the UNSC. He never flinched. Whether he would convince or annoy, he took the Security Council's reaction in stride. He was a consummate diplomat, as his long-awaited book *Centres of Power* amply demonstrates, page after page.'

—Karl F. Inderfurth
U.S. Assistant Secretary of State for South Asian Affairs 1997–2001

'Few people get a ringside view in the world's most powerful body, the UNSC. Fewer got to enjoy this view as world history turned a corner, when the Cold War ended. Chinmaya Gharekhan was truly privileged to be in the latter lot. Now, he's generously sharing all his inside stories, great learnings and wise insights with the world. This book is a must-read for both scholars and laypeople trying to understand the deeper origins of our troubled times. He documents candidly all the mistakes that were made.'

—Kishore Mahbubani
Former Permanent Secretary of the Singapore Ministry of Foreign Affairs

'A candid account by one of India's most respected and admired diplomats, Ambassador Gharekhan's recount of India's Pakistan policy as well as of the Gulf War is factual, honest and informative. The author has been an eyewitness and important contributor to decision-making on several global crises. The book is a must-read for all those interested in diplomacy and international affairs. His record is clear evidence that a career in foreign services greatly contributes to promotion of national interest. *Centres of Power* leaves us craving for more!'

—Fayza Aboulnaga
National Security Advisor to the President of Egypt

CENTRES OF POWER

My Years in the Prime Minister's Office and Security Council

CHINMAYA R. GHAREKHAN

RUPA

Published by
Rupa Publications India Pvt. Ltd 2023
7/16, Ansari Road, Daryaganj
New Delhi 110002

Sales centres:
Prayagraj Bengaluru Chennai
Hyderabad Jaipur Kathmandu
Kolkata Mumbai

P-ISBN: 978-93-5702-233-0
E-ISBN: 978-93-5702-241-5

Second impression 2023

10 9 8 7 6 5 4 3 2

Printed in India

To Rita, my soulmate and true friend

CONTENTS

PART II
DIPLOMACY DURING THE FIRST GULF WAR

INTRODUCTION

This book is based on the diary that I had maintained during the period when the events described in it took place. It is not a memoir in the sense that it is not a present recollection of what happened then. As is well known, memory can play tricks.

The book has been presented in two parts. Part I is a record of my service in the Prime Minister's Office (PMO) in the 1980s. I served in the PMO in two stints while working with both Indira Gandhi and Rajiv Gandhi from 1981 to 1986. I started working with Indira Gandhi in 1981; was recalled to the Ministry of External Affairs (MEA), where I was assigned to the division dealing with Pakistan, Iran and Afghanistan; rejoined the PMO in September 1982 and remained there until August 1986, when I took over as Permanent Representative of India to the United Nations (UN) in New York. I was dealing with the foreign affairs side of the PMO, which, though not too heavy, was the one in which the prime minister (PM) took a great deal of interest.

In most countries, the head of the government prefers to deal with foreign policy issues personally. This is helpful since diplomacy is often discussed and decided at summit level. The minister in charge of the foreign office naturally supervises the functioning of the ministry, and no doubt contributes to the formulation and implementation of the foreign policy. But the policy itself is largely decided in the PMO. Jawaharlal Nehru, India's first PM, was also the foreign minister for all the 17 years that he occupied that office. Usually, the extent of the contribution of the foreign minister depended on their personality and equation with the PM.

The professionals in the ministry belonging to the Indian Foreign Service (IFS) have an important and indispensable role to play in it since it is they who have the institutional perspective and memory so essential to the understanding of a particular situation and the policies to handle it. The political leadership often claims to have all the answers and does not show enough respect for the expertise and experience of the IFS officers.

Indira Gandhi was steeped in foreign relations by the time she became the PM in 1966, after the death of Lal Bahadur Shastri who served as the PM for a short while after Nehru's death. She served as the host for the receptions and banquets held at PM Nehru's residence, Teen Murti. She also accompanied her father on most of his visits abroad. I am not aware if she had access to the official papers, but she had more than a modest acquaintance with most of the issues. She had also met most of the senior officers of the ministry and knew them well.

Part I, 'The Indira–Rajiv Years', is an honest account of what I heard in the PMO as well as the MEA and was involved with. It is written 'with malice towards none', though I am not sure about 'charity for all'. Two of the dramatis personae mentioned in the book are still with us, helping and guiding their successors in the service. They are also active in as much as they continue to write on foreign policy and participate in think tank meetings. Maharaj Krishna Rasgotra escorted my batch to the call of PM Nehru; it was an unforgettable occasion. The next batch was taken to the PM by K. Natwar Singh.

Some of the subjects covered in the book are Pakistan, Sri Lanka, China, Nepal as well as important conferences, such as the 7th Summit of the Non-Aligned Movement (NAM), the Commonwealth Heads of Government Meetings and hijacking of Indian Airlines aircraft. It goes without saying that the issues about which I have written had other aspects of which I would not be aware.

Part II, which I have called 'The Diplomatic History of the First Gulf War', is a running narrative of the first Gulf War of 1990–91. It started on 2 August 1990 when the president of Iraq attacked Kuwait. India was not a member of the United Nations Security Council (UNSC) at the time, but I decided to keep a record of the diplomatic activity from that date, as it was obviously a major event. It was the first of its kind in modern times—a big State swallowing its smaller neighbour in a brazen display of arrogance and defiance of international law. This was what Iraqi President Saddam Hussain did. The fascinating aspect of that crisis was that it was the first challenge faced by the international community—the UNSC—since the Cold War had ended. India, and I, personally, were fortunate in the sense that we served for two years as a non-permanent member of the council during 1991–92, precisely at a time when the Soviet Union had disintegrated and the Pax Americana was ruling the world. One could not miss the high-handedness of the American diplomats and the eagerness with which the Soviets, or rather the Russians, cooperated with their erstwhile rivals. The loss of the 'balancing factor' provided by the Soviet Union during the Cold War was felt most by the non-aligned and the Palestinians and also by some Western countries.

My narrative ends with the conclusion of the formal ceasefire on 28 February 1991, but the actual story did not end there. In the next phase, the UNSC dealt with weapons of mass destruction that Iraq was suspected of hoarding, or concealing, such as chemical, biological and nuclear weapons, or at the least the capability of making them. Iraq did its best to prevent the inspectors of the International Atomic Energy Agency (IAEA) from visiting the suspected sites. The diplomatic war culminated with the adoption of Resolution 687 on 3 April 1991. It had 26 preambular and 34 operative paragraphs, was divided in nine sections and was described as the 'mother of all resolutions'.

The unity among the permanent members witnessed during the Gulf Crisis of 1990–91 has not been seen since. That is because the convergence of interests among the P-5 nations, which existed at that time, has disappeared. While the Soviet Union alias Russian Federation and China did not approve of the American behaviour, they were both anxious not to upset them—their domestic situation obliged them to take that line. There was, thus, at a minimum, a negative congruence of interests among the P-5. This has not happened since, thus rendering the council non-functional in situations of crisis. In fact, today, the national interests of the P-5 are in serious conflict with one another. This has revived, in an insistent way, the debate about the representativeness of the council. Repeatedly, it has been argued, rightly, that the world of today is vastly, unrecognizably, different from the world of 1945 when the UN Charter was hammered out among the 50 participating states in the preparatory conference in San Francisco. Many of them had raised strong objection to the provision of veto, but they were told, in effect, that either they could have the UN with the right of veto or not at all.

India started the campaign for the reform of the UNSC in the 1960s. Positive result was achieved when the Charter was amended to raise the membership from 11 to 15. The campaign has continued ever since to further increase the membership in both categories of permanent and non-permanent members. It would not be difficult to increase the number of non-permanent seats, but to add to the category of permanent seats is going to be extremely difficult, probably impossible. There are two issues there: number and veto. There would appear to be a broad consensus that the permanent category could be increased by six additional members: two from Asia, two from Africa, one from Europe and one from Latin America. The actual identification of the countries from the specified regions is an issue. No country will make it by itself; it will have to be a package deal. The other problem is whether the new permanent members would have veto power. There is zero chance that the new permanent members would have the right of veto. Firstly, the P-5 would not agree—they would not want any new state to break into what is the last exclusive club in the world. Equally, an overwhelming majority of UN members are unhappy with the existing veto provision; they certainly do not want any more veto-wielding members.

The point to ponder is: Will adding new members make the council more effective in discharging its responsibility of maintaining international peace and security? It will make the council a bit more representative, but will that enable it to discharge its primary duty in a better way? The answer cannot be a categorical 'yes'. The council is not a court of justice. Its members are primarily focussed on protecting and furthering their own national interests. As members of the council, they would be calculating the impact their actions would have on their bilateral relations with other countries, especially the rich and the powerful. Principles are invoked only when they are not conflicting with national interests. If that were going to be the case, would not adding new members only lend more legitimacy to the decisions of the council? It would also do nothing to dilute the right of veto. In any case, the veto provision has come in useful for several countries, including India.

I am most grateful to K. Natwar Singh for his constant encouragement and guidance in writing the book. I am thankful to Rupa Publications, in particular to Sri Rudra Narayan Sharma, senior commissioning editor, for his help in bringing out the book.

My wife Rita was a constant source of support for this project. I am sure wherever she might be, she would be thrilled that the book is now out and hopefully being well received by the cognoscenti.

Part 1

The Indira–Rajiv Years

The PMO in India is a very important, perhaps the most important, and most powerful set-up in the country. It was not always so. In the initial years, when Nehru was the PM as well as the foreign minister, the office was small. He had to deal with so many critical issues, starting with controlling the communal riots, organizing the armed forces and so on, that he simply did not have the time to supervise the workings of other ministries. The office was called the PM's Secretariat, not the PMO. It came to be called as 'office' in Indira Gandhi's time.

Over the years, the office has grown, in numbers and influence. The trend of concentration of power in the PMO has continued and gathered momentum. When the number of secretary-level officers increased, the head of the office became principal secretary. Depending on the incumbent, the principal secretary wielded enormous power and influence.

The posting of an officer in the PMO to look after external affairs started with Indira Gandhi. They have been, for the most part, officers of the IFS, except Moni Malhotra, who belonged to the Indian Administrative Service (IAS). K. Natwar Singh was the first occupant. The principal secretary's post has been occupied by members of the IAS, except for P.N. Haksar and Brajesh Mishra, who were members of the IFS; they both proved to be outstanding and highly influential. P.N. Dhar, who was the principal secretary for some time, was an economist.

It is a matter of privilege for an IFS officer to serve in the PMO. The officer might be excused for thinking that they have 'arrived'. In bureaucracy, access is everything. In the PMO, one has access to the highest authority in the country. In the four-and-a-half years in the PMO, I met many people, including politicians. One might get carried away and start feeling that one knows everything, as much as or even more than one's senior colleagues. However, one must be humble and modest. At some point in time, even I had felt that I could influence decision-making process more that the head of the IFS.

One advantage was that one could see all the overseas telegram traffic, including the most sensitive ones. One must resist the temptation to show off and flaunt one's knowledge to others. Highest level of discretion is required.

And finally, with such responsibilities also comes the opportunity to maintain a diary!

1

THE BEGINNING

I was fortunate to have been selected for the IFS in 1958; my record in college had not been particularly impressive though. Like many others, I had the option of either joining the IAS or the IFS. On my father's advice, I consulted a few people in Delhi. One of them was a deputy secretary in the Ministry of External Affairs (MEA). He said that the IFS was an excellent service. But, he said, one might fall in love with a foreign girl and end up submitting a resignation while applying for permission to marry her. The other person I consulted was Morarji Desai, who was the then finance minister. He said, 'The matter is simple. If you want to serve the country, join the IAS; if you want to have a good time, join the IFS.' I asked him if one could not serve the country in the IFS. He said he had given his view and had nothing more to say. A little over a year later, Morarji came to Cairo for an official visit. I was posted as third secretary in the Cairo embassy. As soon as I was introduced to him, he said, 'So, you decided to have good time!'

I still remember when my batch, during our training days, called on Pandit Jawaharlal Nehru, who was the PM as well as the foreign minister back then. He asked each one of us about the subjects we had studied in college. Suddenly, he asked one of us, 'What can you tell me about the Berlin Crisis?' It was not just that batchmate; none of us could talk on the topic. Nehru was most considerate. He said, 'Never mind. I shall tell you about the Berlin Crisis.' And he did so, for about 10 minutes.

I was excited at the prospect of going abroad and working on important issues of foreign policy. I had, of course, no idea what kind of work awaited me and how I would be interacting with my seniors. We had to learn one foreign language, besides English, which was not regarded as a foreign language, for the purpose of official work. I had chosen Spanish as my first choice, being under the impression that it was easy to learn. However, I was allotted Arabic, which was my second choice.

It's a Diplomat's World...

Serving as a diplomat for the first time and that too in an important country such as Egypt excited me. Some of my colleagues, who were going to other countries, and I travelled by the P&O liner called *SS Stratheden*. Family members and friends had come to see us off. The voyage took eight days. I was put up in a hotel in Gazeera, which was not far from the Indian embassy.

I served in Egypt for two years from 1959 to 1961. Gamal Abdel Nasser was the president and India–Egypt relations were at an all-time high. It was said that only two persons had free access to Nasser. One was Umm Kulthum, the legendary singer who was famous for her music throughout the Arab world, and the other was the Indian ambassador.

Congo, my next posting from 1961 to 1963, was in the throes of a civil war, following declaration of independence of the Katanga province by Moïse Tshombe, the leader of Katanga. He was clearly acting on behalf of Belgium and the mining company Union Minière du Haut Katanga. Congo was the personal property of the Belgian king; the country was 70 times larger than Belgium. Congo was rich in minerals, which were for the most part exploited by the mining company.

It was in Congo that my interest in the UN developed; a big UN Peacekeeping operation, including an Indian infantry brigade, was deployed there. In one operation against Tshombe's forces, which were backed by mercenaries, an Indian captain, Salaria, was killed; he was awarded the Param Vir Chakra posthumously, the highest gallantry award of the Indian Army. I think it was my experience in the Congo and seeing the UN in operation in a peacekeeping role that my interest in the UN developed.

This was followed by two years at the MEA headquarters, a stint at the Permanent Mission of India to the UN in New York as first secretary from 1965 to 1968, another stint in Delhi and then on to Belgrade in December 1970 as counsellor in the embassy. My first ambassadorial rank posting was as the chairman of the International Commission for Supervision and Control (ICSC) in Laos during 1973–75. In Hanoi—my next assignment as ambassador during 1975–76—I had the unique experience of presenting my credentials as an ambassador three times: first to the Democratic Republic of Vietnam in Hanoi; then to the Provisional Revolutionary Government of South Vietnam in Saigon, later renamed Ho Chi Minh City; and to the reunified Vietnam, which styled itself as the Socialist Republic of Vietnam. I was the only ambassador to have had this unique privilege. As chairman of the ICSC, I interacted with both sides in the civil war in Laos and was at least partly responsible for arranging and monitoring suspension of hostilities in the country. I was also perhaps the first person from a non-communist country to visit the headquarters of Pathet Lao, the communist side led by the 'Red Prince' Souphanouvong in Sam Neua.

Vietnam had just come through three years of war with two redoubtable powers, France and the United States (US). Their heroism won universal acclaim. What was perhaps unique about Vietnam was the role women had played in the liberation struggle. Men had fought and done the heavy work. But women's contribution was invaluable. They not only worked in the fields, they also drove heavy vehicles, marched on the Ho Chi Minh City trail with supplies for the front and also took part in the war. The Vietnamese behaved as if the whole world owed them a huge debt of gratitude and they also expected to be compensated for all the death and destruction wrought upon their country throughout the decades.

My next posting was in Geneva as India's permanent representative to the European office of the UN as well as the World Health Organization (WHO), International Labour Organization, International Telecommunications Union, etc. I served there for about three years from 1977. It had been a wonderful posting for my family, which included my wife and our two children. My postings in Laos and Vietnam from 1973–76 were non-family stations, quite difficult from a personal point of view but most interesting professionally.

Geneva was a most welcome change since my family and I were all together—we went skiing, played golf, had great food and travelled all over Europe. I was kept busy mainly with work related to the Committee on Disarmament, which met in the Palais des Nations. The other forum involving interesting work was the United Nations Commission on Human Rights (UNCHR). Sadly, it was a highly political body, where no one really cared about human rights. Vijaya Lakshmi Pandit, sister of Pandit Nehru, used to lead our delegation to the commission. She was a dignified lady, gracious, possessing a keen political sense. I enjoyed working with her. One incident in the commission might be worth mentioning here. An Indian woman was subjected to 'virginity test' at Heathrow Airport in London since she claimed that she had gone to London to get married. This rightly created uproar in India. With the permission of the ministry and with Vijaya Lakshmi Pandit on board, I raised the matter in the commission. I mobilized several delegations in support. My British counterpart requested me to withdraw the statement I had drafted to condemn the treatment meted out to the woman. Mrs Pandit was inclined to be accommodative, but I was not. The Brits went to Delhi and Delhi gave in. I was most unhappy.

From Geneva, I was transferred back to the MEA in May 1981 as head of the UN division in the ministry since I had gathered quite a bit of experience in dealing with the UN over the years.

Short Stint at the PMO

The UN division was much sought after. The main benefit, it seemed, was the possibility of frequent official travels abroad. But I soon realized that the ministry did not have much time for the UN. The only time when the UN division got attention was when some issue, usually that of Kashmir, came up for debate in the UNSC, which was mostly attended by the foreign minister.

One fine day, in February 1981, I was told that I was posted to the PMO as joint secretary. It seems that the then incumbent officer, Kamal Bakshi, had taken ill due to his prevailing heart problem. Indira Gandhi was quite comfortable with Bakshi. For reasons that I still do not know, I was selected to replace him. I was excited and nervous at the same time. Indira Gandhi was reputed to be tough and one with a temper. I consulted a few senior colleagues as to how I should conduct myself in the PMO. The best advice I got was from Shilendra Kumar Singh, widely known as S.K. Singh, a senior colleague, 'Be yourself.'

I had been in the PMO for a few months when I was told that I had to go back to the MEA. I was shocked and disappointed. The only conclusion I could draw from this sudden change was that I was found wanting in that high office. I felt very bad about it. Before returning to the ministry, I called on the PM to take leave of her. She was quite friendly. She said, 'They say you have to go back to the ministry; I don't know why [as if!]. Keep in touch.' I said I would do that, whereupon she said, 'I mean, keep in touch with me personally.' I thanked her.

I asked Foreign Secretary Ram Sathe, a wonderful person, as to what he had in mind for me. He offered me two choices: Europe division or Pakiraf–Pakistan, Iran and Afghanistan. I told him that was a no-brainer. Of course, I would take the latter.

I had been keeping a diary for most of my postings, but somehow did not do so in the PMO. I regretted that and decided I will definitely keep a record of whatever I would be involved with while working with the Pakistan division. As it happened, I was recalled to the PMO after about a year, in 1982; I told myself then that I would surely keep a diary.

2

DEALING WITH PAKISTAN

As joint secretary in charge of Pakistan, Iran and Afghanistan, I dealt with all these three countries. I visited Iran and Afghanistan and wrote reports of my visits. In my mind, I was clear that of the three, Pakistan was the most important country for India; this was reflected in the fact that I maintained details only about Pakistan in my diary.

Countering the Pak Propaganda

Ever since the mutual security arrangement was concluded between Pakistan and the United States (US) in 1954, India had increased concerns about the supply of advanced military hardware by the US to Pakistan. Pakistan had joined the Western military alliance and reaped substantial benefit. As far as the US was concerned, its assistance to Pakistan was meant to be used for containing the Soviet Union and China. But Pakistan was quite clear: It had only one enemy—India.

Ambassador K. Natwar Singh once described Pakistan's policy pithily: 'When in doubt, blame India, when not in doubt, blame India!'

It was, therefore, no wonder that when, on 16 September 1981, Pakistan foreign office released a statement announcing the formal acceptance of the US arms package consisting of F-16 fighter aircraft, India was deeply concerned. Let alone Pakistan, even the Americans had not informed us about this deal. The acquisition of F-16s would impact the balance of forces between India and Pakistan. We were firmly opposed to it, but the announcement had already been made and that was that.

In order to soften the negative fallout of the deal, the Pakistan statement included a paragraph at the end, offering to conclude a no-war pact with India. This was a propaganda ploy and an effective one. The natural reaction of the international community, including the Indian media, was to welcome the offer as a token of Pakistan's good faith. We had to counter the propaganda.

We got the text of the statement from our then high commissioner to Pakistan, K. Natwar Singh, on 16 September. As usual, he had addressed the telex only to the Foreign Secretary and to the Principal Secretary to the PM. When I got the text, I prepared a draft statement for our spokesperson in response to his Pakistani counterpart's statement the previous day. In my draft, I recalled the fact that we had made a 'no-war pact' offer to Pakistan in as early as 1949, that we had repeated it several times in subsequent years and that Pakistan had consistently rejected it. I also included some words to the effect that Pakistan's proposal did not carry anything new, but we would welcome any explanations they had to offer. The draft was approved by Foreign Secretary Ram Sathe and even by the PM.

When it was shown to Foreign Minister P.V. Narasimha Rao, referred to as PV by many, he decided against issuing it. He said that there was nothing much in the statement. When the press asked our spokesperson about Pakistan's proposal, he replied, under instructions, that it was under study. This initial mistake of not responding immediately to Pakistan's offer cost us in terms of propaganda advantage that Pakistan derived at home, across the Western media and even among the Indian public opinion. We lost credibility not only abroad but, worse, within our own country, too. Most people agreed with our assessment that Pakistan's move was propagandist and was directed at the US Congress, which was to commence hearings on the arms deal on 26 September.

But it was argued that even if it was a propaganda gimmick, even if Pakistan was not serious, why didn't India call the bluff? After all, the idea of a no-war pact was India's originally. Why should India bother about the motivations? How can India not agree to its own proposal?

The fact was that there was deep distrust between the two countries. Pakistan had been humiliated as a result of its defeat in the 1971 war, which led to its loss of East Pakistan and the emergence of the independent state of Bangladesh. India had harboured 90,000 Pakistani troops as prisoners of war. This was a serious blow to the prestige of Pakistan's military. India remained convinced that Pakistan would seek to avenge that defeat someday. It was because of this reason that India was wary of Pakistan's acquisition of the F-16s.

Our formal position was that the 'offer' of no-war pact was not communicated to us. Governments are not expected to react to each and every press statement by another government; we take cognizance only of whatever is communicated to us through proper diplomatic channels. However, this argument did not carry conviction, even with our own media. Our refusal to react in a formal way was made worse by several statements by the PM in the press to the effect that Pakistan was not serious, that the proposal was a trap, that Pakistan's actions, particularly the acquisitions of massive arms, were in contradiction to its own offer, etc. But Pakistan and others reminded us that India had also been engaged in arming itself heavily. The result of all this was that Pakistan's media went to town. They, along with many Indians, drew the conclusion that India was not grasping the hand of friendship proffered by Pakistan as India had aggressive designs. My own feeling was that Indira Gandhi was reacting out of pique. Though the offer was first made by India 32 years ago, the whole world, even including the Indian media, was now applauding Pakistan's initiative. We could have neatly turned the tables against Pakistan had we come out with a suitable response on 16 September itself, instead of dithering for two-and-a-half months.

Pakistanis played smartly. To blunt India's official and diplomatically correct line, Shah Nawaz, the secretary general in Pakistan's foreign office, handed over, on 22 September 1981, a *note verbale* to Natwar*, in which the Pakistani government formally conveyed its proposal for negotiations on a non-aggression pact. Evidently, Pakistan realized that while it had scored public relations advantage over us, it needed to do more to establish its bona fides, particularly with the US. So, it decided to throw the ball back to us. Its game plan was to make it difficult for us to reject something that we ourselves had proposed in the past.

In early October of the same year, I prepared another draft. PV said it was a good one but did not agree to its release.

---

*A diplomatic note that is more formal than an aide-mémoire and less formal than a note. It is drafted in the third person and is never signed.

When I told him about the propaganda benefit that Pakistan was deriving, he asked me not to worry about it and to leave the matter to him. He asked me to prepare a statement for Parliament. When I said that Parliament was not to meet for another five weeks, his reply was, 'Good, it gives you more time.' But I did not want more time—'I am ready,' I said, whereupon the foreign minister summarily asked me to do what he had instructed and not to worry about other aspects.

The Foreign Minister made a statement in Parliament on 25 November. It was a clever statement, but not a good one. I had prepared draft, but he had rewritten several paragraphs. It was lambasted by the Indian press, to the great glee of the Pakistani media, which reproduced our editorials with much pleasure.

I could never understand Narasimha Rao's reluctance to make an early and positive response to Pakistan's offer. We knew that Zia-ul-Haq, President of Pakistan, was not sincere, and that this was a propaganda exercise. PV said that we could never win the propaganda war against Pakistan, since the media in the West would always favour Pakistan. Our own media also relished in criticizing the government, rightly or wrongly. So, he said, don't worry much about propaganda.

The War of Public Perceptions

During the Foreign Minister's visit to Pakistan in June 1981, it had been agreed that Pakistan's foreign minister, Agha Shahi, would come to India before the end of the year. Natwar kept reminding us of this commitment and kept pressing our Foreign Minister to invite Shahi, but for some reason, he was reluctant. His argument was that the present atmosphere was not propitious, and that Shahi would have a rough time in

India, facing questions on F-16 aircraft, etc. We told him that it was for Shahi to face the music. The consensus among all of us was that the Foreign Minister did not feel comfortable at the thought of taking on Shahi in serious negotiations on the no-war pact.

Natwar came to Delhi in December. We held many meetings. I had recorded a note in November, using which I suggested that we should accept the offer to negotiate and that we should take the initiative and put forward a concrete draft treaty of our own. I even prepared three alternative drafts and sent them to PV. I pointed out that, apart from anything else, we were losing credibility with our own people; nearly three months had gone by without our considered response to Pakistan's proposal. Most people tended to welcome such positive-looking initiatives. This was true even about Pakistan and particularly in North India. The South tended to be somewhat passive about Pakistan, just as people in the North were not much interested in Sri Lankan affairs. He agreed with me: Meetings were arranged and Natwar was called.

I proposed another draft treaty, which underwent several versions. It was decided that the matter would be submitted to the Cabinet Committee on Political Affairs (CCPA) on 22 December. Before the CCPA meeting, we discussed the matter with the PM. There was a difference of opinion among us. I was in the favour of giving a draft of the treaty to Pakistan. My objective was purely based on public relations. Sathe was against the idea of giving anything in writing at that stage. The Foreign Minister had no particular view—at least, he did not express any. We then went to the PM. PV did not say anything except to ask me about the difference between no war and non-aggression. I told him that aggression could be short of war. He did not seem convinced, but did not press the point.

Natwar started the discussions with a short introduction and looked at me. Having worked with the PM for about six months, I was perhaps less nervous than others to talk in her presence. So, I gave my views—if Pakistan gave a draft, Natwar should also forward our draft. If they don't give anything in writing, he should make a little speech and hand over a paper containing elements of a possible no-war pact. The PM seemed to agree. Natwar and S.K. Singh, who was the additional secretary and my boss in the MEA, were of the same view as that of the PM.

Sathe expressed his view of being against the idea of giving anything in writing. When the PM asked him why, he said we should not commit ourselves to anything in writing at this stage. But the PM said, there was nothing in the proposed paper which she herself had not said publicly ad nauseam. Sathe persisted in his view, and I stuck to mine. In the end, we decided that we should hand over a paper listing some points. One referred to the need to prevent diversion of resources for the acquisition of armaments. When I pointed out that this would apply to us too, the PM said the point should be deleted. The paper was considered by the CCPA and approved after a 45-minute discussion with a few changes. It was also agreed that Shahi would be invited by PV. Natwar produced the letter of invitation for signature in the PM's presence and PV obliged, though with not much enthusiasm.

Natwar handed over the aide-mémoire and the Foreign Minister's invitation to Shahi on 24 December. Both, particularly the aide-mémoire, came as a total surprise to Pakistan. They never expected that we would prepare any concrete, written proposal of our own in counter to theirs. Natwar reported that Zia had included nasty references to India in a speech he was to deliver on 24 January, on the occasion of Jinnah's birth anniversary. On being informed of our aide-mémoire, he scored out the offensive parts. In India, too, the press said a few nice things about the government and there was a change in the atmosphere. Anti-India stories saw a decline in Pakistan media.

Shahi was scheduled to come on 29 January 1982. He was supposed to come on 30 January, but Abdul Sattar, the Pakistan high commissioner in Delhi, suggested that Shahi should see the ceremony of Beating Retreat. Apparently, the PM was not enthusiastic about this suggestion (according to Natwar), but when I checked with her, she did not express any displeasure.

3

THE PAKISTAN TALKS

We had frequent meetings to prepare for the talks with Shahi in Delhi in 1982. I produced a paper every day! Our task was not easy, especially because of Shahi's formidable reputation. I was very sceptical and approached the exercise as a game in diplomacy. Sathe, on the other hand, gave more benefit of the doubt to Pakistan and was inclined to trust them to an extent. He felt this might be a genuine opportunity to establish durable peace between the two countries. He described his approach as 'visionary'. However, PV did not trust Shahi at all. Sathe tended to be defensive and not too sure of himself or his side; he saw more merit in the other side's case.

Position on No-War Pact

The position of the two countries had taken a 180-degree turn. Until 1980, we were the ones to suggest, from time to time since 1949, a no-war pact. Pakistan had never agreed. Now, Pakistan had taken the initiative and we were hesitant. Until recently, Pakistan had said that a no-war pact was not necessary, since the Simla Agreement of 1972 was virtually a no-war pact and we had agreed with them. Now, we were asking about the need for a no-war pact even though the Simla Agreement contained all the essential ingredients of one.

PV told us several times that he objected to the manner in which Pakistan gave out the proposal on 16 September. He was not bothered much about its timing (eve of Congressional hearing on the arms package with Pakistan), but the public announcement, tagged to a statement devoted primarily to acceptance of the US arms offer, created grave doubts in his mind about Pakistan's intentions. Sathe believed that it was merely a case of bungling on the part of Pakistan's foreign office. He held this view because Shah Nawaz, and Riaz Piracha, foreign secretary of Pakistan, had told him so. I asked PV, the day after Shahi left, whether he was now satisfied. He said he was beginning to be convinced that it might have just been bungling. But personally, I was not convinced. Pakistan derived maximum propaganda advantage and now wanted us to believe that it was all a case of faulty handling by their foreign office. Sathe believed in the bungling theory because he felt that Pakistan was sincere and, by going public, they damaged their credibility with us.

Shahi arrived on 29 January and left on 1 February. He was accompanied by two generals—Yaqub Khan, a retired general, senior to Zia, and Arif Khan, chief of staff to Zia-ul-Haq. Yaqub was a highly successful ambassador in Washington, and a very charming and polished diplomat. Arif was the second-most important man in Pakistan. In addition to being Zia's chief of staff, he commanded the loyalty of other senior generals. Though technically only No. 4 in the team, there was no doubt in anyone's mind about who the effective No. 1 was.

We were informed of the composition of the Pakistani team for the talks just two days before the visit. Naturally, there was a lot of speculation. Yaqub's inclusion was explained by the rumours of him replacing Shahi, who was genuinely ill due to high blood pressure. About Arif, PV was of the view that his inclusion indicated lack of trust in Shahi. Sathe believed that this would be officially explained as evidence of the personal interest of Zia in this exercise, and this was what Sattar told us. Shahi told PV that he had personally requested Arif's inclusion, so that he would sell whatever was agreed to the army. Be that as it may, the fact was Shahi's style of functioning was cramped by the presence of the generals. On 29 January, the generals accompanied him during his protocolaire call on our Foreign Minister half an hour before the dinner. Some of us were also present. Normally, this should have been a tête-à-tête. The conversation was entirely about Bengal Lancers, Skinner's Horse and the 63rd Cavalry! The following morning, we were hoping for a private meeting between the two ministers. But Sattar said that would not be possible. So, once again there were four to five people on each side; this time the talk was about office accommodation for the two foreign offices of India and Pakistan and the training programmes for IFS officers. Apparently, Zia had agreed to revive the practice of sending Pakistan probationers to the Fletcher School of Law and Diplomacy in Boston. Eventually, the ministers did meet alone for an hour on the morning of 31 January, though we were hoping for a two-hour meeting.

Anticipating Pakistan's Moves

When Shahi called on Indira Gandhi, she proposed a Joint Commission to him. We had earlier suggested this to her, and she had agreed. Shahi looked at Arif, who nodded assent, whereupon Shahi expressed his agreement.

We had prepared the proposal for a Joint Commission with two objectives. It was a public relations move, and it paid off handsomely. Some of us were of the view that it was only by creating a vested interest of peace among the two countries that peace would have a good chance of lasting. The Joint Commission was meant to help in this process. The Pakistani side did not expect us to come up with something like this. But Sattar put on a brave face and said that they also had a somewhat similar proposal in their draft agreement. But my young colleague, Neelam Dhamija, who at that time was the undersecretary handling Pakistan, might have been right: Sattar might be pulled up for failing to warn his bosses about the Joint Commission idea.

We had anticipated that Pakistan might bring a draft agreement. So, I had prepared a draft in consultation with S.P. Jagota, our legal expert, and G. Parthasarathi, who was a close advisor to the PM and had been my ambassador in New York during my posting there in the 1960s. I had recorded a note, suggesting that we ought to present our own draft in case Pakistan gave us theirs. I had said that even if Pakistan did not, we should give a draft to retain the initiative and for the sake of one-upmanship. PV had accepted the first part of my recommendation, but everyone had disagreed with the one-upmanship angle. We should have got the draft approved by the CCPA in time, but inertia at the level of the foreign secretary and the foreign minister came in the way. Perhaps, they were reluctant to face the PM; the draft ought to have been submitted to the PM well before the visit, not at the last minute.

As it happened, Shahi told us that he had brought a draft agreement. What were we to do now? We could not give ours, since it had not been cleared by the CCPA. Sathe and Natwar said that they would speak to Pakistan and ask them to postpone an exchange of drafts since we were not ready with ours. I took a very strong stand against this advice. I said it would be humiliating for our foreign office to have to request Pakistan not to embarrass us by proposing an exchange of drafts. I was particularly upset since I had taken the trouble of keeping a draft ready, which the others did not have the courage of processing. The blame for lack of preparation would be laid at the door of the ministry. After 16 September also, the ministry was blamed for mishandling the response to Pakistan's offer, while the truth of the matter was that PV did not accept our advice.

So, on the morning of 30 January, Ashok Mubayi, special assistant to the PM, and I went to Sathe's residence. He was entertaining Yaqub and Arif to high tea. Soon after they left, I spoke with him, quite passionately, that I would not let the ministry be humiliated again. If Shahi produced a draft, PV must not be on the defensive, and he too should offer him one of his own. We then went to the Foreign Minister. We suggested that in case Shahi proposed an exchange, PV should, in turn, propose setting up a working group to go into both the drafts, instead of exchanging drafts, since we did not have ours cleared by the CCPA.

The following morning, PV asked the PM about all this, to which she said said there was no problem: She would convene the CCPA and get the draft approved the same afternoon. It was great news and immediately all the brains involved in the talks sat down and gave final shape to the draft by 1.00 p.m. In the meantime, PV and Shahi had their private one-hour meeting. As expected, Shahi proposed an exchange of drafts. PV told him that he also had a draft and added that it might not be advisable to exchange them, since they were bound to get public, needlessly committing the two governments to their respective papers. To our relief, Shahi agreed. Thus, we did not have to rush through the CCPA. This was a major diplomatic 'save' for us, otherwise both Pakistan and our media would have gone to town about it.

On the afternoon of 31 January, the two sides met in a restricted session. Pakistan had suggested three members on either side. Our Foreign Minister wanted Sathe, Jagota and me, but Natwar could not be kept out. S.K. Singh was my boss, and it would be odd if I was in and he was not. I did not want to be left out and PV, too, wanted me in. So, we were six and Pakistan matched the number. Shahi and PV talked about the aide-mémoire. About the US defence connection, Shahi said that India was also getting its military training assistance from the US, clearly implying that they were on par with India on this score. He also referred to the Indo-Soviet Treaty of 1971, in defence of the US Pakistan's 1950 security agreement. PV did not react to it. Shahi proposed that the officials from both sides should try to go into specific formulations in the afternoon and report about them the following morning.

On the very first day, Shahi told PV that they would abide by whatever pace India would set. 'We will proceed as fast or slow as you decide,' he told PV. In fact, however, it was Shahi who was setting the pace. He was the one who proposed the drafting group exercise, he set the date for the official visit to Islamabad in February itself and he maneuvered us into agreeing that the meeting should be at the level of foreign secretary. Shahi was not confrontational in his approach with us; he prided himself on his diplomatic expertise and his ability to get the other side to accept his view—a trait he had acquired during his stint in the UN.

During Shahi's visit, neither side mentioned Kashmir, which was at the root of the problem. Pakistan did not really want to settle on the question of Jammu and Kashmir (J&K), except on their terms—which meant us handing over the entire state to them. It was and is my belief that we should be willing to convert the Line of Control (LoC) in Kashmir into a permanent border. According to media reports, this was considered informally during the Simla talks in 1972. It was also covered by media that the former President of Pakistan, Zulfikar Ali Bhutto, had said he would be willing to consider it but needed time to prepare public opinion for it. All reasonable people in India and elsewhere agreed that this was the only possible solution. Of course, we could not offer it publicly; the matter had to be negotiated and approved confidentially first. And we, too, would need to explain it to the public and Parliament. The argument had been advanced—a no-war pact had no meaning unless the territory to which it was to apply was clearly identified in the provisions of a future treaty whereby it would be clear that the LoC would be respected for all time to come.

Sathe checked with the PM regarding this and she was very clear that we should not make any such proposal, but also added that the Foreign Secretary could try to throw a feeler on his own during his visit to Islamabad. PV had a clear stance—and it was against the proposal.

4

THE PAKISTAN CONUNDRUM

When India had asked the Americans for help in 1962, we were reeling under China's aggression. They and the British used the opportunity to put pressure on us to settle the Kashmir question with Pakistan. We had to agree to open negotiations with Pakistan. Six rounds of negotiations were held within a period of six months. We had made a sincere effort to settle the issue. According to Y.D. Gundevia's* delightfully readable book *Outside the Archives*, Sardar Swaran Singh, who was the then railway minister, had made an offer to finalize the ceasefire line in 1949. In addition, we had offered more than 1,500 sq. miles, including important areas in the Valley. But Pakistan had insisted on the whole state, with the exception of Kathua district and a small area near it. We, of course, could not accept that. Pakistan did not mention the UN resolutions on Kashmir issue at that time.

*Y.D. Gundevia was a senior officer in the Indian Civil Service and a senior secretary in the MEA in the early years of Independence.

Prime Minister Nehru had explained all this to President John F. Kennedy and British PM Harold Macmillan, but the latter were not satisfied and wanted us, essentially, to part with the Valley. Lord Mountbatten, who was supposed to be a great friend of Nehru, had told the latter when he was in London in April–May 1963 for the Commonwealth Conference that because of Nehru's policy on Kashmir, his image and prestige in the world had been shattered! The Secretary of State for the Colonies, Duncan Sandys, insisted on undertaking shuttle diplomacy between Delhi and Karachi. Gundevia, in his book, noted that Sandys had neither any finesse nor any tact. George Ball, the cerebral undersecretary of state in State Department, also appeared on the scene once and Gundevia noted that we certainly did not want to play ball with Ball.

Pakistan was anxious about whether we would agree to the exchange of drafts at the next round of negotiations in Islamabad in February. It had been decided that we would not agree in view of the PM's directions. I was looking forward to the Islamabad visit where only Sathe and I were allowed to go. I had come to the Pakistan division at a time when, professionally speaking, exciting developments were in the offing. Indira Gandhi, however, was a bit upset, as she felt we had agreed to go to Islamabad too soon. She wanted us to go slow and did not want to sign anything with Pakistan. One consequence of this go-slow decision was that we lost the propaganda game once again. When we were talking about propaganda with the PM a few days before Shahi's visit, she had said that we would never get the better of Pakistan in that game. Our own press, of course, would be the first to lambast us.

Parthasarathi highlighted a gap, which we were asked to cover up—we had inadequacies in anti-tank as well as defence systems against air attacks. Therefore, in Islamabad, we would have to confine ourselves to generalities. Accordingly I revised the draft brief.

On 16 February 1982, Shahi's resignation was announced in Islamabad. It was not unexpected at all. Yaqub Khan replaced him. It transpired that Shahi's departure from the foreign ministry had been decided even before he had come to Delhi. The man had been genuinely battling hypertension and, according to Natwar, doctors had given him only six months if he continued working with the same intensity. Still, there was speculation about his differences with Zia, which I didn't believe because I did not think Shahi was a man who had any views other than those of his master for the moment. Shahi was certainly distrusted by the Americans (and everybody else). Yaqub was a successful ambassador in Washington. To that extent, Zia may have acted to please the US. Shahi had told PV earlier that he was the only one in Pakistan cabinet who favoured non-alignment for Pakistan. Zia himself had spoken to Shahi mockingly about his enthusiasm for non-alignment.

There could be another reason. Zia admitted at a press conference in Paris that Pakistan should not have handled the no-war proposal through the press. The suggestion to make the offer through the press must have been made by Shahi, it was added. This was the single most important grievance of the foreign minister. Zia might have come to realize this, and it might have contributed to his decision to accept or demand the resignation. There was more than an even chance that our visit to Islamabad might be postponed.

The Heated Exchange at Geneva

Indira Gandhi, in any case, had not been enthusiastic about the visit to Islamabad. She seemed to have picked on an incident in the UNCHR, which was then meeting in Geneva. Agha Hilaly, Shahi's brother, who led Pakistan's delegation to the commission, had told our representative to the UNCHR a few days previously that he would not raise any bilateral dispute in the UNCHR. However, when he spoke about the report of a Latin American expert named Héctor Gros Espiell on self-determination, he mentioned Kashmir. Espiell's report included J&K in the list of territories where the right of self-determination was yet to be exercised. Hilaly expressed his hope for the settlement of the Kashmir question in the spirit of the Simla Agreement. His reference to Kashmir was not couched in offensive terms. But B.R. Bhagat, our representative in the UNCHR, took great offence and gave a rather provocative reply, which, in turn, led to a return reply by Hilaly and another by Bhagat. The latter should have confined himself to the legal and constitutional position and to the Simla Agreement. Instead, he also spoke of the martial law regime in Pakistan. When we got the telex from Geneva, I advised against leaking it to the press. My concern was that it would provide Pakistan with an excuse to bring the whole story about Espiell's report into the open and that won't look too good for us. I was overruled and the next day's papers gave the news front page coverage.

Naturally, the PM was upset. She always reacted very strongly each time Pakistan mentioned Kashmir at an international forum. So, there were consultations among the PM, Sathe, PV and Natwar. Sathe was asked to summon Sattar and convey our strong protest. Should the Foreign Secretary's visit be postponed? The PM suggested that the level should be lowered. Natwar suggested my level. Sathe did not agree. And it was left at that. The PM let it be known that she did not want to sign anything that had to do with

Pakistan. She believed that Pakistan would attack India one day, as soon as it felt strong enough to do so. Her belief, shared by many, was likely based on her conviction that Pakistan military would surely be looking for an opportunity to seek revenge for their humiliation in the 1971 Bangladesh Liberation War.

Post our meeting with the PM, Sathe called Sattar and spoke to him firmly (but I suspect, without his heart in it). The ambassador asked about the visit. Sathe said it would depend on the explanation given by Islamabad. If the visit was postponed, the whole world would draw only one conclusion: India was never sincere about the no-war pact offer and has used the UNCHR event as an excuse for putting off the talks. Natwar was not in favour of postponement.

The day after Shahi left, PV confided in me that he felt so tired after the former's plane had taken off that he wanted to flop down then and there. He talked about being very nervous and mentally tense during the visit. PV spoke frequently of Shahi's unreliability. 'How can you trust a man like that?' In contrast, he said, he had the greatest confidence in Shamsul Haq, the Bangladesh foreign minister. I could appreciate his feeling. He felt exhausted probably because he was apprehensive about how the visit would go and what the PM and other politicians might think of him. He would not say anything in the PM's presence. After the visit, PV was very pleased with himself; he received encomiums from the press and from his fellow politicians. He, in turn, was very appreciative of my work. My colleagues in the division and I had tried to anticipate all the queries and points that Pakistan might raise and had prepared responses to them all.

Sathe said he had established 'empathy' with Arif, whom he met thrice privately. Yaqub did not like it and conveyed the same to Sathe. Arif, on the other hand, conveyed a clear message: 'Don't bother about the civilians. If you have any problems, come to me, I am the man and I will settle everything.'

Pakistan was anxious that we should exchange drafts at the next round in Islamabad. In view of the PM's directions, we would not agree. It would be an interesting experience in the Islamabad talks. Only the Foreign Secretary and I would go. There was more than an even chance that our visit to Islamabad could be postponed. The PM, in any case, had not been enthusiastic about it.

Islamabad Visit Called Off

On the morning of 24 February, PV asked me as to what he should say in Parliament in reply to calling attention notice on the reference to Kashmir at Geneva. The essential point for decision was whether the Foreign Secretary's visit should be postponed. My view was that the visit should not be postponed and that we should derive propaganda mileage by saying that despite the exchanges in Geneva, we had decided to go to Islamabad. In the afternoon, PV called Sathe and me, and discussed the matter again. He asked whether we could make for a good case if we decided on postponement. Sathe felt that if the political decision was against the visit, we could make a reasonable case. I said that our case was not a good one and that everyone, including the Indian press, would accuse us of using this as a pretext for cancelling the talks on the no-war pact, about which India had not been enthusiastic from the beginning. PV spoke to R.K. Dhawan, the PM's special assistant, on the RAX (confidential phone line for senior officials) and asked for an appointment with the PM. Obviously, this was not a matter on which he was going to take any decision on his own.

Sathe, PV, Natwar and I met the PM at the Parliament House at about 5.30 p.m. At that time, Finance Minister Pranab Mukherjee, was present in the room. He must have proposed some tough taxation measures, which would provoke a storm in the House, and because of this, the PM was in a sharp mood. She said, 'I have very little time, the finance minister is here for very important business. So be quick with what you have to say.' Sathe started the proceedings by mentioning the Espiell report. When the PM asked, 'What report?', Sathe looked at me. Fortunately, because of my Geneva background, I knew all about it and I explained about it briefly to the PM. Her reaction was, 'We don't accept such reports.' I told her that indeed we did not accept the report, but it was formally on the table in the UNCHR.

Sathe then invited the PM's attention to the verbatim text of the Bhagat–Hilaly exchange. I handed her the transcript. As she started to glance through it, Natwar said that Hilaly's reference to Kashmir was not as bad as we had thought.

'What do you mean it is not as bad?' the PM retorted. She started quoting from the transcript, pointing out how bad it really was: 'self-determination, comparison with Namibia, Palestine and Afghanistan, ridiculing the general elections, etc.' She said she had already read the transcript (I had sent it to her the previous day). There was an uncomfortable silence in the room for a few seconds.

Natwar looked at me. I said, 'Madam, the point to decide is whether the Foreign Secretary's visit should be postponed or whether he should go as scheduled.'

She replied, 'I had thought we had already taken the view that he should not go.'

Someone asked, 'Should we say that the visit has been postponed for the time being?'

To this, the PM replied, 'He can go, but not now.' She seemed very upset with the developments. She recalled that Hilaly had seen her in Delhi just a few months ago and told her how it was his life's ambition to work for peace between India and Pakistan and how he dreamt about it. 'And look what he has done now.'

Natwar said that Sattar had informed us that a letter from Zia would be delivered the following morning.

The PM said, 'What will he say? He will talk about how much he loves us, how much he desires friendship with us; that it was all a misunderstanding, etc. In any case, I have no time to see Sattar or anybody.' Sathe said Sattar would deliver the letter to him to be passed on to the PM. She thumped the table and said, 'I don't have the time to even read a letter. We are all missing our lunches and dinners because of the pressure of work, and I certainly am not going to read any letters.'

A few days earlier, when I had asked her about the Foreign Secretary's visit, she had said, 'What will he do there?' I had suggested that Foreign Secretary could convey our protest at the highest level.

Her reply had been, 'Then what? What happens if they raise Kashmir again after a few weeks?' I had no answer to that. She was really upset with the Hilaly incident. She might have been equally unhappy with Bhagat for his handling of the situation. Or perhaps, she was preoccupied with other political or party matters. She might also have thought that Sathe was keen to go for personal reasons; she did not approve of officials seeking publicity for themselves.

We then went to PV's room and discussed the contents of his statement for the Lok Sabha the following morning. Soon,

Amitabh Banerjee, special assistant to the foreign minister, came to me and said that the PM wanted to talk to me on phone. This was the first time she would speak to me on the phone. I thought I had landed myself in trouble since I had made bold to suggest to her that the decision to postpone the Foreign Secretary's visit because of the incident in the UNCHR would be interpreted as an excuse to cancel or delay the talks. However, she only said that we should include a couple of points in the Foreign Minister's statement the next day. I came back and told the others about what the PM had told me. Sathe had to ask me a couple of times whether it was actually the PM who had spoken to me. This was the PM's style; when she got used to someone, she would only deal through them, irrespective of that person's seniority. I felt reassured after her telephone call to me.

I had already prepared a draft on the assumption that the Foreign Secretary's visit would be on, but that could easily be altered. It was decided that Sathe would summon Sattar and convey our decision; he was to be told that the visit had been deferred, without adding anything about the time frame. Sathe called Sattar; Natwar was present for moral support, and he later described the meeting as 'chilling' and 'freezing'. Sattar started off with Zia's letter to the PM, which was expected to reach him at any time. Sathe interrupted him and said that before the ambassador went any further, he was instructed to tell him that his visit had been deferred. Natwar said that Sattar's face fell hearing that.

Natwar, PV, Sathe and I went to the Foreign Minister's office in South Block and worked on the statement till 2.00 a.m. The end product was quite satisfactory. Natwar dropped off a copy at the PM's office on his way home.

Next day, when I went to the Foreign Minister's office

to check about the final text, Natwar was there. The PM had made three small but significant changes in the draft. In fact, the changes were done in her own handwriting. She had added 'peace and friendship treaty' somewhere in the statement. More important, she qualified the reference in the statement to deferment of the visit by adding the words 'for the time being'. This was crucial because it softened the blow and the harshness. Lastly, she replaced 'never' by 'not' in the statement in the last paragraph where we had suggested her to be saying that pact or no pact, India would never attack Pakistan. I informed Sathe about the changes, and he was mighty pleased since Sattar was seeing him at 10.30 a.m. with Zia's letter to the PM.

I saw PV briefly before he went into the House. 'So, Chinmaya, you have seen the changes made by the PM.'

'Yes', I said, 'They are most welcome.'

'Indeed. But, I think Indian press will not like this softening,' PV said. The statement, however, was almost not delivered. The Opposition did not permit any business in protest against some issue and walked out after shouting for 20 minutes. When PV started to speak, the Opposition benches were empty, but they returned before the debate was over.

Unlike my expectations, the Indian press did not come out with screaming editorials against the government. On the contrary, *The Indian Express* supported the government, though they all said that the door for dialogue must be kept open. The Pakistani media reacted violently; they wrote that India had used this excuse to get out of the no-war pact talks. Their argument was that India was not at all enthusiastic about Pakistan's proposal but was forced into it by domestic and international pressure. The exchanges on Kashmir in Geneva came in handy for India as a justification for wriggling out of the talks. Most people in India would also feel the same way and I thought that this was, in fact, so.

Irrespective of the PM's motives, the decision was good. The Pakistani calculations must have been that these Hindu baniyas and Brahmins were incapable of doing anything more than verbally protest, and that the domestic and international pressure would not permit India to take a more drastic step of not proceeding with the talks. Pakistan would have never imagined that we would go to the extent of cancelling the talks.

It was not going to be easy to pick up the thread. We had raised a very fundamental issue. We were the ones to insist on delinking the question of Kashmir from the talks on no-war pact. By postponing the Foreign Secretary's visit, we had, in fact, brought the Kashmir question right into the centre of the discussions. This was perhaps a good thing. I had always felt that we should have a head-on discussion with Pakistan about Kashmir. We were quite ready to settle the question—it was Pakistan that could not afford it because of domestic compulsions. In the context of the no-war pact, it was all the more important to clarify the territory or borders to which the pact would apply. What kind of reply did we expect or want from Pakistan? An assurance that they would not talk about Kashmir in international forums? Could Zia afford to give such a commitment? Could we afford to resume the dialogue in the absence of such an assurance?

5

STALEMATE CAN SOMETIMES BE A SUCCESS

An opportunity to resume the talks with Pakistan presented itself to us again in 1982. The source was Geneva and the UNCHR. In his report on self-determination, the rapporteur of the commission had mentioned Kashmir. Our delegation took up the matter with our Pakistani counterpart who had obtained instructions from Islamabad to agree to delete the reference to J&K 'without prejudice to Pakistan's position on the matter'.

I put up a note for Sathe, suggesting that we should take note of this development. Earlier, we had presumed that Hilaly had spoken on instructions from his government: This time we knew that he had acted on instructions. I said that Pakistan had given us a signal. If we were looking for a reasonable 'reply' from Pakistan, this was it. No one would fault the government, in case we decided to resume the dialogue. In any case, I recommended that we should acknowledge this message from

Pakistan, preferably publicly. With a suitable twist, we could even exploit the incident to add to Zia's trouble at home. Sathe did not react at all to my note. Many of us got the feeling that Sathe did not want to do anything during the last six weeks of his service, which might blot his most impressive record. This was understandable, given his unblemished record in foreign service.

On 17 March 1982, I dropped in on Sathe and asked him what was cooking. He agreed that Pakistan's consent to delete the reference to Kashmir in the report of the UNCHR was a powerful signal to us. But he showed no inclination to act on my note for two reasons. First, the domestic situation in Pakistan was not conducive for resumption of the dialogue—there was considerable internal turmoil, imposition of martial law, etc.—and second, our Parliament was scheduled to debate the demand for grants for external affairs and defence ministries, where harsh things were likely to be said about Pakistan.

There was a suggestion that I should talk with an officer from Pakistan's foreign ministry either in Geneva or Bangkok on a confidential 'hush hush' basis. The idea was to have a frank exchange of views on the concept of a no-war pact and related issues. It was probably S.K. Singh who had come up with the idea. It was favoured by Natwar as well as P.C. Alexander, principal secretary to the PM. A few days later, S.K. told me that nothing had come of the suggestion. Sathe told me on 17 March that I should be asked to undertake this mission after Parliament had dealt with external affairs and defence ministry grants. We would have to take the PM's orders, of course.

On 23 March, Pakistan Day, Indira Gandhi sent an approved message from herself to Zia-ul-haq. It was rather a substantive message, the draft of which was prepared by

Kishan Rana, who had replaced me in the PMO. S.K. had brought this up with Sathe on 17 March when I was with him. I had said that Rana had read out the draft to me and I found it to be very good. The only thing I had told him was that the PM should not say anything at this stage that may amount to personal support to Zia in view of the disturbed situation in Pakistan. Sathe, however, had disagreed with my suggestion and said that personal support to him at the time of his weakness could pay rich dividends later. I saw merit in his point.

Later, the same evening, Rana told me that Sathe had telephoned him and sounded very excited about the text of the message. He had said that while he agreed with the draft, he hoped the PM was aware of its implications. He had added, contrary to what he had told me just a few hours earlier, that the phrase about personal health and happiness to Zia, at this stage, was not advisable. He had even recorded a note on the subject and sent it to PV. Rana had convinced him that the PM never signed anything, let alone a message to Zia, casually. In any case, the message had been sent, enclair, to our embassy in Islamabad. So, any change would be seriously misunderstood (or rather, understood correctly!) in Pakistan.

For a few weeks, it appeared as if things were heating up in Pakistan. The appointment of Majlis-e-Shoora, nominated body as it was, turned out to be a mistake on Zia's part. He created the Majlis with the expectation that it would satisfy the desire for democracy. It was a purely cosmetic step, which did not fool anybody. It had no real power to legislate or to question the government. Even puppet politicians are politicians first and puppets later. The members of the Majlis created enough noise for Zia to not convene it every month, as he had promised. In fact, it had met only for four days so far.

One positive fallout from the Majlis was the lifting of pre-censorship of the press. The Pakistani press took full advantage and started reporting extensively about the activities of the political parties. The political parties, too, exploited the opportunity for openly demanding an end to martial law and for holding early elections. Meetings between political leaders were held to form alliances. A 'grand alliance' of all parties was talked about. If all the political parties united and presented a common front, it could make things awkward for Zia. But, he knew his politicians well and nothing came out of the 'grand alliance'.

Sensing danger, Zia acted. Following a sudden 'discovery' of a booby-trapped copy of the Quran, which was allegedly meant to kill a high dignitary, the regime arrested between 10,000 and 14,000 people. The jails of Sind and Lahore could not contain all the detainees. Military courts were set up at a number of places. But the unrest continued. Thousands of teachers in Lahore struck work. The students in Karachi and other places made things generally difficult for the regime. Arbab Sikandar Khan, ex-governor of Northwest Frontier Province, had been assassinated a few weeks ago by a Muslim fanatic. Wali Khan held a meeting to mourn the death of Arbab Khan. The meeting was fired upon. Wali Khan, along with his wife and a few others, was arrested by the police for a few days.

Pakistan's economy was also not doing too well. The crops were poor compared to the harvests of the previous three years. Trade deficits had increased, exports had fallen and imports had increased. Remittances from Pakistanis working abroad had leveled off. There was increasing unrest among the labour force.

All in all, it appeared as if Zia was in for some trouble. Even right-wing Islam Pasand parties called for elections.

One newspaper wrote that in normal course, even an elected government would be obliged to go to polls after four-and-a-half years. So, Zia decided to nip the trouble in the bud. He reimposed pre-censorship and restricted movements of political leaders, arresting some of them. He might have realized, with or without American advice, that letting things slide might take them completely out of his control, as had happened to the Shah of Iran, and that there was no half-way house between dictatorship and democracy. His choice was obvious. He declared that he had no intention to hand over power to the civilians 'at this critical juncture'.

Here in India, there was a calling attention notice in the Rajya Sabha about the postponement of Sathe's visit to Islamabad. I had briefed PV and in answer to supplementaries, the external affairs minister acknowledged that Pakistan's agreement to delete the reference to Kashmir from the report of the UNCHR had been noted by the government as a positive sign.

I had two sessions with Rasgotra, who was supposed to be understudying Sathe from whom he was to take over on 1 May 1982. He was the senior-most officer, very distinguished and highly experienced. We talked only about Pakistan. His view was that we should let things cool down for the time being, that there was no hurry to resume the dialogue, and he might be going to Islamabad that year in October–November. He said we must get a commitment from Pakistan that they would not make nuclear weapons. When I pointed out that such commitment would apply to both sides, his reply was that we should not give any commitment; only Pakistan should. He asked me what we should try to get out of these negotiations. My reply was short and swift: the final settlement of the Kashmir question. He agreed.

During April and May of 1982, things were rather quiet. There were several changes in dramatis personae. Natwar joined on 1 April as secretary in the MEA. Rasgotra took over on 1 May. In Pakistan, Yaqub became the new foreign minister and Niaz Naik's appointment as the foreign secretary was announced. Riaz Piracha was coming to Delhi as the next ambassador. Sattar had gone back after a highly successful tenure of four years. Inder Malhotra, a respected columnist, in an excessively generous mood, described Sattar as the most successful ambassador ever in India.

Zia had prevented things from becoming altogether dull by making statements on Kashmir and on the so-called 'Northern Areas', such as Gilgit, Hunza, etc. Nearly all the statements were made to visiting Indian journalists whom Zia made a point of meeting with great charm and warmth. He spent hours with them, talked to them quite candidly and even sensibly and coherently. In the process sometimes, he committed faux pas. Zia appointed three observers from the Northern Areas as observers to the Majlis and said that these areas were not part of Kashmir and, hence, were not 'disputed' territory but that of Pakistan. We protested and asked for authentic version of Zia's remarks. Of course, we neither got it nor did we really want it. Then Zia told Kuldeep Nayyar, a respected senior journalist with many contacts at high levels in Pakistan, that he was prepared to discuss all the problems with India on a bilateral basis except Kashmir, which was an international issue. This was a much more serious matter and once again we asked for an authentic version of Zia's remarks. When Rajendar Sarin, another highly respected journalist, asked Zia about it a few days later, he said he was prepared to discuss Kashmir bilaterally. Zia was adept at making statements geared to appease his Indian interlocutors.

In the meantime, we in the MEA were having a quiet and not-so-open exchange with Pakistan about the Joint Commission, the no-war pact and the friendship treaty. The Pakistanis said that they would consider the Joint Commission only after the conclusion of a no-war pact. The friendship treaty idea, the new foreign minister declared, was premature. When we asked Sattar, who was the high commissioner at the time, about this, he said they stood by the joint statement issued in Delhi on 2 February. Neither Natwar nor Rasgotra could pin him down on their position on the Joint Commission. We took the line that Agha Shahi had agreed to the Joint Commission proposal without preconditions; therefore, its consideration should not be made subject to prior conclusion of a no-war pact. As for the friendship treaty, Pakistan maintained that it was not even on the table, since India had not offered it formally; PM Indira Gandhi had only referred to it en passant to Shahi and had only proposed it rhetorically during her meeting with Pakistani journalists.

Eventually, Natwar acted as the catalyst. Zia had written a letter to the PM on 21 March 1982. It was received on 24 March (the same evening we decided to postpone the Foreign Secretary's visit to Islamabad). I had been suggesting to Natwar that the PM should reply to Zia, and he had been in touch with the PM. My idea was that the PM should write before her Saudi visit, but she was very clear that she would write to Zia only after coming back from her Saudi visit. Personally, I did not understand this linkage to the Saudi visit. Anyway, when she returned, she gave the go ahead to Natwar. When asked if she wanted anything particular in the letter, she said, 'No, the usual.' Natwar's interpretation of the 'usual' was: 'the usually tough letter', though, in fact, she had not been sending tough letters to Zia. I prepared a draft, Natwar and

Parthasarathi worked on it, got it approved by PV and sent it to the PM, who made a few changes and sent the duly signed letter to the MEA, to be sent to our embassy in Islamabad for delivery to Pakistan's foreign office. So far, so good.

But then Alexander got into the act. Parthasarathi called me and said that Alexander thought the letter was too strong. Natwar said that Alexander was peeved because he had not been consulted in the drafting of the letter. Parthasarathi spent several hours with Alexander and a revised letter was prepared. The PM approved it again after a few changes. Sharada Prasad, the PM's information advisor and speech writer, called her a compulsive sub-editor! (But her changes were almost always for the better, both stylistically and substantially). The question arose: how to deliver the letter? Natwar suggested that he should hand it over personally to Zia in Islamabad. The PM agreed and Natwar took off with the letter on 31 May.

He met Zia on the same day at 6.45 p.m. His mission had been kept a secret. He wanted to show (he told me) that things could be done quietly. Of course, this had exactly the opposite (and desired) effect, with next morning's newspapers' banner headlines on Natwar's visit as the PM's special envoy.

Zia read the letter aloud in the company of Gen. Arif, Secretary General Shah Nawaz and Piracha. As soon as he finished reading it, he turned to Natwar and said in Urdu, 'Is this what you have brought with you? This?' There followed 40 minutes of blunt talk in which Natwar also gave as good as he got. Zia told him he was expecting Natwar would bring the draft of a no-war pact. Pakistan was ready with their draft, which they had planned to hand over to Natwar the next day. Natwar talked about the Joint Commission. Zia described it as 'frills'. He showed a distinct lack of enthusiasm for it and said that he was prepared to consider it, but only after the no-war pact. In any case, he asked, where the Joint Commission draft was. The best Natwar could do was to promise to give it to Sattar within a week.

Natwar came back to Delhi on 2 June, carrying Pakistan's draft. Pakistan had upstaged us once again. They forced the pace by giving the draft of no-war pact to us. They did not immediately disclose this fact to the public, but we were not wrong in our assumptions that they would do so within 48 hours. Natwar claimed that he had saved us by going to Islamabad since otherwise Sattar would have given us the draft in Delhi. Basically, he was claiming success for his mission. It was true that handing over the draft to us in Delhi would have been embarrassing for us.

We authorized the spokesman to say that Pakistan's draft would be carefully examined, and we would react in due course of time. Rasgotra told me that Mani Shankar Aiyar, official spokesperson of the ministry, could also say that the draft would need substantial changes. With his usual penchant for flowery language, Aiyar spoke of substantial modifications, amendments and changes as well as, for good measure, of seminal principles, which should guide Indo-Pak relations. Rasgotra was clearly upset the next morning, when several dailies came up with banner headlines saying India had rejected Pakistan's draft. He called me and asked me about it. I told him that this was generally in line with his instructions. He said all that bit about amendments was purely for internal discussion and not for the media. I told him I had misunderstood him and accepted full responsibility for what had happened. Aiyar was also called in. We thought he should have another briefing session with the press and explain that we had not rejected the draft—how could we when we had not had the time to examine it? I expressed doubt about the wisdom of explaining our own statements, as it might lead to further confusion. So, it was decided to let the matter be.

Having done his bit to stir things up, Natwar left on a month's junket to London, New York and Geneva. Not bad at all!

From One Draft to Another

We had internal discussions on how to react to Pakistan's draft. Of course, they had scored one over us, although it was just a point and not the whole game, certainly not the set. I felt that we should give them our draft of the friendship treaty, which we had kept ready since February 1982. Parthasarathi agreed. He and I went over the draft once again and made a few changes. He said he would speak to the PM and asked me to tell Rasgotra that he should also speak to her. Parthasarathi seemed to be in some hurry about the whole thing. Rasgotra counselled restraint and patience.

Then one day, Rasgotra called me and asked me to prepare a new draft of the friendship treaty, which would incorporate the entire Pakistani draft, our proposed draft of the Joint Commission as well as other provisions on non-alignment, etc. He said he had discussed the entire matter with Alexander and the latter had welcomed the idea. I myself was not enamoured of the idea.

A few days later, Rasgotra gave me a document. It was a draft treaty, different from the one I had prepared. He had a triumphant look on his face and asked me what I thought of it. I had a quick look and told him it was clear he had worked hard on it. He said it was the third draft he had prepared. I made appropriate noises. In my mind, I was thinking of Parthasarathi's possible reaction. He was not likely to take kindly to the fact that his draft was not found good enough.

We had the draft vetted by the Legal and Treaties Division, and kept it ready.

Simultaneously, we prepared a draft agreement for the Joint Commission. When we sent it to PV for approval, he called me saying, 'What is so special about this draft? It is absolutely colourless. How is it different from other Joint Commissions?' I told him it was not our intention to have any special Joint Commission with Pakistan. He was not satisfied. He was particularly worried about the subsequent scenario on the no-war front. Had anyone explained to the PM, he asked, the probable end result of the negotiating process? That it would lead to our signing a no-war pact of some sort? PV added that the PM had already said that she did not want to sign anything with Pakistan. She would then blame the ministry for not pointing out all the implications to her.

I conveyed PV's point to Rasgotra. His view was simple: If we had to sign a treaty, we should sign it, provided it took care of our concerns. He talked to PV and got his approval for the Joint Commission draft, which Rasgotra handed over to Pakistan Charge d'Affaires on 26 June. I then prepared a draft note for Rasgotra, suggesting the line he would take in his talks in Islamabad in August. The note made it clear that while Pakistan was not likely to accept our draft, we should be prepared to sign it, in case they did. Rasgotra made a few changes in the note and sent it to Parthasarathy, PV and Alexander.

Natwar returned on 9 July and now things began to move. Rasgotra and I were scheduled to go to Islamabad in August for bilateral talks. We had to go in any case for a meeting of the South Asian countries to discuss cooperation; we would stay on for additional two days on 11 and 12 August. Natwar told me he would join us for the bilateral talks if necessary. 'Let Rasgotra handle the South Asian meeting.' I had my doubts if the Foreign Secretary was going to like it if Natwar came to Islamabad.

Rasgotra said Parthasarathi had cleared the draft. I was surprised and a bit sceptical. Parthasarathi told me that he was not very happy with the draft and the covering note. Both countries were sparring with each other. Our attempt was to give Pakistan drafts of agreements on friendship, etc., which Pakistan was not comfortable with. We had also prepared a comprehensive draft treaty, covering all aspects of bilateral relations. In particular, our draft called for denying any kind of military base or facility to anyone, which would violate the core principle of non-alignment.

Rasgotra, Parthasarathi and Natwar were busy preparing for the PM's visit to the US, which was scheduled for 27 August the same year. They were all going to the US ahead of her, and so there was not much time for Pakistan.

On the 19 July 1982, Alexander sent a note to Rasgotra, saying the PM did not approve the idea of a comprehensive treaty, which would include elements of non-aggression and friendship. He added that Pakistan had, in principle, agreed to our two proposals of Joint Commission and friendship treaty, and we should hold them to their commitment. So, he said that the MEA should prepare the draft of a friendship treaty, and the Foreign Secretary should hand it over to Pakistan when he went there in August.

Rasgotra showed me Alexander's note on the same afternoon. He was obviously upset that the PM had rejected his draft or his concept of the draft. He told me to prepare a new draft and get it approved by the PM before she left for Washington on her tour. He himself was leaving for

Washington the same evening, and so was Natwar. Hence, I had very little time left.

But there was a problem. Alexander's note did not make much sense to me. He was labouring under the impression that we would, eventually, sign two documents—a no-war pact and a friendship treaty. But a friendship treaty had to have all the elements of non-aggression, along with other related elements. Our offer to Pakistan was not additional to, but in lieu of, their proposal of a no-war pact. So, how to proceed?

I looked to Parthasarathi for help. He held a very grim view of Alexander on his understanding of Pakistan. We decided that the draft we had prepared in January at the time of Shahi's visit was a very good document and that we should get it approved by the PM. So, Parthasarathi called Alexander on the RAX from my room. Alexander told him, 'I have already conveyed the PM's instructions.' But, Parthasarathi was not letting it go; he eventually persuaded Alexander to agree to discuss the note with him the next day.

Next day, Parthasarathi saw Alexander at about 6.00 p.m. Before that I had already given him all the papers. I had told him it would be for the best if he could get the PM's approval to which Parthasarathi replied that he did not want to go over Alexander's head. He added that Alexander was a fighter and won't give in easily. However, after half an hour, I was called in—Parthasarathi had done his job and indicated the lines on which a note for the PM should be prepared. A few minutes later, Parthasarathi came into my room and said that they had a very heated argument for 15 minutes, but ultimately, Alexander came around. 'He just does not understand these things.' Finally, I prepared a draft note, included Parthasarathi's name in it, got it approved by Alexander and prepared a fair note for the Foreign Minister.

Now, tackling the Foreign Minister was not going to be easy. P.V. Narasimha Rao was a gentleman, and I did not like the persistent rumours about him going to some other ministry. But he had been left out of all the discussions so far, not because I wanted to keep him out. I was racing against time, and it was part of good tactics to get things cleared by Parthasarathi and Alexander, two people whose voices carried great, almost decisive, weight with the PM. But PV's signature on the note was equally indispensable.

I saw PV the next morning. He said, 'We shall discuss those things [drafts for talks with Pakistan] when PM is away.' I told him we had to obtain the PM's approval before her departure. In that case, he said, 'Let us discuss it the following day', but it was a holiday. We met on 23 August in the ministry and PV was clearly unhappy at having to rush the whole thing. He said if Natwar had not gone to Islamabad, all this would not have been necessary. By giving the draft to us, Pakistan had thrown the ball in our court. They were forcing the pace. The PM had said very clearly last year that she did not want to sign anything with Pakistan. But once we gave them our draft, the negotiations would start, and we would not be able to avoid signing a treaty. I told him Natwar could not have refused to accept the draft.

He flashed back, 'Why not? I had made Agha Shahi agree that we would not exchange drafts.'

I told him we could drag on the negotiations easily into the next year. Eventually, if we obtained a treaty to our satisfaction, we should sign it.

We went over the draft. We were introducing three elements that were important for us. Our idea was to present the Pakistanis with a draft, which they would find extremely difficult to accept. Nevertheless, the draft was very reasonable and easy to justify to everyone. The three crucial points were: overriding importance to Simla Agreement as the basis of our relations, exclusively bilateral settlement of disputes and non-granting of any military facility to outside powers. In addition, we titled the treaty as one of peace, friendship and cooperation. Parthasarathi said the word 'friendship' would stick in Pakistan's throat since it would remind them of our friendship treaty with the Soviet Union.

There was one other point of great importance for us—we wanted a categorical reconfirmation of the LoC in J&K. At the time of Simla Agreement, we had tried hard to negotiate with Bhutto to get the LoC formalized. Bhutto did not agree but later did try to incorporate Pakistan-occupied Kashmir into Pakistan, though without success. We had one more opportunity now, not for a formal conversion of the LoC into an international boundary, but something close.

The principal difficulty we faced was about the article in the draft dealing with non-alignment and granting of military bases. We wanted to make it as watertight as possible. We were quite clear in our minds that we were not going to give any bases to the Soviets or anyone else. At the same time, Pakistanis made it no secret, during their visit in January-February, that they could not accept any restrictions on their sovereignty. This suited us since we could legitimately press for inclusion of such a provision. But we wanted to draft the treaty in such a way that it did not enter into a conflict with the Indo-Soviet Treaty of 1971. We had numerous discussions on this point. The Foreign Minister was most anxious that the treaty with Pakistan should not dilute our relations with the Union of Soviet Socialist Republics (USSR) in any way. Under the 1971 Treaty, the two countries were required to consult with each other in case either was threatened by a third country and wished to take steps to remove the threat. What would happen if either the Soviets/Afghans were to attack Pakistan or if Pakistan/US were to intrude into Afghanistan? Also, a no-war pact with Pakistan would effectively freeze the situation on Indo-Pak border, thus leaving Pakistan with a free hand on their northwestern borders with Afghanistan. How would the Russians react to it?

Immediately after Shahi's visit, it was decided that the Foreign Secretary and I would go to Moscow to keep the Soviets informed of our discussions with Pakistan. Somehow, we could not go. Now, PV felt strongly that we should talk to the Soviets before leaving for Islamabad in a week's time. Practically, this was not possible, since the foreign secretary was in Washington with the PM. We thought of sending Jagota, head of the Legal and Treaties Division, to Moscow, but he said he was a closely watched man because of his involvement with the Law of the Sea negotiations. So, we decided to call Vishnu Ahuja (our ambassador in Moscow) to Delhi. We would brief him, and he, in turn, would brief the Soviets. All agreed that the briefing should not be done with the Soviet ambassador in Delhi.

This aspect had been examined and many learned notes had been written. The draft had been subjected to close scrutiny from the Soviet angle. In the article dealing with non-alignment, we included a ban on granting military bases or facilities to anyone in any form 'which brings tension to the area, or which adversely affects the security of the other party'. Some of us felt that this qualifying phrase diluted the obligations on Pakistan. Jagota, on the other hand, argued very strongly in favour of retaining this phrase. He said that in the absence of this phrase, the article would be weak and Pakistan might even accept it. This phrase protected our interests since it gave us the right to decide what affected our security interests. Further, the phrase would also protect our interests with the Soviet Union. In any case, the Soviet Union, being by far the stronger power, was hardly likely to invoke the treaty, in case they were in trouble. PV raised various scenarios. Finally, we amended the article, and everybody was satisfied. The new phrase was: 'particularly those (bases and facilities) which adversely affect the security interests of the other party'.

Having resolved all doubts, I prepared a covering note for talks with Pakistan, got it signed by PV and sent it to Alexander. Parthasarathi was rather keen that his name should be mentioned in the note, which I did. I also referred to Jagota, Rasgotra and Natwar. Let everyone's name be included for the sake of history!

On the morning of 26 August, Parthasarathi came into my room. The PM had consulted him about the treaty the previous night at 10.00 p.m. 'I told her that it was alright, Pakistan would not agree because of three things: reference to friendship in the title, exclusively bilateral settlement of disputes and the denial of bases. I read out to her the relevant articles. She has agreed.' Within a few hours, I got the papers from Alexander with his minute of the meeting: the PM had agreed. We could give the draft to Pakistan.

The draft was now ready. Rasgotra would give it to Naik early next month. My idea was that we should hand over the draft only during the last round of talks before our departure, so that they would not have the time to study and react to it while we were still there. Let them come to Delhi after a few months with their counter proposals.

One more thing about the draft: We wanted to get the LoC reconfirmed. So, we included reference to Para 4 (ii) of the Simla Agreement* in such a way that our point of view would be taken care of.

We returned from Pakistan after spending a week there and holding bilateral talks. The new Pakistani team had put their best foot forward. The hospitality was excellent and expressions of friendship exuberant. Naik acted smoothly; years of multilateral work had given him good command over putting across his point of view in a persuasive and inoffensive manner.

Rasgotra performed excellently all throughout. I thought that during the second session, he was perhaps rather soft on Pakistan, but he had a game plan and he stuck to it. At the first night of the bilateral talks, I reminded him of the PM's instructions and of her letter to Zia, which was sent on 25 May. We also had to keep in mind the political realities back home. I drew his attention to the Foreign Minister's statement in the House that our position on Kashmir would be reiterated at the talks. Rasgotra was, of course, fully aware of all this, but I felt it was my duty to draw his attention to it again. However, on Kashmir he would not go beyond saying, 'You know our position and we know yours.'

When he presented our draft on friendship treaty to Naik, it came as a surprise to Pakistan, judging from the reaction on their faces. Perhaps, they never expected that we would go so as far as to hand over a draft of a friendship treaty.

Pakistan took the line that we should concentrate on the non-aggression pact and the Joint Commission; the friendship treaty could be considered later. 'We should first build the two pillars of non-aggression and joint commission; the super structure of friendship can be constructed once the pillars

---

*Para 4 (ii) of the Simla Agreement said that in J&K, the LoC resulting from the ceasefire of 17 December 1971 would be respected by both sides without prejudice to their respective position on either side.

are built.' This was stated by Zia during our meeting and I had kept a record. This was a clever way of putting aside our draft of the friendship treaty. We were certainly not thinking of two separate documents—a non-aggression and a friendship treaty. In fact, we envisaged the friendship treaty as swallowing Pakistan's non-aggression pact, though we did not want to put it quite like that for the time being.

On the matter of the Joint Commission, Pakistan expressed disappointment at the restricted mandate suggested by us. They said it should provide a consultative mechanism to enable the two governments to discuss political and military matters, too. We were opposed to this idea since Pakistan would certainly raise their pet themes of force reductions, nuclear weapon free zone, etc. As it happened, Naik himself had earlier stated that we should elaborate confidence-building measures, which could include meetings between our defence secretaries. In the end, we asked them to send their suggestions to us in writing.

On the third day, Rasgotra asked them pointedly whether they were rejecting our draft out of hand. Naturally, they said 'no', but Naik repeated his story of a step-by-step approach. We told them we were not against such an approach, but which step would come first? We felt that the easiest first step would be the Joint Commission.

The talks ended in a stalemate since no agreement was reached on any of the drafts or on the approach to be followed in subsequent meetings. That meant our mission was successful. We had not conceded anything. We bought time to test Pakistan's intentions and we regained propaganda initiative—we had two drafts in the ring as against one of theirs.

6

BACK IN THE PMO

I regretted that I had not kept a diary when I had served in the PMO earlier. Well, I got another opportunity from 1 September 1982. For some reason that I was not aware of, Kishan Rana, a brilliant officer who had replaced me as joint secretary in the PMO, was coming back to the ministry. Alexander asked Rasgotra for names and my name was in the list of four to five probable candidates. When Alexander discussed the matter with the PM, she asked, 'Why not Gharekhan?' She asked him to speak to Rasgotra and PV. Rasgotra said Alexander had slight hesitation in my going back to the PMO, but he eventually told Rasgotra that they would be ready to consider my name if he was willing to spare me.

'I Am Very Glad to Have You Back'

Alexander called me on 23 August 1982 and asked me to join on 1 September. I was happy since it was a complete vindication for me. But it meant that I was getting into a delicate situation. I could sense that Alexander was not happy. Quite unwillingly and unwittingly, I had become a pawn in the power struggle between Dhawan and Alexander. Rasgotra advised me to make a special effort to remove any prejudice that Alexander might have against me, and at the same time, to work well with Dhawan. There were rumours that Alexander himself was not on a good wicket with the PM and there was even speculation about his successor. What a messy situation for me to get into. Natwar, however, was very happy and told me he had a lot to do with my return to the PMO.

Arjun Sengupta, a distinguished economist and additional secretary in the PMO, told me something quite extraordinary. He said he and many others did not understand why I had to leave the PMO in the first instance. He added 'in strict confidence' that I was regarded as progressive and that this was perhaps an important consideration in the PM's decision to call me back!

When I met the PM for the first time after rejoining in the PMO, I made appropriate noises about the privilege of working with her again. She said, 'I am very glad to have you back. But you would have to work hard. I don't mean only in terms of hours, but in terms of thinking what I should say and so on.' I did not know what she meant. I asked Parthasarathi and Natwar about it—they, too, were clueless.

I had always found the PM a gracious person to work with. She was very polite and would not fail to thank you for the tiniest things (giving her your pen for an autograph, for example). She did not frown upon dissent. Most of us working in the PMO did not hesitate to state our views. She treated us courteously and never raised her voice. She was known to have a sharp temper, but seldom displayed it to the officials. I remember one occasion when she lost her temper—in Nairobi in August 1981. Alexander came back, white with terror, and said, 'She is very angry.' It was about some minor matter. In fact, she usually got upset about small things (distribution of gifts, invitation cards, etc.), but she maintained her calm on the bigger issues.

My first encounter with the PM was back in 1972 in Belgrade where I was posted as counsellor in the embassy. She had come on an official visit. For the banquet in the evening, a speech was prepared in Delhi. When I saw the speech, I was aghast. The very first paragraph spoke of 'a young man from Macedonia', referring to Alexander the Great. Now, Alexander was from Macedonia, but the Macedonia in Greece, not the one which was a province in Yugoslavia. This had to be amended. I spoke to my ambassador P.A. Menon, who agreed with me. He spoke to Rasgotra, who, in turn, spoke to the principal secretary to the PM. The question was 'Who will tell the PM about it?' None of the senior officers were willing to tell the PM that there was a grave error in the speech. Finally, I was asked to see her. I went to her suite, where she was resting, but I was ushered in. I mentioned the problem to her.

She asked, 'What does the ambassador say?' I said he agreed. 'Then change it.' That was the end of the story. She was quite cool about it.

During my earlier stint in the PMO, I had accompanied her to Geneva, where she was invited to deliver the main address to the WHO. There was a transit halt in Bahrain. Someone from the local press had asked her about the Gulf Cooperation Council (GCC). She had said something negative. During the onward flight, I had told her she could have answered that question without causing offence to the members of the GCC. She did not say anything, but when asked the same question in Geneva, she gave a more diplomatic answer and threw a glance at me.

She loved to talk in French, which she had learnt as a student in Switzerland years ago. She had an excellent accent. On the flight, she had invited me to work with her on the few sentences that she would say in French after landing in Geneva.

I must confess I had felt nervous in her presence. Neither did I make any effort nor did I have any ambition to get close to her. It was not possible, and it would have only destroyed me. Maintaining low profile in any case suited my temperament.

All the PM's Men...

Alexander and I got along well. Six months back, his position was shaky. There were reports about his removal and even about his possible successors—Abid Hussain, commerce secretary; P.K. Paul, finance secretary, and Natwar. My return to the PMO was hinted as indication of his weakened position. This was not so, and I told my friends the same. But Alexander was worried. So, Sharada Prasad, PM's information advisor, with his excellent contacts in media, got a couple of newspapers to write about the matter to set his mind at peace. And it did. He seemed to enjoy the PM's confidence, as I had witnessed. When Gen. Hussain Muhammad Ershad, President of Bangladesh, and Indira Gandhi had met in November 1981, she had called Alexander alone for 20 minutes before calling other ministers. She had included him in the breakfast meeting with Margaret Thatcher. These were her ways of showing her confidence in public. Had Alexander lost the PM's confidence, she would not have included him in the breakfast meeting.

Alexander did not exude friendliness. I thought his coldness was only for me. But I found that he behaved like that with everyone. The only time I saw him break into a smile was when I had congratulated him for his first grandson.

Dhawan was the kingpin of the office. He was most able and astute. He was completely loyal to the PM, in or out of office, so for him, matters were simple: 'Whatever helped her was good.' He had a sharp memory. He had to have one not only because the PM might ask him about something or the other at any time, but also because she herself had an incredible memory.

Dhawan was almost always relaxed. I thought he was the only person among all officials who appeared really relaxed in her presence. I found him very useful and helpful. He travelled with her in her car most of the time and thus had access to her more than anyone else. I did not know anything about his private life, except that he was a bachelor. He enjoyed his whisky and smoke, but did not indulge in either in the PM's presence. He was fond of naughty jokes, of which he had a good stock, mostly in Punjabi. He was—had to be—very hard working, but would still let his hair down in the company of a few friends. He said he had not seen any movie in years and the only game he played was the political game. He was closely involved in all election strategies, ministerial changes and state politics, though he did not accompany her on internal tours. Any aspiring politician had to first establish his credentials with him. The PM listened to his advice more than to anyone else, except, of course, Rajiv, her son.

But Dhawan had a rival in Makhanlal Fotedar, a Kashmiri small time political worker, who, for some reason, was influential when it came to political matters. The two disliked each other intensely, though in public, they displayed friendship for each other. Fotedar worked exclusively at 1, Akbar Road, which served as the PM's political office, whereas Dhawan operated from 1, Safdarjung Road, the PM's residence, as well as from the office in South Block and Parliament House. Fotedar was brought in by Sanjay Gandhi, the PM's younger son who had died in a plane crash in June 1981, and worked closely with Rajiv. Fotedar was supposed to plan the party's election campaigns. I had met him only once or twice. He might have been a good person, but I found him a bit slippery.

Rajiv, at the time, had not made a mark in the political life of the country, as his brother did. He had a much cleaner image than Sanjay and was often referred to as 'Mr Clean'. Somehow, he did not appear to have the drive, dynamism or ruthlessness that his brother possessed. He was reported not to be an influential speaker. Natwar said that Indira Gandhi did not rely on Rajiv as much as she did on Sanjay. Rajiv campaigned in the state elections in Karnataka and Andhra Pradesh. He spoke about the Asian Games and dangers in the Indian Ocean. The PM, too, campaigned tirelessly, but lost both elections ignominiously. She recovered some sympathy and prestige when she won the Delhi election in early February, even though Delhi was known to be a Jan Sangh or the Bharatiya Janata Party (BJP) stronghold.

I had no doubt that a very large number of people would support the PM without any hesitation, provided she made it convincingly clear that she was not preparing the *gaddi* (throne) for her son. Her obsession, or what most people perceived as her obsession, to ensure the succession in her family, had cost her a lot of support. People were just not ready to automatically endorse the son's claim to the leadership. Rajiv had worked very hard to organize the Asian Games in 1981. All those who had worked in the Asiad spoke very highly of him. The PM herself had mentioned this to some foreign visitors. This was undoubtedly true. But people, certainly outside Delhi, were not impressed with all this talk.

'I Would Stay, I Never Quit'

We hosted the 7th Summit of the NAM in Delhi in March 1983. Our preference was to host the eighth summit, but we were running into problems because the North Koreans, and particularly the Libyans, were also strong contenders for it. Fortunately or unfortunately, the Iran–Iraq War and Iran's strong opposition to Baghdad hosting the seventh summit created a groundswell, which we did nothing to stem, in favour of Delhi hosting the seventh summit. It was a good opportunity for the political leadership to project themselves on the international scene for three years as chairman or chairperson of the NAM. (Indira Gandhi was very particular about the use of the gender-neutral terms. 'Mankind' always had to be referred to as 'humankind', etc.) If she won the 1985 election, the NAM would provide a good platform to the heir apparent to project himself as a leader at domestic and international fronts.

The NAM conference itself was a 'success' as far as conferences go. There was, in fact, a tremendous euphoria in the MEA and in the circles around the PM. After the conference, there were talks about the follow-up action. Rasgotra set up a new NAM division and I was given two officers to assist me in the PMO. Rasgotra did not look too happy when Alexander told him that my office was being strengthened for the follow-up work.

It was a taxing experience for me. The PM took her chairmanship seriously as indeed she should have. She insisted on chairing and sitting through all the late-night sessions of the conference, all of which usually ended at 3.00 a.m. Her stamina impressed everyone. I suggested she need not stay for the entire duration of the night sessions, but she said, 'I would stay, I never quit, and I am used to it.' This meant that I spent 16–17 hours a day with her for five days.

She never lost her cool during these sessions. She only got irritated on the last day when the conference documents were not ready, but she did not explode except once on 11 March 1983. What had transpired was as follows.

The Sri Lankan President J.R. Jayewardene presented a proposal that the PM, as chairperson of the NAM, should constitute a committee of a few heads of state and lead them in a delegation for talks with others, mainly President of the US, Ronald Reagan. Now, Indira Gandhi had strong views about Jayewardene and, if I can say, detested him. The meeting between him and her was a delight.

He asked for the PM's support for his proposal.

She said, 'But we have already talked to him [Reagan] at Cancun.' He said there was no harm in talking to him again; new voices were being heard in the US.

She said, 'Yes, but they were all outside the administration.'

In his reply, he said, 'Anyway, we would lose nothing by talking to him. I am confident he would respond.'

She responded by saying, 'I am not sure.'

It went on like that. When he expressed hope that she would visit Sri Lanka, she replied, 'Well, let us hope so one of these days. Actually, I am still catching up with visits promised in 1980.'

This was met with retort from his end, 'Same here.'

I was present at all these bilateral meetings.

Meanwhile, Chancellor Bruno Kreisky of Austria wrote

to Jayewardene about Sirimavo Bandaranaike, the former PM of Sri Lanka. Jayewardene replied to him, 'I am glad you do not wish to interfere in the internal affairs of my country because in that case, I should have known what to do.' Kreisky sent a copy of Jayewardene's letter to the PM who wrote to Kreisky that now he would have a better idea about Jayewardene's democracy! She also told Kreisky that Jayewardene had been carrying on a venomous propaganda against her and her family.

Now, under those circumstances, one could easily judge Indira Gandhi's reaction to anything coming from that man. She made no secret of her opposition. She carried on effective lobbying against Jayewardene's idea with all the leaders she met. 'I find it quite humiliating to go with a begging bowl to Washington. I have already talked to all of them, etc.' In any case, she said, 'This was a stupid proposal* but even if it was not, I am not going to support it since its author is Jayewardene.'

Given this background, I could well understand the way she exploded when she saw a conference paper in which the conference welcomed the proposal and asked her to take a team to different countries. She told Muchkund Dubey, my senior colleague who was chairing the economic committee of the conference, 'How could this proposal be included without my clearance? Do they expect that I, Indira Gandhi, would go with a begging bowl to Reagan?' She asked Dubey to kill it. It was not Dubey's fault, as we learnt later that Sengupta had told him that the PM had approved the text. Natwar and Alexander also received their share of displeasure from the PM.

---

*Jayewardene's proposal of forming a small committee to go meet Reagan.

The Many Hues of World Leaders

I saw all the leaders since I was present at all the meetings with the PM. There was Sergeant Samuel Kanyon Doe, head of state of Liberia, who had personally shot his predecessor President William Tolbert. Then there was Col. Desiré Delano Bouterse, leader of Suriname, who got 15 intellectuals and trade union leaders executed in cold blood in December 1982. There were other leaders from Africa about whom we knew very little. Looking at most of them, one would not suspect them of possessing such ruthlessness, though Doe did give me that impression as did Bouterse, whom I did not like at all. Regrettably, we had to ask Bouterse to chair the conference a couple of times; he was one of the vice chairmen. He was most willing since it earned him opportunities to get himself photographed as the chairman. Then there was Zia-ul-Haq of Pakistan, too. Looking at him, talking to him, who would suspect that he had Bhutto, the man who made him Chief of Staff and asked him to take over as Martial Law Administrator, condemned to what Indira Gandhi called 'political murder'? A motley crowd it was.

For instance, take Yasser Arafat. He was supposed to be a freedom fighter and a revolutionary leader. One would not expect him to be too concerned about protocol matters. But no, the chap was more protocol- and status-conscious than the authentic heads of state. On the opening day, Arafat was listed to speak after the Yugoslav and Zambian presidents. He protested to the extent of even boycotting our President's reception. We had a situation on our hands and the PM had to call Fidel Castro, leader of Cuba, for help, and he said, 'If Arafat is a friend, he should not behave like this.' We had to send an emissary to call the sulking Arafat from his hotel.

The PM and Castro jointly appealed to him and suggested a compromise. His ego having been flattered, he said, 'Whatever you say, my sister!'

The Libyan leader Abdessalam Jalloud had kept his arrival time such a secret that nobody knew about it until literally half an hour before his landing. The same was true of Arafat. The President of Iraq wanted to send several hundred commandos, but he did not come in the end. The Iranian PM also did not announce his arrival schedule. The PM went to the airport once, but he was not there yet. And when he did land at about 1.00 a.m., only the Chief of Protocol was there to meet him. What kind of revolutionary were these people, who were so afraid for their lives? Arafat was not only scared, he was also highly protocol conscious.

On the last day of the conference, Arafat did his best to complicate matters on the Iran–Iraq question. He instigated the Iraqis to increase their demands, even though a compromise had been reached the day earlier with the Iranians. At about midnight, the PM herself got personally involved in this affair. Arafat was called. The PM suggested some formulation to him; he agreed and managed to sell it to both sides. Having created the problem, he was only too willing to help with the solution.

For all that, Indira Gandhi seemed to like him. She remarked to me once: 'Arafat is a real brother; he had inquired 10 times about my cold today.' There was no answer to this logic.

There were very few leaders in whose company I saw the PM relax. These were Julius Nyerere of Tanzania, Kenneth Kaunda of Zambia and Forbes Burnham of Guyana. The meeting with even Apollo Milton Obote, President of Uganda, was not completely informal, as it was with the other three. With the three, the atmosphere was totally free of tension, with banter and jokes. They teased her about the issue of using chairman, chairwoman, chairperson. There was exchange of advices. She was also relaxed around Samora Machel of Mozambique. He was a hearty person, who smiled and laughed all the time. Of course, all of them asked her for increased assistance, credits, scholarships, etc., as did many other leaders. She did not make any commitment to any of them, not even to Nyerere and Kaunda. This was a great quality she had—to refrain from agreeing to requests on the spot. It was not easy for the PM not to make at least friendly or sympathetic noises when another leader made a request. One usually overstated friendly sentiments. But this lady was most cool about such things. She would only say, 'We would look into it, please give us a note.'

It was interesting to witness the talks between the PM and Burnham. He said something about pressure to devalue his country's currency. She said, referring to the devaluation of the rupee in 1966, 'I don't mind confessing that that was the biggest mistake of my life.' About Reagan, Burnham said he was an obscurantist. Also, he just skimmed over subjects—it was difficult to engage him in a serious conversation about anything. I found that Reagan was the favourite whipping boy of most leaders—Reagan, not the US. Once the PM said something about 'until the next American election', to which Burnham quickly added, 'or until Reagan's death, whichever is earlier.' They were all extremely wary of Reagan.

Soviet ambassador Vasily Nazarovich Rykov brought a letter for the PM from Yuri Andropov, general secretary of the Communist Party of Soviet Union. It was a reply to her letter after the NAM Summit, suggesting he go to New York for the General Assembly session for a few days. Andropov's letter was silent over this point. But Rykov conveyed an oral message, which was a definite disappointment. He said that the PM's letter had been carefully considered by the leadership. Andropov was always ready to meet Reagan, provided it would lead to positive results. Reagan's actions did not give ground to think that he wanted such positive results. Also, Reagan might use such meeting for his own political ends and the Democratic Party might interpret it as interference in America's internal affairs. For all these reasons, the leadership had come to the conclusion that Andropov should not go to New York.

Andropov's message came as something of a shock to the PM, particularly since Andropov's letter was warm and promised cooperation to her in her responsibility as the Chair of the NAM. Rykov would have expected some reaction from her because he pointedly asked if she had any message for Andropov. She smiled and said, 'Give him my greetings and good wishes.' Very cool.

Our general assessment was that Andropov would decide to go to New York because the Russians were not on the defensive at all on the question of nuclear disarmament. The peace movements in the West were quite strong and the North Atlantic Treaty Organization's (NATO's) decision on the deployment of new Pershing II ballistic missiles was due for implementation in December 1983. A visit to New York would have provided an excellent platform to the Soviets to air their views about disarmament.

7

WORKING WITH MRS G

'It is unfortunate that in every sphere, the United States administration takes an anti-India stance. We have gone out of our way and at the risk of political alienation within India, to be friendly and accommodating to the United States, but to what avail?'

The above text was the PM's minute of the meeting on 28 March 1983, which she added to a note I had recorded during my talks with a visiting State Department official. The issue at hand was the granting of a visa by the US to Jagjit Singh Chohan, the Sikh leader who had been campaigning for an independent state of Khalistan. By inclination, the PM found it difficult to be genuinely, instinctively friendly with the US, as she was with Britain (but not with the Soviets). During the previous two years, she had tried hard to be friendly with the Americans. Her visit to the US in 1982 was successful. Evidently, she found Reagan to be a charming person. But charm did not take one far. There had been no concrete benefit to us from the Americans. Fuel for the Tarapur Atomic Power Station near Bombay (now Mumbai) was a major irritant, but it was somehow settled with the French agreeing to replace the US as the supplier. But this in no way had helped matters with the US, which refused to give the spares for Tarapur. More than these individual differences, it was the attitude of the US administration that was the bigger obstacle. If one wanted to have good relations with them, it was possible only on their terms. No self-respecting nation would accept that kind of arrogance.

Reagan and Indira Gandhi exchanged polite letters, and that too frequently. But I had a feeling that they were both maintaining this show only for the sake of records; neither's heart was in it. Reagan did not care for any other country, including the Western alliance, barring his own. He believed in 'Fortress America'. India was nowhere in his priority list. American officials referred to us as the dominant power in our region. (And regrettably, some of us got flattered at being so described.) He was not bothered much even about the Chinese.

We had a one-hour briefing meeting with the PM on the visit of the American Secretary of State, George Shultz. The length of the meeting was unusual. Also unusual was the fact that not once during the one hour did she send out a note to Dhawan or otherwise engage herself in any small activity, such as filing her nails. Even when she did that, she was all ears. The Foreign Secretary had carefully prepared a list of subjects for the PM to raise with Shultz. She simply said, 'I am only going to talk to him about bilateral political relations and you, PV, deal with everything else.'

As our discussions progressed, she agreed to take up a few

more subjects. As always, she took a commonsensical view of things. If anyone made a 'learned' or 'profound' analysis, she would say, 'But what role can we play?' or 'What has that got to do with this?'. She did not seem to have a high opinion of the MEA. Half the time, we talked about the Middle East, Arafat's difficulties, Soviet's role, Reagan's letter to her on 7 June and what she should tell Shultz about it. At the end, she asked me to give her a note on what she should say. She herself had very clear ideas about it.

The PM visited several countries in June that year—Yugoslavia, Finland, Denmark, Norway and Austria. Before we returned from the European visit, American ambassador Harry Barnes had said something to the effect that he could not understand why Indians got so upset about the grant of visa to Jagjit Singh Chohan; after all, people advocating independence for Puerto Rico also came to India. The press and political parties as well as the PM were all very upset with the ambassador. One of the Congress general secretaries asked for his recall as did, for some reason, the Bihar assembly. Inevitably, inference was drawn that the ambassador was not speaking entirely on his own. Wisely, the government decided not to give any official reaction. Barnes came to see Alexander, who told him he had added insult to injury. I told Barnes that the analogy with Puerto Rico was particularly unfortunate from the American point since it would generate pressure on the Indian government to change its vote on Puerto Rico in the UN from abstention to affirmative.

For some reason, the secretaries in the MEA had a soft corner for Barnes. Alexander also felt the same way. He once said, 'We all know what a sincere and warm-hearted person Barnes is!' Rasgotra tried to help Barnes out of the situation. His idea was that Barnes would make a press statement that he did not mean to draw an analogy between the two situations, etc. Barnes merely issued a statement through his press officer. He and Alexander were pressing the PM to host a lunch or at least a breakfast for Shultz. She was not keen but felt the pressure. My worry was that the Canadian deputy PM, Allan MacEachen, was coming soon after Shultz and the discrimination would be blatant. When I mentioned this to the PM, she said she had not yet decided on the lunch. She agreed with my suggestion of tea.

The name of Prince Norodom Sihanouk, the mercurial ruler of Cambodia, came up during the meeting about Shultz. He wanted to stop by to talk to the PM. She was not unwilling. Rasgotra suggested that Sihanouk could be persuaded to break with the coalition government in Phnom Penh. I said he might ask for a quid pro quo. The PM retorted, 'From me? Never, he would never ask for quid pro quo from me, he knows me too well for that, long before I was in the government, when I was only my father's daughter.' She added that it was not that Sihanouk was not intelligent, but he had no political sense at all. 'His voice is so shrill that it gets on my nerves.'

Shultz arrived in June 1983. The PM met him alone for 75 minutes, whereafter PV, Rasgotra, Alexander and I joined them for about 25 minutes. Someone asked about their tête-à-tête. All Shultz said was that he received insight into several issues from his talk with the PM. The PM, meanwhile, had a triumphant look on her face as if she had really enjoyed giving him lessons about international affairs. She said, 'Oh, we just wandered around.'

This was our problem. After others left, Alexander and I asked her again about her talk with Shultz. She mentioned a few points, but was generally not very communicative. She said she spoke to him about India's image in America as a Soviet client and other related issues. Ideally, she should have dictated the gist of her conversation like her father Jawaharlal Nehru always did. Indira Gandhi did not seem to share her father's ideological affinity with the Russians. She was certainly more at ease with them and other socialist and progressive countries. But she was by no means sold on the Russians. I personally saw her giving hell to the Soviet ambassador in Delhi. For her, the Soviet connection was an important factor in India's political scene. To the extent that the Soviets influenced the communist parties to support her, they were useful. But the communists had stopping supporting her for some years. The communist parties bitterly opposed Emergency and voted against her during the 1977 elections. She never forgot or forgave the Russians for that. She frequently told the Russians that it was strange that the extreme Left should join hands with the extreme Right in weakening her position. She accused the communists of supporting the Indo-Soviet Cultural Society, rather than the newly established Friends of the Soviet Union. She continued to send very warm messages about time-tested friendship and all that. But there was no illusion on either side. She knew that the Soviets had equally good relations with Morarji Desai, once a very important leader of the Congress party, who was known for his Right-wing views. And the Soviets knew that the same Indira Gandhi had broken up with the Communist Party of India under the influence of Sanjay, her son, who openly advocated free enterprise. Both countries needed each other. This was as it should be. It was only with mutuality of interest and benefit that friendship could last.

The people she was really anxious to please were the British. She would go out of her way to give time to visiting Lords and minor nobility, even on Sundays. She quite genuinely enjoyed talking to them. She was extremely keen to attend Prince Charles's wedding and was so disappointed she could not because President Neelam Sanjiva Reddy insisted on going. She even wrote to all and sundry how Reddy decided to go even though he had told her that he would not go. I had never seen the extent of her bitterness as on that occasion. She took great care in selecting the present for the royal couple. But then she was always very particular about the gifts for foreign dignitaries.

When Margaret Thatcher, the British PM, came to India on a visit in 1981, I remember what the PM had to say about her. As her aircraft was taking off, I asked the PM what she thought of Thatcher. She said, 'She is still not sure of herself, she lacks confidence.' Here was a senior woman PM, talking about her junior counterpart! But later, they got along quite well, though they did not address each other by first names (as the PM did with Kaunda and Nyerere).

Indira Gandhi, the Person

Indira Gandhi loved to write letters. Rather, she loved to amend drafts of letters, speeches and messages. The moment she would get a draft, she would reach for her pencil and start amending. Sharada Prasad called her a compulsive sub-editor. The end product would be invariably better than the draft. She preferred simple and direct expression, in the spoken medium. She did not even read the MEA's drafts. They came to me, and I tried to reword them in her writing style. My efforts did not fare too badly.

Another thing she took great pains about was the menu and seating plans for her dinners. During the NAM Summit, she hosted daily lunches for a few heads at a time. Every morning, during the meeting, I would give her a table plan, which would have been prepared by Hamid Ansari, chief of protocol. She would make a few changes and suggest some more. I would give her a revised plan. More changes would follow, followed by another plan and then another. This would go on until about half an hour before lunch and the table plans would then be printed. Fortunately, the Rashtrapati Bhavan, known for hosting state lunches and dinners, was quick with the job.

One day, French President François Mitterand called her from Paris. I prepared for her a few phrases in French (which she found no opportunity to use). The talk was all about the Williamsburg Summit of G-7 (the seven industrialized countries, namely, the US, Canada, Japan, the United Kingdom (UK), France, Italy and Germany) and the president of European Commission. Mitterand had suggested an international monetary conference within the framework of the International Monetary Fund (IMF). We, the non-aligned, had also made a similar proposal. He promised the PM to take this up in Williamsburg. She was quite pleased with the conversation and with herself because she neatly slipped in a sentence about Reagan, which Mitterand would have liked to hear, owning to his dislike of Reagan. He promised to come to New York for the General Assembly session. I was convinced that Mitterand was making all those pleasing noises about North–South cooperation and dialogue because he wanted concrete gains for France in the commercial field. Simultaneously, with his call came a pressing plea to us to buy a certain number of Super Puma helicopters!

I was surprised that the PM loved to receive honours, particularly international ones. She was awarded a medal by the International Olympic Committee, which was made much fuss of in the media. Then, after some months, some woman from Chandigarh suggested that she should be nominated for the UN Population Award. To my surprise, the PM showed interest in it. I was asked to speak to the health secretary to organize the acceptance of the honour. I got a message from New York that the jury had selected her and the Chinese minister for family planning. The award consisted of a citation and $10,000. I thought it would be beneath her to be on the same podium as a minister from China and suggested that our permanent representative might be instructed to accept the award on her behalf, but she did not agree. She received the award in person during her visit to New York.

G.K. Reddy, an influential journalist, told me that the PM's great ambition was to get the Nobel Peace Prize. I did not believe him. But a few weeks later, Alexander told me that there was a proposal or a move by some people to nominate her for the Nobel. Kreisky had apparently suggested it to her and promised to gather support for it. Was that the reason she was keen to go to Austria? She had said a number of times that she wanted to go to Austria only to talk to Kreisky. Alexander also said that he would talk to me about this matter later and that we would have to plan out the campaign for the Nobel Peace Prize very carefully.

Yes, Prime Minister!

We went to Yugoslavia, Finland, Denmark, Norway and Austria from 8–18 June 1983. It was a hectic tour. We had delicious food and excellent wine everywhere. The leaders in all five countries went out of their way to be nice to her, devoting a lot of time to her. Particularly in Denmark, PM Poul Schlüter and his wife spent nearly all the time with her, being very attentive to her needs. The latter absolutely charmed the PM to the extent that she was the only spouse to whom the PM wrote a personal letter after returning to Delhi. The tour was undoubtedly a big success for her. She received ovation and adoration fit for a world leader, and enjoyed every minute of it.

On one occasion, during the visit to Denmark, the PM said something to the effect that she was not angry every time she raised her voice. Thereupon, Alexander mumbled something. So, she immediately told him loud and clear, 'But you know when I yell at you!'

These prime ministerial visits were a great strain on the ambassadors. There was tension all around in the Indian camp. The ambassadors were scared about things going wrong. Natwar had told me that earlier that was not the case. But now she was getting older. The other, more important factor was that the grandchildren often accompanied her on these tours, and she was most particular about their programme. When the children would not go with her to official functions, she would personally go into great details to ascertain how they would spend their time. She showered love on them in public. During one week in Belgrade in the same tour, we were taking a little walk in the garden when Priyanka, Rajiv's daughter, came to call her for dinner. The PM linked her arms with hers and walked away, marching in military steps. Indira Gandhi really enjoyed playing like that with her granddaughter.

While her family gave her joy, there were some small matters that would upset her. In Oslo, Sonia Gandhi was seated below the ambassador. The PM blew her top. She asked Alexander to convey her deep disappointment to the ambassador and said she would not go to any other function unless the correct protocol was ensured. She was right about the protocol; Sonia Gandhi was the No. 2 in the party. But it was not totally the ambassador's fault. He did tell the hosts about Sonia Gandhi's precedence, but they insisted that in Norway, the ambassador took precedence over everyone except the PM. The ambassador could have tried harder. He could have mentioned it to me, and the ire would have fallen on me.

After the incident of the seating plan at the dinner, the PM became rather cantankerous. She strongly objected to the return dinner in Vienna to be hosted by her. She had personally approved the return dinner and even selected the menu. Her answer to Dhawan was: 'So what? Why did you put up such a programme to me at all?'

But the worst was in Austria. Kreisky had decided to give up office; his relations with his successor Alfred Sinowitz were not very cordial. The ambassador in Vienna reported this, saying Kreisky would not be in Vienna but would meet the PM in Alpbach. All this was known to her before we left Delhi. But while in Oslo, she asked Dhawan to call the ambassador. The ambassador said the situation was similar to one if Morarji Desai was to become the PM when Nehru was still alive. She got angry. She dictated a devastating note, lambasting the species called ambassadors and condemned the entire ministry. She said the ambassadors did not understand the Nehru family. 'We are not bureaucrats, we don't care for office, etc.' She concluded the note by saying that the ambassadors were all ill-informed not only about India but also about the countries of their posting and that the government would function so much better if the MEA was more effective and cooperative. Fortunately, she did not sign the note (for which Dhawan took credit). In general, I found that she treated the ambassadors with indifference and even contempt. My advice to them had been: 'Don't try to get close to her, keep as far away from her as possible, but be available.'

But there were several aspects of her personality which can be described as concerning, unpredictable and, at times, humorous. For instance, I sent a note asking for her approval that the Mathura refinery might be commissioned during Soviet Deputy PM Ivan Arkhipov's visit. She returned the note with the following comment: 'I suppose we have no way out of this refinery, but I am worried (in spite of various reports from experts) about its effect on the Taj.' Then, in the last week of June 1983, Arafat sent an urgent message to the PM, asking for help between the Palestinians and 'our Syrian brothers'. This was after Syria had thrown him out. The PM's remark on the telegram was, 'I hope the ancient monuments of Baalbek do not get caught in this crossfire.' Here was Arafat's SOS and she was worried about Baalbek! She had concerns for Arafat, but did not do anything.

A cabinet meeting was held to discuss the related television programmes and about extending those to different cities. The quality of programmes was freely criticized. When someone suggested that Satyajit Ray should be asked to prepare new programmes, the PM said, 'No, he does not want to work for the government.' Alexander spoke about the BBC series 'Yes, Minister', which had just been aired. The PM asked him, 'Is this the first time you were watching the series?' He replied with a yes. She continued, 'I hope you can recognize yourself there!'

8

TROUBLE IN SRI LANKA

The Sri Lanka trouble blew up in July 1983. The Tamil community in Sri Lanka formed about 20 per cent of the population. They resented the discrimination practised by the government against them. In July, they revolted under the leadership of a man called Velupillai Prabhakaran. The Tamil militants called themselves 'tigers' and called for an independent state of their own under the banner of 'Eelam'. The PM was so worried, she told Parthasarathi that she could not sleep the whole night.

Blowing Hot and Cold with Jayewardene

She had never liked Jayewardene, and she was right in her instincts. This fellow had really shown himself up for what he was: a second-rate politician. He told PV that his primary and only concern was to make the Sinhalese people happy. Not a word of sympathy for the Tamils. He was trying to convert a domestic, communal, law-and-order problem into a foreign issue, essentially an Indian threat. A United Press International correspondent reported from Colombo that Sri Lanka had approached the US, the UK, Pakistan and Bangladesh for military assistance. This had been confirmed to us by those governments. The British had even publicly admitted this. Yet, the Sri Lankan government described the report as baseless. Besides, the help was requested not to deal with the law and order situation, but to deal with possible foreign invasion. The President was quoted by the official press as saying that if invaded, they would fight. 'Maybe we would lose, but with dignity.'

This bogey of foreign invasion was difficult to understand. Jayewardene had won massive support in a referendum just a few months ago. He had no challenge from his party. He was a virtual dictator. And now he had outlawed three political parties on the ground that they advocated separation. These parties were leftist. He was always very pro-US, but now he seemed determined to establish his credentials beyond all possible doubts with the Americans. And the latter were thrilled at the prospect of getting some berthing rights in Trincomalee Port of Sri Lanka.

We were in a difficult spot. There was tremendous pressure from Tamil Nadu for some action. Someone suggested raising a complaint with the UNSC. But there was also a demand for more drastic action, such as sending troops. On the other hand, we did not want to appear to be interfering in another country's internal affairs. The cooked-up bogey of foreign invasion made things a bit easier for us to take some action.

In our statements, we had been talking of cultural and ethnic identity, violation of human rights providing grounds for concern. In my view, we should have confined ourselves to the plight of Indian nationals, as well as the repercussions in India by way of a possible refugee influx. I was sure Pakistan was keeping a careful record of our statements for possible use in the future.

We asked the four governments of the US, the UK, Pakistan and Bangladesh to not send any military assistance to Sri Lanka, since we did not want them to get involved in this region. This was our Monroe Doctrine, though nobody had thought of it in those terms so far. I mentioned it to Parthasarathi and Shankar Bajpai, a senior officer and secretary in the ministry, and they both agreed with me. But we went a step further. We asked the UK to tell the Sri Lankans to ask India for help. I thought this was not wise. If our troops went there, they might have to open fire on the Sinhalese or the Tamil people, which would not make us very popular within India. In fact, Jayewardene himself should have asked us to send troops, so that we could get involved in the messy situation in the island. But then, he would not be able to persist with the Indians. He did ask to send ships to transport the Tamils from the Jaffna region to the capital, but he withdrew even this request, along with those for medicines and oil. He wanted the British to help him with the air ferry.

The Sri Lankans renewed their request for ships, which we readily complied with. We also started sending food and other essentials, 10 tonnes a day.

India's Stake in Sri Lanka

The single most important element for the Indian government was Tamil Nadu politics. The PM had been cultivating M.G. Ramachandran (MGR), the chief minister of Tamil Nadu. This was the only or most reliable hope for her to get a few seats in the South in the next general elections. The Sri Lankan events had come in handy for the Dravida Munnetra Kazhagam and others to resurrect themselves. One person burnt himself to death in support of the Sri Lankan Tamils. M. Karunanidhi and other leaders resigned from the Assembly. Two went on hunger strike. Several hundred undertook a march to Rameshwaram, with the threat of crossing over to Jaffna by boats. All this worried the PM and the Indian government. This weighed so heavily on her mind that she talked about it even with foreign visitors.

Jayewardene spoke to the PM on 5 August. The call lasted just about 10 minutes. He asked the PM to control MGR's speeches. The PM asked him about seeking foreign assistance; he simply said that the Americans were giving some wheat and the British had offered money of which Sri Lanka did not have much need then. The PM told him that India was not just any country, and that India and Sri Lanka were the two principal countries concerned with the situation. He said he would send a special envoy, perhaps his brother, the following week to discuss the Tamil situation.

We thought this was a great victory for us. For the first time, Sri Lanka had recognized at the highest level that India had a legitimate locus standi in Sri Lanka's Tamil question. A statement was drafted with great care by Alexander, Parthasarathi, Bajpai and me, the punch line of which was to be in the last paragraph, announcing Jayewardene's decision to send someone to India for discussion over the Tamil issue. As it happened, Indira Gandhi, who sat through a long debate in the Lok Sabha, forgot to read the last paragraph! By the time she realized her mistake, the Speaker had adjourned the House. She rushed to the well of the House, the Speaker returned, but the House could not be reconvened. She asked Atal Bihari

Vajpayee and some other Opposition leaders whether they would have any objection if that last para graph was given to the press. They all agreed.

The events were unfolding fast and Jayewardene's brother, Harry Jayewardene, who was a lawyer by profession, was to arrive in Delhi in four days' time as Jayewardene's special emissary. We had to be ready with our proposal.

We had a strategy session for about 70 minutes in Alexander's room. Parthasarathi, Bajpai, Thomas Abraham, joint secretary in the MEA and a couple of officers from the ministry were present, including Meera Shankar, a bright young officer at deputy secretary level. Alexander asked whether we were clear in our mind that we did not favour Eelam, a separate Tamil state. There was general agreement on this point. Alexander said that an independent Tamil state would have profound implications for us and çould lead to secession of the South. That was a pretty conclusive argument.

We then concluded that we should work for a federal set-up in Sri Lanka, with autonomy for the constituent states along the lines of the Constitution of India. It was also felt that we should secure for ourselves a continuing role in this matter. Sri Lanka should ask for our good offices in the search for a lasting solution and not just a fire-fighting role. I said we would have to take positive steps to convince them of our bona fides, such as preventing the Tamils in India from going in boats to Jaffna to help the rebels, as it was alleged was about to happen. Alexander said we had already taken measures to deal with that possibility.

We agreed on three points for the PM to put across to Harry Jayewardene: We would not tolerate, or, there should not be any foreign presence, not even in the form of training personnel for counter-insurgency operations; there had not been a single statement of condemnation of Tamil losses, etc.; we had a legitimate interest and were ready to help in discussions with the Tamils in the search for a lasting solution.

I asked whether we were really bothered at the periodic communal disturbances in Sri Lanka. I said, 'What does it matter if a couple of hundred Tamils lost their lives every three to four years?' Alexander immediately said that the Tamil question was of great importance to the entire South Asia, and that it was a very explosive situation and the whole thing would blow up if no solution was found to the problem. I asked no more, though my question was, in any case, rhetorical.

Bajpai observed that Jayewardene's brother was coming only for eyewash and that Jayewardene had no intention, no real intention, to give us a continuing role.

Incidentally, the PM in her statement in Parliament the previous week had said that other governments had recognized our special interest in Sri Lanka. She was referring to the fact that the US and the UK had decided not to send military assistance because we had made it clear to them that we would find it intolerable. Rasgotra had also told me a day before the PM's statement that we should, in due course, evolve our own Munroe Doctrine. He had said that we should help the Eelam Tigers to get their independent state (and also work for a separate state in the Tarai area in Nepal).

Meanwhile, Natwar was getting concerned that the Foreign Secretary was handling the no-war pact file when he, Natwar, was the secretary responsible for dealing with Pakistan. When Yaqub and Naik were in Delhi in early August 1983, Rasgotra agreed with them to go to Pakistan for the no-war pact talks. Natwar was very upset. He told me that Yaqub had told Naik that the PM had agreed to resume the dialogue. Satinder Lamba, joint secretary incharge of Pakistan, told me the same thing. I was surprised because it was not the PM's style to agree to such things in a hurry. I asked the PM about it. She told me, 'I said no such thing and I have agreed to nothing. It was only a social call; I just generally agreed upon talks for improving economic relations. I am not going to sign any no-war pact.' Natwar was thrilled.

The Tamil–Sinhalese Conundrum

In all the talks with Harry Jayewardene, the PM and PV tried to convince him that Sri Lanka should accept our good offices for mediation between the Sinhalese and Tamils. We told him that the basis for talks with the Tamils had to be widened to include any proposals, short of a separate state. Harry finally agreed but clarified to the PM that our good offices also had to be used with the Tamil terrorists who operated from Madras (now Chennai). He said it was quite clear that the whole Eelam-independent Tamil state movement was being orchestrated from Madras.

Apart from talking to Harry, our principal exercise was to draft a statement for the PM for Parliament. I had attended all the talks except for the first one between her and Harry, where only Alexander was present. As I had come to know, she had spoken to him very firmly and frankly but with her usual charm.

The statement was discussed in the CCPA. Bajpai and I had prepared a draft. Harry wanted some endorsement of the various proposals, including offers made in the past to the Tamils. I told him that this was out of question; the PM could not do it for political reasons. Bajpai suggested some drafting changes to accommodate him with words to the effect that these proposals were to be welcomed but were not adequate.

In the CCPA, these words were deleted. PV was not happy. He told Bajpai later that the statement would not take us anywhere.

The statement was delivered on 13 August. During the final discussion, someone said that the Sinhalese were not with us. The PM observed, 'With us? They hate us.' The PM showed understanding for J.R. Jayewardene's difficulties. The statement as finally drafted was accepted in substance by Harry. We avoided, even by implication, endorsing the Sri Lankan government's position; neither did we reject not did we condemn it. We also got them to welcome our offer of good offices.

One interesting point to note was that the statement had one reference to Sri Lanka's independence, unity and territorial integrity. But the PM and others would not agree to say that we did not support secession anywhere. Harry wanted us to say that the various offers were subject to the condition that the demand for a separate state would be given up. However, there was great resistance, not from the PM but from other ministers and the cabinet secretary. We seemed to want to keep all options open.

Parthasarathi was to leave for Colombo the following week. The PM made the announcement and at the last minute, she deleted 'most' from her statement, where she had referred to him as one of our 'most experienced diplomats'. It was very typical of her. Parthasarathi was very proud. But the day after this announcement, J.R. Jayewardene told the press in Colombo that India had no role to play in this exercise. Her telephone talk with him was interesting. (I was not present but read the verbatim record of the conversation present with the MEA.) It was cold, proper and completely devoid of any warmth from either side.

She asked, 'How are you, Mr President?'

'Quite well, thank you,' replied J.R. Jayewardene.

She said the talks with his brother were very useful and hoped that he would continue in this role.

'I would do that.'

'From our side, I am nominating Mr Parthasarathi,' and with that, she went on with some rigmarole about her talks with Mr Appapillai Amritalingam, the leader of Sri Lanka Tamils.

He asked, 'Yes, what is his name?' She repeated Parthasarathi's name and said she would write to him about it. He said his brother was going to be away for two weeks and asked again, 'Would you write to me giving the name of your special envoy?

The PM asked, 'Would it be alright if he comes at least for a short while before your brother's return from abroad?'

He asked whether he should wait for her letter before replying. The PM said, 'I will say the same thing if I write.'

Whereupon, Jayewardene said, 'If you want to send him, there is no objection. He can come straight away.'

The PM said, 'Not straight away, but in a few days.' She offered to send any relief assistance needed. He thanked her in return saying he would let her know if something was needed.

Meanwhile, Rasgotra was very worried about Sri Lanka. He had told me that the country was bound to break up into two at some stage. But he was not bothered about this aspect too much. What worried him was that next time there was communal violence in India, the entire Muslim world would be at our throat. He said our politicians in the South and the Opposition could not care less about the embarrassment they were creating for the government by their selfish and short-sighted demands.

About Parthasarathi's mission, PV said we might be getting ourselves into a very messy situation. The Jaffna Tamils regarded themselves superior to the Tamils in India, let alone the Indian Tamils in Sri Lanka. He said, 'I know for a fact that our Tamils do not care at all for the Sri Lanka Tamils; in fact, they hate one another, but they are using the situation solely for political purposes, without giving the slightest thought to broader implications.' I wished PV would have expressed his views to the PM and others.

9

THE HANDS-ON PRIME MINISTER

In Pakistan, a civil disobedience movement started by the Movement for the Restoration of Democracy (MRD) was going on since 14 August 1984. The MRD was established in 1983 mainly at the instance of Bhutto's Pakistan Peoples Party, which formed an alliance with opposition parties to oppose Zia's oppressive rule and restore democracy. Zia came down heavily on the MRD. Several hundred political leaders were arrested, including Tikka Khan, Mumtaz Bhutto, Ghulam Mustafa Jatoi, and others. Scores of demonstrators were killed. The agitation was mainly confined to the Sind region initially, but soon Jamaat had also joined in. And with Jamaat really throwing in its lot with the MRD, Zia's days were undoubtedly numbered.

I sent a note to the PM, saying that the movement was now 10 days old and showed no sign of abating. I suggested it was time for us to make some statement, expressing sympathy for the democratic aspirations of the people of Pakistan. We would make it clear that we did not want to interfere in Pakistan's internal affairs, but we should say something at this stage. If Zia was to be toppled, our statement would earn us goodwill with the future leaders. If he rode the storm through, he would not be able to find fault with our statement. It was all a question of drafting. I suggested this could best be done in the form of an answer to a Parliament question.

The PM sent the note back to me, saying that it was too late for a Parliament question. I found out that PV was due to answer a starred question on Pakistan in the Lok Sabha. So, I took the note with the PM's comment to him. He said the PM had discussed the note with him. The idea was good but what to do? I reminded him about the starred question. He said he would try to bring it up during the supplementaries. But he did not speak about the agitation in Pakistan during his reply to the Parliament question. He did make a statement about Abdul Ghaffar Khan's arrest, expressing the deep concern of the House. He went on to express India's 'uneasiness and distress at the recent events in Pakistan' and affirmed our commitment to democracy. The PM decided to write to Zia, conveying Parliament's concern about Ghaffar Khan. I gave her a draft. There was an unconfirmed rumour that five Pakistan generals had resigned. Was this the beginning of the end for Zia?

Newspapers quoted the PM as having said that she would speak up against injustice anywhere. She emphasized that India believed in democracy and that she will always speak up in favour of democracy. Bhutto was not her friend and opposed her all throughout, but India still spoke against his execution.

She received praise from many quarters, citing that she was the chairperson of the NAM and the world expected her to show leadership and initiative. While she enjoyed these compliments, she did not get taken in by them.

Plain Speak about Nepal

The PM was angry with the Nepalese. They were making things difficult for the Indians in the Tarai area—not allowing them to work, sending them back to India, and so on. She noted that there were plenty of Nepalese in India and they should be sent back in response. The former Nepalese PM Surya Bahadur Thapa had got some straight talk from her earlier in 1982. The two PMs had met alone in Delhi in 1982, but at some stage, she had sent for me and asked me to talk about the harassment of the Indians in Nepal.

Fortunately, I was ready with facts and figures. Thapa had tried to give some explanation, but she had cut him short and said she had received independent reports of such harassment. She had told him bluntly, 'We are always doing things for you, but there is absolutely no reciprocity from your side.' The atmosphere had become a bit uncomfortable for me, so I excused myself. Thapa had asked for concurrence to the Joint Commission proposal. He was very keen and nearly begged her for it. She did not readily agree. Only the following morning, when PV was having breakfast with Thapa, she had called him over the phone and given her nod. She had told me that PV and the MEA believed that Thapa was very well disposed towards India, but foreign minister Padma Bahadur Khatri was not so friendly. I had suggested that perhaps Thapa and Khatri had divided these roles between them, to which she had said, 'Well, it may not be quite like that, but I do not agree that Thapa is our best bet.'

During the NAM Summit, somehow a meeting between

the PM and the King could not be arranged. One was fixed, but had to be cancelled because she had to rush to the airport to receive Castro, whose arrival was announced only 45 minutes before the actual time. Thereafter, I suggested many times to the Nepalese to arrange a meeting with the PM, each time at somewhat short notice. This was inevitable, since she was chairing the conference. All other appointments were fixed like that. The King and the PM could never meet.

Downing of South Korean Airliner

On the midnight of 31 August and 1 September 1983, the Soviets shot down a South Korean airliner with 269 passengers on board. The plane was well inside the Soviet airspace. There was an uproar, particularly from the Americans. The Soviets neither, until a day later, admitted that they had shot down the aircraft nor did they say that they had not. On 1 September, we had to make some statement. I told Alexander that we did not have to say anything, but that was not possible. Bajpai drafted a brief statement. It had a sentence to the effect of 'We hope it was not shot down, which would be deplorable.'

Parthasarathi did not like it at all: 'Why should we deplore some hypothetical situation?' I said if it was established that the Soviets shot down the plane, we would have to deplore it. He agreed with my logic. Our statement finally merely expressed our distress and regrets at the loss of lives and added that we did not have all the facts.

The Soviets issued a detailed statement giving all the circumstances and admitted that they had shot the plane down. They said the plane had intruded 500 km inside the Soviet airspace, refused to identify itself or respond to the messages and signals to force land or to leave the Soviet airspace; its navigation lights were off and it was flying over sensitive Soviet naval installations in Kamchatka Peninsula. The Soviets accused the Koreans of spying. The Americans also admitted that an RC-135 reconnaissance plane was in that area and its configuration resembled that of the Boeing. Also, the weather was bad.

The Soviets did not enter the plea of error—they agreed that they had shot down the plane. Had they said that they did so thinking it was a spy plane and offered compensation, large part of the criticism would have been defused. But they only expressed regret at the loss of lives and affirmed that they would always do whatever was necessary to protect and defend the Soviet territory.

We had good fun for the better part of the day, drafting a statement for the spokesman, primarily because the PM was the Chair of the NAM and was expected to share the widespread condemnation of the incident. Bajpai and I told the PM at the airport (the Maldivian President was coming on a state visit) that we would have to say something. She agreed. Bajpai drafted three brief paragraphs, but there was no condemnation or deploring. I reacted strongly that if we were not going to deplore, it was better we did not say anything at all. Alexander agreed. We three went to the PM with a draft, which had a sentence deeply deploring the extreme step. She generally agreed with the idea.

Parthasarathi, however, was most unhappy. According to him, the draft was not balanced, as it ignored the Soviet point of view. He was also against mentioning the Soviet Union by name. We then went to the PM with Parthasarathi's suggested changes. The key change would now read: 'We deeply deplore the incident, which caused the loss of so many innocent lives.'

The reference to the Soviet Union was dropped. None of

us were happy at having to deplore the Soviet Union's action, but we were all convinced that we had to. Bajpai pointed out that this would be the first time we would be publicly censuring the Soviets. The PM said we had to do it. After all we had condemned Israel's shooting down of a Libyan plane with many civilians in 1973. She said we should explain to the Soviet Union that we had an additional obligation to say something because we were Chair of the NAM. She said Andropov had told her that as the Chair of the NAM, India could do this and that. 'But I told him that, on the contrary, we would be less of a free agent than before.'

The PM said, 'If a foreign military aircraft flew over India and did not heed the warning, I shall certainly order it to be shot down.'

On being told about all this in the evening, my wife Rita's wise comment was, 'So now you are taking on even the Soviets!'

New York Visit

In the third week of September 1983, we were discussing with the PM the New York get-together. She was very keen to organize a small meeting where a few invited leaders would discuss, in an informal setting, the global economic situation and the difficulties they faced in their respective economies' development. Reagan was to address the General Assembly on 26 September. The question was whether we should ask for a meeting with him for the PM. I suggested that we should. Should we invite him for a lunch with the PM the day after his address? Alexander was not sure whether it would be proper for us to ask for a meeting. But Parthasarathi must have spoken to him because at the meeting with the PM, he said we must ask for the call. As Parthasarathi said, Alexander had a lot to learn.

The PM thought Reagan won't give more than five minutes to her.

Alexander protested, 'How can he give only five minutes?'

The PM said, 'Well, not more than 10 minutes, of which five would go to photography.'

The opinion was that Reagan's aides did not allow him to have one-on-one with any foreign leader, least of all with the PM.

Protocol wise, the PM would call on presidents. But she was used to other leaders, even presidents, paying court to her. She really expected others to accept her as the world's elder stateswoman and to give her due respect as such. She enjoyed all that attention.

The delegation for New York had to be decided. Everybody from the MEA wanted to go. Alexander asked me for my opinion. I suggested names of Rasgotra, Parthasarathi, Bhandari, Sengupta and Natwar. He asked about Parthasarathi. I said he would be useful. He did not seem to agree, but when he passed my note to the PM, he added Parthasarathi's name in his own handwriting. Games people play! She did not agree to Natwar's name, as a result of which he was upset, but Bhandari was thrilled.

The PM decided that nobody from the MEA would travel with her in her aircraft. Even Rasgotra must travel separately. She would visit Cyprus and Greece en route New York. Rasgotra was disappointed. Such things were important at that level.

For the UN speech, during the PM's New York visit, the PM drafted two to three pages herself: '[...] out of the ashes of each civilization, a new one is born, out of the industrial revolution were born capitalism and Marxism. Both have different approaches but have the same materialist ethos. The next order must be free of the evils of the existing one, the world needs a new international order of humanity [...]' Parthasarathi and Sharada were not at all impressed. They made a mild effort to dissuade her, but to no avail. So, they modified it as best as they could, keeping to her main ideas. For example, her original draft suggested that a new civilization would emerge out of the ashes of the Third World War, almost saying that a Third World War was inevitable. There were two sentences there, to the effect that everything that had a beginning must have an end. I asked Sharada to explain this to me. His reply was classic: 'Every politician thinks that by such phrases, he or she would become, and get recognition as a philosopher.' Parthasarathi was convinced that many of these phrases were given to her by others

Sharada was a bit unhappy. He and the PM had worked very hard on her inaugural address to the World Energy Conference on 27 September in Delhi. Suddenly, the previous night, she decided to shorten it and struck off several pages. The speech was already printed and distributed, but she insisted. Sharada's grievance was that she would be saving no more than about five minutes of the conference time, but she had personally expended several hours of effort on that portion. I suggested she must have felt the impulse to do something at night and correcting drafts was the best form of relaxation or release of nervous energy for her. He agreed and said if she engaged in other activities like arranging her hair, it would give her something to do, besides working on drafts. P.N. Dhar, economist and secretary to the PM, used to call it 'substitute activity'.

It was amazing and sad how many comparatively minor

matters had to be taken to her for decision and how much time she had to spend on them. The Korean airline incident, for example. She spent at least an hour on drafting the statement in which we deplored the incident. Our delegation in International Civil Aviation Organization had to make a statement on the same issue. The draft was prepared in the MEA. I suggested a couple of substantive changes, but Alexander thought it prudent to submit it to the PM who found time to go through it and inevitably make a few changes.

She would even approve the over-flight messages that were sent in her name to the leaders of countries over which her plane flew. These routine messages were my nightmare. She insisted on using different words in each one, though the basic idea remained the same. Her attitude was laudable—she wanted to add a personal touch where possible, but I was not sure the effort was worth the result. But the drafts always came back with improvizations.

10

AN INSTINCT FOR FOREIGN POLICY

Indira Gandhi was not an expert on foreign affairs, in the sense of knowing about nearly all the issues facing the international community at a given point of time. Even professional diplomats do not have that kind of expertise. But she had a keen sense or instinct about what position should be taken to protect India's interests. She was proud of India's policy of non-alignment. Once she was asked at a news conference whether she was left- or right-inclined. Her reply, which went on to become widely recognized, was, 'I do not lean Left or Right, I stand firmly in the centre.'

We had a briefing meeting with the PM about China on 23 October 1983. It was a rambling session, with the officials talking at cross purposes and the PM carrying on, as usual, with other works, making a comment or two and occasionally asking questions. The idea was to get her instructions on whether we should give a hint of some flexibility on our side in the fourth round of Sino-Indian official-level talks starting the following day, 24 October. Her main concern was that we should not appear to be the obstinate or unrealistic ones in the eyes of the world. We should not give the impression that our position was 'take it or leave it'. She said the West, particularly America, was with China and would support China on all such issues, which was not the case a few years ago.

A suggestion was made that we might propose the setting up of an expert group to go into the historical evidence of the question related to boundary. Alexander was not sure. The PM asked whether such a group might not rake up old controversies, thus vitiating the atmosphere and hardening positions. Bajpai saw no harm. The final conclusion was not clear to most of us.

Bajpai then said he wanted to raise one or two 'small matters'. One was our embassy property in Beijing, which the Chinese had taken away in 1967. Later, they had offered us a plot of land, but we had not built on it for a few years and then the Chinese had given it away to the Romanians. We didn't receive any compensation for this loss of land and now we wanted to acquire the premises that we held at lease at present. But the Chinese contention was that it was too much to ask. Bajpai wanted to know whether he could take up the issue with the Chinese.

The PM strongly felt that this was not a minor matter at all and that it should be taken up with the Chinese. She argued that we had given 30 acres to China in New Delhi and, if necessary, we should tell them that we might have to take over a part of that land. At this stage, someone pointed out that there might be legal complications which made the PM explode, 'What legal difficulties? What the hell does the law have anything to do with it? National interests must come first. No country in the world functions like this. Every time the central government wants to do something, the Supreme Court says we can't do it. The West Bengal government does something illegal and the court does not say anything. What the hell is this? My own officials tell me this can't be done! Nothing must come in the way of national interests, neither the government nor the laws. If national interests demand it, we must have the Emergency or anything else.' Bureaucracy always frustrated us.

Once her angry tirade against the system was over, she seamlessly spent 40 minutes with Bajpai discussing the menu for the Commonwealth Heads of Government Meeting (CHOGM) dinner!

The heads of the governments of the Commonwealth meet at summit level every two years in a different country. The seventh CHOGM was hosted by India from 23 to 29 November 1983. The main part was held in Delhi in Vigyan Bhavan, and the 'retreat' was held in Goa. It was chaired by Indira Gandhi.

As the CHOGM event was nearing, the PM's anglophile nature came to be in full display because the Queen of England and the Prince Consort were coming to India on State visit in November for the CHOGM. The PM looked into every single detail of the programme herself. She wanted to see the menu for the Queen's breakfast, lunch and dinner every day. She wanted to ascertain what sarees to wear on what occasion.

The Queen was due to attend dinner at the Indian High Commissioner's residence in London at 9 Kensington Palace Gardens on 25 October 1983 before her arrival for the CHOGM in India. The PM spent one whole day in London on her return from New York, inspecting the Gardens and selecting and arranging the furniture. Mrs Prakash, an interior decorator, was flown from India to assist in the selection of the curtain material. The High Commissioner was given instructions on how to behave in the Queen's presence (never turn your back to Her Majesty).

The most difficult part was the guest list. The table was to seat 18. The British had decided their guest list. On the Indian side, the PM decided, after returning to India and after giving the matter a deep thought, to send two couples from India: the governor of Assam, Prakash Mehrotra, and his wife, and Madhavrao Scindia and his wife. She wanted to send Mehrotra as the next High Commissioner in London and so the dinner trip to London would give him the much-needed opportunity to get to know the place and, hopefully, to like it. The selection of Scindia, from what I understood, was in recognition of him controlling 20 MLAs in Madhya Pradesh. Besides, he was an educated and articulate person. These four people were to keep company to the Queen for at the most two hours. They would stay at the Savoy. The dinner was going to cost quite a packet. There was no question—the PM loved the British, particularly the royalty.

I had a ringside experience of the CHOGM conference. Normally, the executive sessions were attended only by the heads and two aides. But being the host, Natwar arranged for him and me to stay in the hall all the time, except when the heads discussed Sonny Ramphal's reappointment as secretary general of the Commonwealth.

The CHOGM Event

As the CHOGM was coming to a close, the PM started showing her unhappiness with the Commonwealth. She was obviously not enjoying the company of so many of her peers who were not exactly conservatives or reactionaries, but rather afraid to express their views freely out of fear of the rich members of the club. Though not physically present, the American presence was all pervasive. Nearly all the countries depended on the US for economic help or for support with the IMF. Even if they might disapprove of the American action in Grenada, they would content themselves with as mild an expression of their position as possible. The standard of debate reached great heights when Grenada was discussed. The tiny Caribbean nation was invaded by about 2,000 US troops on 25 October 1983. Six Caribbean nations had joined the operation code named 'Urgent Fury'. President Reagan's justification was that Grenada was about to be taken over by Cuba with Soviet help. This would endanger the lives of about 800 American citizens, most of them medical students.

The three veteran stalwarts of Africa—Julius Nyerere, Keneth Kaunda and Robert Mugabe—led the attack on American invasion. Their argument was that the US action would establish a dangerous precedent in Africa. South Africa might use the same logic to justify punitive action against Namibia. They all spoke effectively and sincerely.

But the tiny East Caribbean countries' PMs were not to be awed by Kaunda and co. They argued their case (talking about the communists and leftists taking control of the country) so well that at the end of the debate, most people in the hall were clearly inclined to agree with them. So much so, the Australian premier, who had earlier said that he would have advised against the invasion if consulted, declared that he was now convinced of the rightness of American action. Lee Kwan Yu, Singapore's PM, said that Singapore had voted against the US at the UN, but he was glad that the US did what they did.

Tom Adams, the PM of Barbados, in support of the intervention, cited the analogy of Bangladesh's and India's intervention there. He clarified he was glad that India had intervened but still it was not legally defensible. He also drew a parallel with Tanzania's intervention in Uganda. Indira Gandhi came down heavily on poor Adams. I had seldom seen her so sharp. She was very angry and said she strongly resented the comparison with the Bangladesh situation and outlined all the details—her visits to Western capitals, 10 million refugees, attacks on nine of our airfields, etc. The vehemence of her reaction surprised me as well as Natwar. Adams was not exactly apologetic, however. He clarified that he had not meant to disapprove Indian action. Lee Kwan Yu said Adams surely meant no disrespect. The PM who chaired the conference with great charm combined with firmness became even more anti-Commonwealth after the CHOGM.

Bob Hawke, the PM of Australia, was known to be abrasive. But he was at his impolite best on the last day when he and Indira Gandhi had differences over a paragraph on Lebanon. He proposed an amendment that we could not accept. The PM was firm but polite. Hawke, on the other hand, was positively rude. He threw up his hands in disgust and derision and passed remarks such as 'your inflexibility on principle is incredible'. She stood her ground but was most bitter that none of her friends spoke up on her side. (This was one of the incidents which convinced her of the one-sidedness of the Commonwealth and of the pressures on its poorer members who were afraid to speak up.) Even the members of the Australian delegation were embarrassed at Hawke's offensiveness.

At every CHOGM conference, there is what is called a 'retreat'. The idea is that the leaders go away somewhere all by themselves; they could take only one aide with them. They would use the opportunity to iron whatever differences might have emerged during earlier discussions. We had our retreat in Goa. At the retreat, the leaders were talking about Cyprus, about the unilateral declaration of independence by Northern Cyprus under Turkish occupation. Every time someone criticized the Turks, the Malaysian foreign minister, Ghazali Shafie, would bang his fist on the table and mumble something. He was stone drunk and was making a nuisance of himself. Kaunda warned him once gently, 'My brother from Malaysia may not please disturb others.' After about half an hour, when the Malaysian did not stop, Kaunda exploded, 'First of all, you have no right to be here, this retreat is meant for only presidents and prime ministers. We have allowed you only because your Prime Minister is busy and could not come, and you keep disturbing when serious discussions are going on…'. When Ghazali mumbled something, Kaunda shouted at him, 'Shut up!' Everybody in the meeting was stunned.

The most impressive thing about CHOGM was the frankness, the candour with which the leaders spoke. Most of them were on first name terms with one another. The fact that they all spoke English was of great help. When Namibia was under discussion, Thatcher kept quiet for a long time. So, Kaunda said, 'I am sorry Margaret has not spoken, I am not asking her to speak. I merely wish to record my disappointment.' She still did not speak.

Pierre Trudeau, the Canadian PM who was active in campaigning for nuclear disarmament and had established a reputation as being against nuclear weapon, came with a much-publicized initiative for a conference of the five nuclear weapon states (the US, the UK, China, Soviet Union and France) for injecting political will into disarmament negotiations instead of leaving them to technicians and generals. Thatcher had no hesitation in speaking her mind, rejecting Trudeau's idea in no uncertain terms, reminding him that the generals had broken off talks in Geneva under instructions from political leaders. All her hawkishness came out unalloyed when she spoke about the threat from communism and the need to defend democracy. She had done her homework well. She spoke without faltering. She was never at a loss for words, which our PM was at times.

Ramphal, the secretary general of the Commonwealth, had included a paragraph on Non-Proliferation Treaty with which we had great difficulty. I suggested some changes to the PM. She tried them out but ran into expected difficulties from Trudeau, Hawke and Thatcher. They suggested alterations that the PM was inclined to accept, but I advised against accepting them since they were still bad from our point of view. She did not seem to see through their game. I was not sure if she had ever negotiated anything in detail the way she had to at the CHOGM. The result was that I negotiated directly with Trudeau. He did not seem to mind, but this was clearly against the Commonwealth tradition. The PM started getting restless and even annoyed with my stubbornness. She said, 'But they would never agree to it.' I told her we also should make it clear that we would not agree to it. She argued, 'But why can't we accept, since in any case we are not going to make atomic bombs?' In the end, we agreed to a form of words, which I still did not like, but she said we had to accept something. She later explained to me that continued objections on our part would have made them suspicious of our intentions. She was right, but I thought she did not wish to continue the fight. Also, as she told the meeting, she felt a bit handicapped being in the Chair, since she did not wish to appear difficult or obstructionist.

She was a perfect hostess—charming, spending a few moments with each guest, taking enormous interest in details of the menu, flowers, etc. She mixed easily with everyone but felt comfortable with only a few, as mentioned before. She and Thatcher met quite a few times, but they were still not on first name terms.

She almost never raised her voice while talking to officials. For the 26 odd months I worked under her, she did not once shout at me.

She was a modern person, though she was also religious compared to her father who was agnostic. When she went to temples, she seemed to be quite sincere about praying. Of course, she visited mosques, churches, gurdwaras, too. She was genuinely secular in her approach. She had *shraddha* (faith) as a Hindu, but she was not an obscurantist.

She had commonsensical approach to events and issues. The following is a quote from a minute that she recorded after witnessing a children's community singing programme on 14 November 1983.

> I was disappointed with the children's community singing programme. What I had in mind was not a formal programme, but to encourage people and children to learn common songs and be able to sing them joyfully and spontaneously together. I was especially worried to learn that the children were made to come three hours before the appointed time. It is obvious that if they were made to wait and to conform to certain patterns, their programme cannot be joyful or full of zest. It is not at all important that they should all sing absolutely in tune and together. Nor is it necessary for them to stand in rows. That is better of course. But the aim is something else and it seems to me that we have bypassed the main purpose of this programme.

11

1984: THE YEAR THAT WAS...

In 1984, Indira Gandhi turned 67. She was still in the pink of health, still walked faster than all of us, sat erect, refused to take the lift, worked hard and did not keep a file pending for more than 12 hours. However, she started complaining of tiredness to her physician Dr Krishna Prasad Mathur after returning from a three-day trip to Himachal Pradesh. I wondered how she would stand the rigors of the next general elections and the impossibly hectic campaigning and grueling schedule.

The Election Heat

1984 was election year in the US and in India. The PM had several invitations, including from some of the most prestigious universities in the US. To all, she replied that 1984 was the election year and that her travels abroad would have to be kept to the minimum. To some, she also said that no one could count on the outcome of an election.

The Opposition had been clamouring for months that the PM would hold a midterm poll to cash in on the good crop situation and before the Opposition parties could manage to organize themselves. She, however, had been insistent that the polls be held only when they were due, i.e., end of 1984. I myself tried to test her reaction by bringing to her notice the stories in foreign press that were predicting early elections. Her response was consistent: 'This is Opposition propaganda.'

From her point of view, she needed time to unsettle the governments in Karnataka and Andhra Pradesh, to give them enough time to make a mess of things.

In Karnataka, the toppling game was in full swing. The Karnataka Kranti Ranga of Sarekoppa Bangarappa, who had supported Ramakrishna Hegde's Janata Party government, had already withdrawn support and merged, or was about to merge, with the Congress. The infamous Moily tapes, which the Hegde government claimed contained evidence of the Congress giving ₹2 lakh to each defecting MLA, did not seem to have caused much harm to the Congress image. There were deep differences within the BJP about continuing support to Hegde, though the BJP would not support the Congress.

The situation in Tamil Nadu was a little bit easier, especially since Parthasarathi had succeeded in persuading all the parties in Sri Lanka to participate in a round table conference, which started in Colombo on 10 January 1984. However, it was the most difficult assignment. When J.R. Jayewardene was in Delhi for the CHOGM, he took back with him a package of proposals. The PM met Jayewardene a couple of times. The first time they met alone, the PM had assured him of her complete support. Recalling her conversation with him, she said, 'I told him bluntly that we would deal with you rather than with someone else whom we don't know at all and who may be an extremist.' Jayewardene was convinced that the PM was not after his blood personally. She had also told us several times that he feared not only for his position but for his life, and that, left to himself, he would try to accommodate the Tamils.

But there was a last-minute hitch to the roundtable conference when S.W.R.D. Bandaranaike's Sri Lanka Freedom Party refused to take part on some pretext. The real reason was that Bandaranaike wanted to win back Sirimavo Bandaranaike's civic rights that Jayewardene had taken away from her. Jayewardene was an old bandicoot (which is why Parthasarathi got along with him!) and was certainly not going to give in to Bandaranaike. Parthasarathi got the Sinhalese Buddhist Mahanayakas to appeal to Bandaranaike and the trick worked.

Even in Andhra Pradesh, the game was on. I asked Parthasarathi as to why they did not strike a deal with N.T. Rama Rao (NTR), the CM of Andhra Pradesh. His reply was typically enigmatic, 'I know but can't tell you!' My guess was he did not know anything.

And then one fine day, Andhra Pradesh Governor Ram Lal sacked NTR on his own without getting the Centre's authorization. No one was prepared to believe this. The total collapse of the government's credibility made things much worse for the PM. There was initial jubilation in the Congress camp at NTR's ouster. But the backlash was stunning. All the Opposition parties and normally pro-establishment press severely criticized the Andhra Pradesh developments. NTR was losing his hold anyhow. Apparently, his son and son-in-law were involved in many property scandals. The government servants as a class were very unhappy because NTR reduced the age of retirement by two years. He had also launched some eye-catching schemes, which could not be implemented.

So, his popularity in urban areas had greatly diminished. But in rural areas, especially among women, his sway was strong because of his image as Lord Rama. The Governor's action of sacking him and getting him arrested, even if only for two hours, completely rehabilitated NTR. On top of it all, he had just come back from the US after a heart surgery and had developed chest pain. If he died, he would be a martyr, fighting the Centre's authoritarianism. If things had been allowed to take their course, the Congress's position would have improved a great deal, but Ram Lal's antics had ruined it all.

Oppositions Galore

The Andhra affair became a major headache for the Congress. The PM declared in both Houses that she had no knowledge of the Governor's action and that she came to know about it through a press report. While she was making inquiries about the press report, she learnt of the dismissal of the NTR ministry.

Dhawan was most worried about the fallout of the Andhra episode for the PM. Vijay Tripathi, an IAS officer posted in the PMO and who seemed to enjoy confidence of the PM, agreed that this was the most serious setback for the party. For the first time, I saw the PM showing preoccupation when talking to a visitor. The Opposition organized a public rally at the Ramlila grounds in Delhi and newspapers described it as massive. NTR paraded his 167 MLAs in front of the President who refused to enter into the counting game. Bhaskar Rao, leader of the Congress party, also paraded his own strength in Hyderabad. As many as 35 MLAs were common in both lists. But NTR clearly had the majority. He returned to Hyderabad, took no chances and kept his flock in a hotel in Karnataka.

The Economist came out with a critical editorial about the PM, which made her upset, as she very much cared about what the press, particularly the Western press, wrote about her. I could not understand this weakness in her; the Brits or the Americans did not care what the Indian press wrote about them.

The Andhra Assembly met on 11 September 1984 and adjourned after a few minutes because of the extremely unruly behaviour of Rao's men. Even the condolence resolution on the death of an MLA could not be put to vote. There was even attempted arson in the Assembly. People were expecting the PM to announce withdrawal of support for Rao. However, she was not able to act decisively.

An acquaintance of mine who was an industrialist had told me that Rao had told him that all he needed was two days with the MLAs, and that he guaranteed majority support. One million rupees per person was the going rate!

Maimoona Sultan, a Congress MP in the Rajya Sabha, told me:

> After the 1977 election, the Congress was finished. By a stroke of good luck, we were back in power. If we lose the next election, we will be finished forever. We have only Mrs Gandhi, she should change the Constitution and become the elected president, which is our last chance because never again can we hope to get such a majority. Next election would be very messy. 10 per cent of candidates would get killed. Please ask Madam not to hold elections.

The general conviction was that she had become the prisoner of third-rate advisors—people who had no scruples and no principles except to grab and remain in power and to make money at any cost.

She also needed time for Rajiv to establish himself in the party. His 'Mr Clean' image was unsullied. He was supposed to be engaged in reorganizing and cleansing the party. The by-elections in Uttar Pradesh, where the Congress lost all the three seats, portended a very unfavourable trend. Prices were high, whereas they had been traditionally low after the harvests. Even if the next crop was not good, there were enough buffer stocks to absorb any shortages and check prices. Also, as Dhawan had told me, 'Why should we voluntarily give up a year or even a few months of our power since we can't be sure of the results of an election?' Nearly everyone agreed that the Congress would emerge as the single largest party in the next House. Equally, there was consensus that the Congress simply could not repeat the 1980 performance. Elections everywhere, especially in India, were an anti-establishment affair. With the South almost hopeless and the Hindi heartland uncertain, with intra-party feuds in almost all the states, I felt that the Congress would be lucky to get 250 seats compared to over 350 as it did in 1984.

There was a widely held theory that the PM was concentrating on the Hindu vote. Her popularity with the Muslims and Dalits had declined. These two classes had generally supported her in the past, but now they were supposed to be alienated from her. Mir Qasim in Kashmir left her in disgust to start his own party. Hemwati Nandan Bahuguna in Uttar Pradesh got along well with the Muslims, but he was too keen on the prime ministerial gaddi to join up with the PM. (She really hated him. I heard her once say that Bahuguna was unreliable and told lies. He had apparently told Jagjivan Ram, a significant Congress leader representing the backward class, that the PM was not prepared to give him a seat, while she had said nothing of the sort.) The Opposition had got Syed Shahabuddin (he and I were in the same batch), my erstwhile colleague in the IFS, who had resigned from the service and jumped into politics. Vijay Tripathi said he told the PM that Shahab was doing extremely well in Bihar and was cultivating the Muslim vote in the entire country. He added it would not be difficult to get Shahab to come over to the Congress. I did not agree with him at all. Shahab could not be bought. Also, his dislike for the PM was far too intense for him to work with her. So, she had to depend on the Hindu vote. This explained her success in the Delhi election in 1983.

12

THE BURNING PUNJAB

In the 1970s, a Sikh leader by the name of Jagjit Singh Chohan had emerged in Punjab. He had started the movement for the establishment of what he called Khalistan, meaning the state of Khalsas. He had been an active politician of the Akali Dal and had been the finance minister of Punjab at one point of time. He did not seem to have received much support in the beginning, but things changed when he went to Pakistan. General Yahya Khan, the strongman of Pakistan, gave him some precious artifacts, which helped Chohan attract a large number of followers as well as significant financial support. In 1982, he went to Anandpur Sahib gurdwara and declared the independent state of Khalistan. He went to the UK and Canada to propagate his goal and received generous support from the Sikh communities there.

By the 1980s, the Khalistan movement had grown in Punjab and engaged in acts of terrorism. Jarnail Singh Bhindranwale, the new firebrand leader of the Sikhs, was advocating violence.

Most people believed that he was the creation of the Congress party in the hope that it would divide the Akalis, but he turned out to be the Congress's Frankenstein's monster. The state government was unable to control him and the killings of innocents continued. The PM made several attempts to arrive at a truce with the moderates among the Sikhs. At times, the talks came close to a conclusion, but at the last minute, the extremists would manage to scuttle the talks with threats against the moderates. Bhindranwale received open support from Pakistan and fortified himself at the Golden Temple in Amritsar. Not a day passed without a couple of people getting killed. A retired deputy superintendent of police, his wife and guard were killed in an autorickshaw.

Then one day, government forces had to lay siege to one or two gurdwaras in Moga in Punjab because the terrorists had made them their operational headquarters. The Akalis gave an ultimatum of 48 hours to lift the siege, or else they would send suicide squads. The war in Punjab was on.

The tragedy was that no one had any idea how all this would end. It was bringing bad name to the government and to Indira Gandhi personally. The diplomatic corps were now talking about it and it was having a direct bearing on her prospects for winning the Nobel Peace Prize.

In spite of the grave pressure of the Punjab situation, the PM looked amazingly relaxed. One could never make out, looking at her, that she had so many worries and concerns. I took the Kenyan High Commissioner to her in early May 1984 and she was absolutely relaxed. She gave him at least 15 minutes and talked about the election system in India and about the Anglo-Indian community citing an incident, 'Many years ago, I was going to Oxford by ship. Many Anglo-Indians were taking Indian names. There was an Anglo-Indian girl named Cynthia. Years later, someone told me a woman called Shanti claimed she knew me and was with me on the ship. I found that Shanti was actually Cynthia!'

Towards the end of May 1984, the headlines in newspapers had become routine, monotonous and alarming: 'Extremists kill 13 in Punjab', '8 killed in car in Ludhiana', and so on. Not a day passed without at least half a dozen people getting killed in Punjab. It was evident that the government had lost total control over the situation. Law and order was non-existent. The Akalis were losing support because of the senseless and brutal killings, but the government was not gaining any sympathy either because of its inept handling. The CCPA met nearly every day to discuss Punjab, exploring possibilities to cause further split among the Akalis. Some negotiations were going on with moderates, but they demanded protection and guaranteed progress.

The PM narrated the Punjab story to every foreign visitor. Once, Sharada scribbled a note to me which read,

> Once we used to have Assam LP (long playing record), now we have Punjab LP. It went something like this, 'The agitation is led by a small Sikh party called the Akali. They were themselves in power in Punjab for three years. At that time, two ministers in the central government were from their party. But they did not do anything to solve the problem; they did not even raise it, let alone try to solve it. But as soon as I came back to power, they started the agitation. Thus, the agitation is aimed only at me. People say I should form a coalition with them because what they are really after is power. But how can I? My party won with a sweeping majority, they were soundly beaten [...]'

The record continued:

> I told those who started the agitation that it is easy to start the agitation but very difficult to control it. This is exactly what has happened, extremists have taken over. We have had many rounds of negotiations, often we were close to reaching an agreement, but when they went back, they were denounced by the extremists who would ensure the collapse of the talks by creating some incident and escalating the demands. I have already accepted most of the religious demands. But the territorial and water demands affect the neighbouring states—how can I accept those unless the states affected also agree? Otherwise, I shall have agitations from those states as well. As for the demand for Khalistan, it exists more in Canada and United States than in India.

Alexander was the principal guiding hand in directing the strategy for the Punjab situation. People were asking, 'What does Alexander know about Punjab, the Sikh psyche, their history?' Romesh Bhandari, secretary in the Ministry of External Affairs and related to Patiala's former ruling family, too held the view that Alexander did not understand Punjab and was a hardliner. People had as much respect for Alexander on Punjab as Parthasarathi and Rasgotra had for him on foreign policy, which was very little. To cite an episode, when Alexander suggested to the PM that she might send Parthasarathi on a secret mission to Sri Lanka for talks with Bandaranaike, Bhandari's reaction was, 'Can anyone think of anything more ridiculous?' On the other hand, one could argue that it was better that the situation was handled by someone who was not emotionally involved; he was likely to be more objective and ruthless, if required.

But Punjab continued to burn.

The army was called in to assist the governor of Punjab. The government played the last card and the PM made a forceful appeal to the Akalis on the night of 2 June 1984 in an address on TV. She was convincing, sincere and well meaning. She more or less played the Punjab long playing record in her speech.

Before the eruptions in Punjab, the PM had everything going for her—a massive mandate, two-thirds majority in the Lok Sabha, personal popularity surpassed only by her father, a reputation of someone who could get things done, of being decisive. However, most of it had dissipated by June 1984. On paper, the country did make a lot of progress. But her own image and credibility had diminished. Punjab gave her extreme worries. She told foreign visitors that she allowed things to drift in the hope that the problem would get resolved on its own. She had no one like P.N. Haksar to advise her. Haksar was her principal secretary during her earlier stint as the PM in the 1970s. Dhawan told me that Haksar was brilliant and did not bother about appointments of additional secretaries or other junior officials. But, Dhawan added: Haksar gave wrong advice at the time of 1972 election, about pre-dating Yashpal Kapur's resignation letter*, which eventually led to her losing the election case to Raj Narain and to the declaration of Emergency in 1975.

Operation Blue Star

The army operation in Amritsar was without question the most difficult decision the PM had to take in her long political career.

*Yashpal Kapur was officer on special duty to Indira Gandhi. He later resigned and served as her election agent.

On 1 June 1984, the PM instructed the army to start preparations for attacking the Golden Temple complex in Amritsar. Operation Blue Star was launched on 6 June 1984. Her television address on the morning of 3 June had sort of prepared the ground. The army was called in and given the task of clearing the terrorists from the temple. A massive operation was undertaken; tanks were brought in. The Sikh terrorists had fortified themselves extremely efficiently and every meter had to be fought for. Causalities on both sides were heavy—about 400 on the Sikh side and 60 on the side of the security forces. The extremists were heavily armed, with enough ammunition to equip a brigade—medium machine guns, rocket launchers, anti-tank missiles, grenades, and hundreds of rifles and stun guns.

Bhindranwale was found dead with 40 others in the basement of the Akal Takht. There was speculation for two days about his fate. Facts about how he died were not clear. It was likely that he was wounded on the first floor of the Akal Takht and was moved to the basement, where he died for want of medical attention. Legend would certainly make him a martyr as one who sacrificed his life rather than fall into the hands of the 'enemy of the Sikhs'.

The chief of Intelligence Bureau (IB), K. Sankaran Nair (popularly known as Shanks), went to Amritsar and saw Bhindranwale's body and other carnage. He was all praise for the defences set up by the extremists and all curses for their ruthlessness and utter lack of humaneness. They had unleashed a veritable reign of terror. They showed no mercy to the security forces, while the latter had exercised great restraint. He found bodies piled up all over the place. Bhindranwale's right side of the face was found blown off.

Fortunately, the main temple, Harmandir Sahib, had not

been damaged. President Zail Singh, who was distressed about the whole affair, flew to Amritsar and satisfied himself about the Harmandir Sahib. This was expected to assuage the feelings of the Sikhs, who were hurt and angry. In Delhi and other parts of the country, the simmering anger of the Sikh community was palpable. Abroad, too, our missions became the subject of demonstrations and stone throwing. Within the country, there was a sense of relief that the government had acted decisively. There was also general appreciation in India and abroad that the PM was right in delaying action to demonstrate that all peaceful avenues had been explored and exhausted. There was a sense that this factor would help her in the upcoming elections; personally, I did not think elections were a factor in her decision.

By coincidence, the officer incharge of the operation Blue Star was a Sikh—Lt Gen. Dayal. There were other Sikh officers and men. The first group of 10 commandos was led by a Muslim officer. And the commandos who led the strike on the Akal Takht came from the Research and Analysis Wing (R&AW).

One theory about Bhindranwale was that he was killed by members of Babbar Khalsa people in an internal fight on the 6 June. Two other important Sikh leaders, Harchand Singh Longowal and Gurcharan Singh Tohra, managed to escape on 6 June in the nick of time; otherwise, they would have been killed inside the complex. Nearly all non-Sikhs believed that there was no alternative. Many Hindus were thrilled that the Sikhs had been thrashed and taught a good lesson. But the Sikhs were deeply hurt. Not one Sikh approved of government action. Some Sikhs resigned from their parliamentary and legislature seats. Some Sikhs, one being Khushwant Singh, the celebrated writer who returned his Padma Bhushan but refused to resign from his Rajya Sabha seat, believed that by this action, the government had achieved what Bhindranwale had sought to achieve, namely the separation of the Sikhs as a distinct nation, alienated from other communities, seething with hurt pride and anger and determined to take revenge on the Hindu India.

Since Operation Blue Star, the PM's approach changed to 'the healing touch'. In several of her public speeches, she said how it should not be treated as a victory or defeat, how the government had to order the operation with a heavy heart, how as a mother, she felt the pain of so many deaths and how the aim of her government now was to win over the Sikhs and restore communal harmony.

The problem was that there was no one on the Sikh side with whom the government could negotiate. She did not have a single Sikh on her side except President Zail Singh who cautiously avoided making any comment. She had Buta Singh, her own creation, but he did not command any respect.

In the meantime, killings were going on in Punjab, as if Operation Blue Star had never happened. Phase two of the operation was to flush out the terrorists from the countryside. The Sikhs were not accepting the government's contention that Harmandir Sahib had not been damaged; the government then decided to telecast a special feature on television every day, showing the unscathed structure of Harmandir Sahib.

Another controversy was about Pakistan's involvement. The major general in charge of the operation spoke categorically of Pakistan's involvement, citing vast quantities of Chinese-origin arms from Pakistan captured as evidence. He also spoke of two Nihangs who were found, on medical examination, to be Pakistanis (they were circumcised). The government itself neither made such an allegation nor did they deny it. When

The Sunday Times asked her what worried her the most, she replied 'destabilization'. Her theory was that there was a master hand guiding and organizing the whole campaign and that this person was operating from abroad. The movement itself was financed by the Sikhs living abroad, mostly in Canada but also in the US, the UK and other Western countries. She told all foreigners that the West, particularly the US, was determined to keep India weak, that we were surrounded by hostile neighbours, etc. Involvement of foreign hand featured too often in her speeches.

The Akal Takht had been badly damaged and was beyond repair. This fact had been kept from the public and this was why the Golden Temple could not be thrown open to the public. The PM went to Amritsar two weeks after the Operation Blue Star; it was the fourth anniversary of Sanjay's death. A friend from the IB told me that there were thousands of people on the streets but not a single Sikh. The security around her and Rajiv had been tightened by 200 per cent. There were reports that the Sikhs abroad had collected huge sums and hired professionals to assassinate the family. There were several army deserters at large who were motivated enough to kill the family. This army mutiny was quite serious as hundreds of deserters had been killed in encounters with the army. There was a report that 23 Sikh soldiers had crossed over to Pakistan. In Rambagh, Bihar, the mutineers had shot their commanding officer, Brigadier Puri.

And now we were to witness another drama.

13

THE HIJACK

On 5 July 1984, an Indian Airline airbus, on a regular flight from Srinagar to Delhi, was hijacked by some Sikhs to be flown to Lahore. We got the news at about 5.00 p.m. They threatened to blow up the plane unless it was permitted to land in Lahore. Rasgotra sent a message to Pakistan, asking them to permit the plane to land, which they did, after the plane circled over Lahore airport for 90 minutes. Somehow, Pakistan did not let out that we had to request to let the plane land. Instead, they said that they had allowed the plane to land because of humanitarian considerations.

The hijackers demanded $25 million, withdrawal of the army from the Golden Temple, release of all the arrested Sikhs and refueling of the aircraft, and their deadline was 2.30 a.m. the same day. Of course, there was no question of conceding to their demands. We offered to send our commandos, but Pakistan said that they could handle the situation.* Nothing

*In 1981, Pakistan commandos had surprised hijackers by dressing up as sweepers.

happened during the night. There were 355 people on board. The hijackers refused to release even women and children. No food, not even water, was allowed to be brought in. In the morning, the hijackers asked to speak to Balbir Singh Sandhu, secretary general of the outlawed All India Sikh Students Federation, and said if Sandhu asked them to, then they would release the passengers. They were still insisting on refuelling, but we requested Pakistan not to do so. Rasgotra even asked Americans to speak to Pakistan not to refuel; Pakistan was only too happy to oblige. Just after noon on 6 July, the leader of the hijackers went out to meet Pakistani officials, returned to the aircraft and announced the negotiations had failed and they would blow up the plane in five minutes. There was panic, with many passengers breaking into tears.

Quarter of an hour later, the leader of the hijackers went out to talk to the Pakistani officials again and declared it was all okay and that they would be releasing the passengers. The hijackers surrendered unconditionally to the Pakistani authorities. The passengers were given a sightseeing tour of Lahore, fed and sent back to Delhi in a Pakistan International Airlines plane. The hijackers were driven to a guest house. The drama lasted 20 hours.

Commando action did not have to be resorted to; otherwise, Pakistan would have made a success story of it and earned our great obligation. Rasgotra was euphoric about Pakistan's helpful and friendly attitude. This was also the general public reaction. Rasgotra suggested that the PM should ring up Zia or at least send a message to him. My feeling was that she should not, unless Pakistan returned the hijackers. The PM was greatly relieved, but she was also angry that we did not press strongly enough to hand over the hijackers' baggage to us. The hijackers were extremely keen to have the passengers' baggage. At one stage, they agreed to let the passengers leave if they left their baggage behind and the plane was refueled. They did not permit our people to be present when they inspected the baggage. The PM told Sharada that Pakistan would surely have been hand in glove with the hijackers; she suspected that they would have made some deal. She did not agree to talk to Zia or send a personal message to him. The spokesman, however, had to make a statement, expressing government's appreciation.

The acid test of Pakistan's intentions was what they decided about the hijackers. The five hijackers of 1981 were still enjoying Pakistan's hospitality. Rasgotra did not even want to ask for the return of the hijackers. There were several unexplained points. Where would the hijackers have gone after refueling? The answer was 'nowhere' because no country would have given them asylum, except Pakistan. Another point was about the security lapse at Srinagar airport. How did the hijackers manage to take revolvers and grenades with them? The 'collusion' explanation was valid. It was convenient to blame the Farooq Abdullah government for it. The hijackers were all young people with one of them only 15 or 16 years old; we were told he was crying when the drama ended. They shouted slogans of 'Khalistan Zindabad' and 'Pakistan Zindabad'.

Amidst the tension inside the aircraft, some humanitarian stories also unfolded, which we came to know about later. There was a child who did not know what was happening and asked one of the hijackers, '*Uncle, bathroom jana hai* (I want to go to the bathroom).' He was allowed. One air hostess proved she was Sardarni, by producing a pocket Guru Granth Sahib from her bag and reciting a few verses in Gurmukhi, whereupon one hijacker touched her feet and said, 'You are my sister, and no harm shall come to you.'

Meanwhile, the Golden Temple was thrown open to the public. But the army could not be withdrawn. A myth was growing that Bhindranwale was not dead and that he had escaped through a tunnel and would reappear at a suitable time.

An interesting point emerged about the hijacking. From all accounts, including that of an English couple, we were convinced that the hijackers were given pistols at Lahore airport. Pakistan, of course, denied it. But the fact was that the hijackers did not brandish any pistol between Chandigarh and Lahore, which they would have certainly done had they had access to the arms then. They displayed the firearms only after taking off from Lahore. The English couple said that they saw a Pakistani man hand over a newspaper package, which contained two pistols. The circumstantial evidence was strong.

The PM told me that when Zia spoke to her on the first day of the hijacking, he was quite rude. He told her that this was the fourth hijacking in recent times and that the Indian government had to do something about it. She told him that the Pakistan government's refusal or failure to punish the hijackers on an earlier occasion or to hand them over to India had encouraged the others. She said to me that Zia did not say anything about the pistols. From a telegram from Islamabad, it was noted that the hijackers had been given chicken for dinner and the passengers had only been given snacks. She also told me that when Zia spoke to her the following morning, he sounded defensive. She asked him about the pistols, and he said that he did not know anything about it, even though he had told her the previous evening that he was in close touch with his people in Lahore.

The hijackers were returned to India; the UAE government handed them over to us. Bhandari had a part in this. He was also called 'Sheikh Bhandari'. His contacts with the Gulf sheikhs came in handy. In the UAE, the hijackers were taken in heavily curtained buses to the aircraft. The plane was American and so was the crew. The hijackers thought they were going to America when they saw the air hostesses were American. They confessed that the pistols were given to them in Lahore.

The Punjab Debate Resumes

The much awaited and much feared (by the government) debate on Punjab started on 24 July 1984. It was not much of a debate though. The Opposition was divided and not in a position to condemn the government's action. They did, however, find fault with the white paper and also made the expected points about not taking timely action, about the Congress having built up Bhindranwale, and so on. But the ruling party was able to answer all the points. The PM firmly rejected allegations of Bhindranwale having shared a platform with her. She made a speech in Parliament, which, though not a great speech or an intellectual peroration, was effective and sincere: 'I might have made mistakes, but I had erred only in order to avoid bloodshed.' She made it clear that she would never think of a separate state or religious places being abused for political purposes. One of the things she said in her speech was that the British had propagated the myth of some communities being martial and the others as non-martial. 'This is not so,' she said in Parliament. 'Any community can become good soldiers with good training.' She said to me, 'Except your state (Gujarat)!' while we were walking back from the House to her office. I told her that the same thought had occurred to me. She probably thought I had been offended. So, she added, 'But in recent years, people of Gujarat, particularly girls, have

14

THE ASSASSINATION

It was a Wednesday and the RAX at my home rang just before 9.15 a.m. I assumed it to be a call from someone in the office about an appointment or a draft, so I left for the office without taking the call.

As soon as I reached office, Natwar called on the office RAX, 'Have you heard?'

I was sure he was referring to some posting or transfer, perhaps my own. I said I had heard nothing. He said that the PM has been shot at. I could not believe my ears.

'How bad?' I asked.

'Very,' he said, adding that she had been rushed to the All India Institute of Medical Sciences (AIIMS). I immediately went to the PM's house at 1, Safdarjung Road. Sharada was present there and so was Dhawan. Teji Bachchan was also there. Both Teji and Harivansh Rai Bachchan were very close to the Gandhi family. The security cordon was tight. I had to cross three barriers, but faced no difficulty going inside, thus become very good mountaineers.'

The only jarring note in her speech was repeated references to 'my family'. This overemphasis on family did not sound decent in a democracy. Thousands of other families had also made tremendous sacrifices during the freedom movement. No family could have a monopoly on patriotism. As an extenuating factor, one could say that her family probably had a greater record in the service of the nation than most others present in the House, including the people in her own party.

As for Punjab, things were not getting settled at all and killings were going on as before. I doubted if the government would ever be able to withdraw the army in such circumstances. A knowledgeable source had told me that the army had completely mishandled Operation Blue Star, which had lasted 36 hours; it ought to have been finished in two hours. He said the army knew that all the defences were facing inward into the temple complex. When the army ran into stiff resistance inside the complex, it should have attacked from the outside, from the lanes surrounding the complex. That way, at least the front façade of the Akal Takht would have not been destroyed.

Whatever it was, the actions of the government in Operation Blue Star did not inspire confidence. The media was kept under censorship for many weeks. Stories were fed to the media that the Akal Takht was damaged only slightly, even though it had been blasted completely.

The general elections, too, were nearing and it meant that I would soon go out on a posting in early 1985. But nobody was prepared for the events of 31 October 1984.

showing that our security chaps could easily be browbeaten into allowing passage.

The PM's Last Walk

I went to the exact spot where she had been shot. The ground was still wet with blood. There were other blood marks on the ground a few yards away from the spot. More than 20 empty cartridges were still lying on the ground. Her chappals—simple black ones—with small heels were lying around. Her umbrella, the one she always carried, was flung on one side. It was a red-and-green, big, striped umbrella, like one of a golfer. I told her once at the airport that it was a golfer umbrella. 'I know,' she had said. I had told her she should have a proper ladies' umbrella. 'Yes, I won't mind,' she had replied. I had thought of bringing one for her and presenting it to her, but never did because I first wanted to check the colour with her. Now it was too late. The sten gun with which she was shot was still there, just a few feet away from her chappals. I think the whole magazine of 30 bullets had been pumped into her at close range, in addition to four to five pistol shots.

This is how it happened. I have pieced the event together from what different people have said, including what Rajiv Gandhi told foreign visitors. An Irish channel team was to record a documentary on her for a new series on world leaders. She was going to be the first in a series of a few. Peter Ustinov, the famous British actor, had come especially for it. He was to be the producer of the recording of the interview. Originally, the recording was to start at 8.30 a.m., but the time was shifted by 15 minutes. Someone from the Doordarshan team had come and applied light make-up on her. The recording was to resume at 11.00 a.m. in the office, so Sharada had asked the make-up person to come to Parliament House at 11.00 a.m. 'Not Parliament House, but Safdarjung,' the PM had corrected.

It was past nine and she was getting impatient, 'Why are they not ready yet?' Sharada had gone to find out. The filming was to be shot in the lawn behind 1, Akbar Road. The Irish TV team had been making a fuss about having flowers, tea tray, and so on in the background.

Dr Mathur, the PM's physician was there. He had seen her at about nine. He hung on for a few minutes and left for the hospital at about 9.15 a.m. The PM, knowing that Sharada would have organized everything, started off from 1, Akbar Road. Sometimes, she would be in a car, but often walked. On that day, she had chosen to walk. Dhawan was with her, while her security officer Bhatt was ahead of her. Her personal attendant Nathuram had been following her. Dhawan and she were talking about the programme for the day. As they had approached within 5 feet of the wicket gate between the Akbar and Safdarjung Road compounds, the security officer at the gate fired at her with his pistol at point-blank range. We still do not know for certain how many shots he fired.

The PM most certainly did not see the gunman open fire because her face was turned right as she was talking to Dhawan. As soon as she fell down, the other gunman opened his sten gun and emptied the entire magazine of 30 bullets at one go.

Sharada and the Irish channel team heard the gun shots. The director, a woman, had remarked, 'That sounds ominous.'

Unaware of the turn of events, Sharada had jokingly said, 'Oh, it must be the last of the Diwali crackers.' But, he soon heard the commotion.

The two hurried outside. The time was 9.18 a.m., Sharada recollected.

Dr Mathur said he had left and had just reached the roundabout close to the house. He had not heard anything but was summoned as soon as he reached office.

She was driven in a car to AIIMS. She had undoubtedly died instantaneously on the spot. But the doctors kept on trying till 2.30 p.m. No miracle seemed possible.

Ill Prepared for Emergency

Both the assailants were Sikhs and members of her own security staff. One, sub-inspector Beant Singh, had been with her for 10 years. The other, Constable Satwant Singh, aged 21, was a fresh recruit. Since the Operation Blue Star, the security had withdrawn Sikh staff, but she had objected. Not only that, she had insisted that they had to be put on duty in the inner circle. She must have had her fears. Barely three minutes before her assassination, she had told Rahul, her grandson, that there were too many Sikhs in her house.

The previous evening, she had returned from a two-day trip to Orissa (now Odisha) at about 9.00 p.m. In her last public speech, she had said that if she were to die, she would want the nation to know that she had worked for the country till the last drop of her blood. How prophetic!

After completing their dastardly act, the assassins threw their weapons. According to one version, they ran towards the wall to escape. According to another, they were overpowered on the spot. They were taken to the guard room. After about 10–15 minutes, a scuffle took place and the commandos, one of whom opened fire, killed one of the assailants and severely wounded the other. At first, everyone had assumed that the assailant was killed by the commandos at the time of the assassination itself. But when it became evident that this was not so, Arun Nehru, scion of the Nehru family, immediately suspected foul play along the lines of Kennedy's murderer Oswald being killed by Jack Ruby. It was only thereafter that the commando who killed one and wounded the other assailant was himself placed under arrest. The fact that the commando had not run away should go against the theory that the conspirators had tried to silence the criminals to do away with evidence. Everyone thought that Satwant Singh had been killed, but it turned out that Beant Singh was the one who had been killed. They had both shouted that they had completed what they had to do.

The PM had no time to utter a single word when she was shot at, unlike Mahatma Gandhi whose last words were 'Hey Ram'. I am sure she had no time to realize what was happening. If she had even a second to think, or feel something, she would have been in incredulity at what was happening and that it was her own trusted security men who had shot at her.

Things were not in order on the morning of 31 October. The Sikh security persons were not supposed to be on duty. They had exchanged their duties with their colleagues. They were from different units and their respective controlling officers did not maintain any liaison with each other. The commandos on duty did not rush to the scene of shooting. The ambulance van could not start, so she had to be rushed in a car. The hospital had not been telephoned, so barring a couple of junior doctors, no senior doctor was available. The roads were not cleared of traffic. In short, all kinds of drills required for such an emergency were of no avail whatsoever.

There was persistent doubt that had the security officer

on duty been alert enough, he could have prevented the sten gun onslaught. Some people were talking of a 40-second gap between the pistol and sten gun shots, but this was simply not true. As soon as she fell, the sten gun opened up.

The doctors put her on an artificial heart and lung. There were rumours that she had revived once for a little while.

The All India Radio kept saying that her condition was serious. It was only at 6.00 p.m. that her death was officially announced with the time of death decided as 2.30 p.m.

Meanwhile, a large crowd had gathered at AIIMS, waiting and seething with anger against the Sikhs. For a while, some people thought that the identity of the assassins should not be disclosed. But it was impossible. The news had spread faster than wildfire. So, as soon as the death was announced, the crowd went for the Sikhs—their houses, their cars and their lives. The spark of the anti-Sikh violence was ignited at AIIMS and soon enveloped most parts of Delhi. Sikhs, several scores of them, were burnt alive. Many more were shot, stabbed and lynched. Instant comparisons were made with the 1947 riots. For three days, there was a complete breakdown of law and order.

The government seemed paralysed for the first 24 hours. There was no one in Delhi who could take decisions. The home minister was in Hyderabad, defence minister was in Moscow and finance minister had gone to West Bengal. The PM's principal secretary, cabinet secretary and finance secretary had left for Bombay for a meeting of the Atomic Energy Commission of India. Rajiv was in Bengal. The President was away on a state visit to Yemen.

Calls for police assistance went unanswered. Hindu mobs went hunting for Sikhs, many of whom were given shelter and protection by their Hindu friends. There have been several instances of Hindus rescuing Sikhs, at considerable risk to themselves. The army was called in rather late, and took 12 hours to get organized and deployed. Shoot at sight orders were issued but carried out only after 24 hours. There was an atmosphere of panic—an ideal fertile ground for rumours. One rumour was that many Sikhs had come from Patiala after shaving off their beards and hair with the motive of taking revenge on the Hindus. What infuriated the Hindus was that there was no word of condemnation by the Sikhs on PM's assassination. Five priests issued a statement on the same day, condemning the murder, but they quickly retracted, denying they had issued any such statement.

At the time, Rajiv was in some village in West Bengal. It was only at about noon that he was informed about the shooting, but was not told about her death. The West Bengal government had an Indian Airlines plane emptied for him and the defence ministry had also sent an aircraft. He had to drive to the nearest town, fly to Calcutta (now Kolkatta) by helicopter and reach Delhi at about 5.00 p.m. Finance minister Pranab Mukherjee and Speaker Balram Jakhar were with him.

The question of succession was uppermost in most people's minds. Parthasarathi and Vice President Ramaswamy Venkataraman were at AIIMS, where Arun Nehru joined them. They discussed how to go about installing Rajiv. On previous such occasions, the practice had been to appoint a caretaker or an interim PM. This time, they did not want to do so. Back in 1964 and again in 1966, there were no clear successors. There were two candidates on each occasion. Indira Gandhi herself had to be elected in 1966 against Morarji Desai. She was supported by the Syndicate because she was thought of as pliant and weak, someone they could manipulate. No bigger miscalculation could have been made.

They did not want to wait for even a day or two. Who

knew if someone might decide to contest. Sharada told me that President Zail Singh himself might have been harbouring ambitions. 'Every president has wanted to become prime minister,' he said.

Normally, the Congress Parliamentary Board would elect the leader. But almost all the Members of Parliament were out of Delhi. So, the Congress Parliamentary Board, which had only six members, met. Two of them were dead. Of the remaining four, only three were in Delhi. They met at AIIMS itself and signed a letter to the President to swear in Rajiv Gandhi. Vice President Venkataraman had some doubt whether President Zail Singh would agree to swear in Rajiv immediately on his return from Yemen. So, he rode with him from the airport, and the President readily agreed.

Parthasarathi told me that the idea of interim PM was difficult. The PM's house was hostile to Pranab Mukherjee; PV had better support in the House. But Pranab had always regarded himself as No. 2 and had, in fact, presided over cabinet meetings during the PM's absence. Parthasarathi said that during the flight from Calcutta to Delhi, Pranab made some noise about his claim to become the interim PM, but was prevailed upon by Jakhar and others to not insist.

Rajiv was met at the airport by Parthasarathi and others. He readily agreed to accept the leadership of the party and the prime ministership. Of course, he drove straight to AIIMS. The President arrived half an hour later. He agreed to fall in line and Rajiv was sworn in at 6.45 p.m. as the sixth PM of India.

The next on the agenda was the issue of which other ministers should be sworn in at the same time. Should the entire previous council of ministers be retained? Rajiv's entourage wanted to exclude some names, and high on that list were names like P.C. Sethi, Vasant Sathe and Kalpanath

Rai. These decisions could not be taken immediately because Rajiv was reluctant to start his prime ministership on a note of discord. So, four cabinet ministers were sworn in along with him—Pranab Mukherjee, PV, Buta Singh and Shiv Shankar. I was present on this historic occasion.

The Funeral

Right from the morning, I had suggested that someone should issue an appeal for communal harmony. Parthasarathi thought that Venkatraman could do it, but he was reluctant. It was decided that Rajiv should issue the appeal at 9.00 p.m. on the AIR and Doordarshan. Sharada came to the South Block to draft an appeal. I had prepared two paragraphs, which Sharada incorporated at the end of his draft. The draft was given to Rajiv at Rashtrapati Bhavan. It was passed on to Amitabh Bachchan (Rajiv's family friend), who used some of the material and produced a new text in Hindi. Sharada and I went to 1, Akbar Road for the recording of the audio message. Amitabh Bachchan was obviously proud of his creation, and it did sound impressive. He then added two longish sentences from the paragraphs I had suggested. The English version of the text was typed out. But Rajiv wanted the Hindi version of the text to be written in longhand in big type which one of the technicians from the AIR did.

It was about 10.30 p.m. when Rajiv was called in for the recording. The moment he saw the Hindi text in four pages, he said, 'My god, this would take at least six takes.' He was nearly right—it took five.

That broadcast recording session brought out flashes of temper from Rajiv. As he sat down for the recording, he objected to the number of microphones and pushed away one. A technician requested him not to remove it since it was indispensable to the recording. But Rajiv objected, saying, 'Why can't there be coordination between the AIR and Doordarshan?' The technician persisted—I admired her guts—and Rajiv relented, but ordered that this must never happen again. He then addressed H.K.L. Bhagat, who was not a minister strictly speaking, midway and said, 'This sort of thing must not happen again.' Many among those present felt that he should not have spoken to a senior politician like that. Some wondered if this was going to be the working style of the new PM.

On the morning of 1 November, Indira Gandhi's body was taken to Teen Murti at around or just before eight. The embalming job was not well done and her face had swollen up, particularly her lips. She no longer looked her charming self. She would definitely have disapproved of her looks as she lay in state at the Teen Murti house. Rajiv was not happy with her appearance at the time and wanted something to be done. Dr Mathur called the doctors at six and they came at 7.30 a.m. The public would have been able to see the body and pay their condolences from 7.00 a.m. on the 2 November, but it was only at about 9.00 a.m. that the public was allowed in. By that time, security arrangements had totally collapsed. The VIP line itself stretched 1 km and two women nearly got crushed. Order could only be restored once the army was put in charge.

Maneka Gandhi, the widow of Indira Gandhi's younger son Sanjay, came to the funeral with her son, Varun. She went up to the pier and spent not more than 30–40 seconds; in fact, little Varun spent a longer time in the company of his cousins.

Arun Singh was the person closest to Rajiv and one who enjoyed his complete confidence. It was clear that he was going to use his position. He took full charge of the funeral arrangements. He would be the single most important and extra-constitutional centre of power.

The funeral was fixed at 4.30 p.m. on 3 November. The Hindu custom is to not keep the body overnight. Nehru was cremated the next day, as was his immediate successor Lal Bahadur Shastri. This time, we preferred a gap of 48 hours, so as to give time to foreign leaders to come for the funeral.

The participation of foreign dignitaries in the funeral was unprecedented. There were more than 110 delegations—nearly 60 presidents and PMs, plus many vice presidents, vice premiers, speakers, and so on. We were expecting a crowd of 2–5 million, judging from the unending line of people at Teen Murti.

On 3 November, Sharada, Gopi Arora, additional secretary in the PMO, and I went over the entire route and hardly found any crowd at all. There was no movement of people, no throngs at important junctions like India Gate. This was a cause of serious concern; we were worrying about how to control crowds, whereas now our worry was the absence of crowds. The riots in the city, the curfew and the absence of public transport, together with rumours of Sikhs threatening to loot houses of Hindu families if they went for the funeral, discouraged people from coming out. We went back and reported what we saw. I suggested to Arun Singh for a slight postponement for the departure of the cortege, but it started on time.

Our worst fears were proved right until the journey to Vijay Chowk. The only people on the streets were those living in nearby houses and servants' quarters. We felt deeply sad. Indira Gandhi, who loved crowds, who gave her all to the people, was practically shunned by the people on her last journey. It was only from India Gate that people started joining us. At the Shanti Van, the funeral ground, the crowd was impressive—about half a million. The foreign visitors were vastly impressed, but we were depressed. Till the previous day, even Rajiv was saying that there would be a crowd of 3–5 million. In the car, we were discussing the size of crowds seen at the funeral processions of other important people. Sharada said that the funeral of S.K. Patil, the 'King of Bombay', was attended by merely 35 people. Gopi Arora said the funeral of Ram Manohar Lohia, the socialist leader, was attended by only 35,000. Sardar Patel drew large crowds in Bombay (Now Mumbai), but with no solemnity on the occasion. Well, Indira Gandhi's funeral was certainly solemn, and the crowds were considerable under the given circumstances.

Indira Gandhi's ashes were strewn over the Himalayas on 11 November. She loved the mountains. But she did not like the sun. She could not bear the sun for one minute. Even on that fateful morning, for the short walk from Akbar Road to Safdarjung Road house, she had covered herself with the familiar golf umbrella. How sad it was to see her on her last journey with her body being carried on the gun carriage under the blazing sun for 12 km, all the way to the cremation ground.

15

RAJIV GANDHI: THE MODERN PRIME MINISTER

Rajiv Gandhi started going to the South Block office from 12 November 1984. On his first day, he was escorted by Alexander to his prime ministerial office. The photographers were there in full strength to record the historic event. The new PM met officers of the PMO the same evening, laid stress on modernizing working methods and asked, 'Why can't our office run electronically? Let us have computers.' As expected, he emphasized that we must follow-up on the implementation of policies. To the MEA also, he stressed on the introduction of computers, especially in the passport offices. Rasgotra said they had been thinking of introducing computers, whereupon the PM responded with 'Why didn't you go beyond thinking to implementing?' He was firm but polite.

Rajiv and the Sympathy Factor

Arun Singh was sworn in on 12 November as parliamentary secretary to the PM. Arun Nehru became general secretary of the party. R.K. Dhawan was appointed special assistant but his arch enemy, M.L. Fotedar, was made political secretary to the PM. Dhawan felt confident that he would regain his influential position in due course of time, and told me that just 15 days before her assassination, Indira Gandhi had told him how she looked upon Dhawan as her son!

Rajiv went to Amethi in the third week of November to file his nomination papers; it used to be Indira Gandhi's constituency. I asked Dhawan whether the time for filing had been fixed by astrologers. He said that unlike his mother, he did not believe in astrology. As for her, even the time for leaving the house for office would be decided by astrologers.

On the morning of 1 November, Sharada told me that at least now, the Nobel Committee should give her the Nobel Peace Prize. I told him that the Nobel was not given posthumously, citing the example of Mahatma Gandhi who was never conferred with the Nobel. The government decided to institute a peace prize in her memory. When the matter was discussed in Alexander's room, I raised reservations. 'We already have Jawaharlal Nehru Award. We have difficulty in identifying worthy recipients for it every year, sometimes we are desperate and give it to just anybody. If you have one more prize, our problem would double.' Everyone agreed with me. But when the matter went to the Cabinet, no one said anything. Alexander said Rajiv desperately wanted it to be accepted.

Then one day, the Soviet ambassador brought a message from his leadership for the PM; they wanted to confer the

Lenin Peace Prize on the late PM. Rajiv immediately agreed. The ambassador was thrilled and asked whether he could convey this to his leadership. Rajiv looked at me. I said in Hindi that he might like to consult his cabinet colleagues first and that he could tell the ambassador that he would let him know later. (The ambassador's interpreter knew Hindi, but Rajiv did not know that!)

Alexander, when I briefed him about all this, said, 'No, no, this is a very important matter to decide, it has many implications, it is always given to fellow travellers, this would have to be decided by the CCPA.'

On the other hand, Parthasarathi's reaction was, 'How can you refuse it? It is the highest honour bestowed by the Soviets. After all, what is there in the Nobel Peace Prize? It was only a conscience money given by a man who made a lot of money selling arms and explosives.' She was given the Lenin Peace Prize.

Elections were declared for 24 and 27 December 1984. The general expectation was that the 'sympathy factor' would help the Congress sail through. Some forecasts even placed the Congress's strength at over 400. The scramble for tickets was in full swing. Everyone talked about seeking help from young professionals who knew how to operate computers because, for the first time, the data about possible candidates was being fed into computers.

In the last week of November 1984, US Senator Claiborne Pell called on the PM. Harry Barnes, the American ambassador, who came with Pell, asked the PM about the elections. The PM said the Congress would do very well, the Opposition was divided and the supporting record was for all to see. I was taken aback by the PM's confident reply; Indira Gandhi would have never said anything like that.

Four more senators called on him after that meeting. All in all, I felt a bit uneasy about the PM's talks with all these senators. They told him they had dinner with Zia the previous evening, that Zia was sincere in his desire for peace with India, that the US wanted to be an important factor in Indo-Pak relations, etc. They also told him that he should try to open a new chapter, use the window of opportunity after the elections. Rajiv said he intended to do just that. He did not say a word about American arms supply to Pakistan or about the latter's nuclear ambitions. The senators spoke to him about Afghanistan. They flattered him by saying that only India and he were in the position to speak to the Soviets and urged that he do so after the elections. He agreed to oblige.

Most tricky of all, they pumped him about his ideas regarding the economy. They asked him whether there would be a shift in favour of free enterprise. When he said something that was somewhat in the affirmative, Senator John Glenn got very excited, 'Prime Minister, this is very important. If, as you say, you were going to move away from the socialist system towards free enterprise, it would be an important incentive for private investment throughout the world.' Rajiv was not categorical about saying any such thing. After I left, I had a feeling that he would like to make such a shift eventually.

Alexander was aghast when I reported to him about the meeting. He asked whether I could have given some advice to Rajiv in Hindi, but quickly added that I could not have, since Barnes understood Hindi. I said even if Barnes was not there, I would not have interrupted the PM.

The election results were out on 30 December. They surpassed the most optimistic forecasts of the Congress itself. The tally was over 400. The Opposition was decimated. Maneka lost her deposit to Rajiv. Madhavrao Scindia bested

Atal Bihari Vajpayee, Amitabh Bachchan humbled the wily Bahuguna and Sunil Dutt, the actor and husband of the renowned actress Nargis, defeated Ram Jethmalani, the famous criminal lawyer. Natwar and K.R. Narayanan, both former diplomats, won. How many foreign ministers were we going to have?

Rajiv was sworn in on 31 December 1984 at 5.20 p.m. The real surprise was not who all were included but who all were dropped. Pranab did not find a place in the new cabinet. The prospective ministers had no idea whether they would be in or out. In the 'Yes Minister' fashion, the aspirants would have literally been glued to their phones. R.N. Mirdha, a Congress politician, got the call at 3.00 a.m. and so did Natwar. While Natwar became the Minister of State for Steel, Mirdha became the Minister of State for Home.

There was confusion at Rashtrapati Bhavan, as nobody recognized the new ministers. A surprise inclusion was Arun Nehru, who was given Power portfolio. The PM kept external affairs, commerce, industry and all the science departments with himself. As soon as the ceremony was over, all the ministers were seen rushing to Alexander to ask him about their portfolios!

The PM Meant Business

By early January 1985, PM Rajiv Gandhi had succeeded in convincing everyone that he meant business, that he was serious and in earnest. He was sending out the right signals. Like his mother, no one would be able to presume on his confidence. Anyone who began to behave as if he was close to or favourite of the PM would be in for a shock. Sengupta was replaced by Montek Singh Ahluwalia for the post of the additional secretary in the PMO. Even Sharada felt that he might have to go, as he was past 60 and Rajiv might not give him extension. However, Rajiv did give him an extension for one year to the delight of everyone at the PMO.

There was a move to transfer me back to the MEA. I asked Arun Singh whether the PM wanted to replace me. His reply was categorically in the negative. He said I was in the panel for additional secretary and that was why I might have to go because the post in the PMO was of the rank of joint secretary. I told him I was already additional secretary and the PM had personally approved to upgrade the post. In that case, Arun Singh said that my going back to the ministry would give the wrong impression.

The Americans were most excited at Rajiv's ascension to power. They were convinced he would correct the tilt towards the Soviets and even lean towards the West. His repeated emphasis on modernization and computerization led them to believe that they alone could supply what India under Rajiv would want. Quite a few senators travelled to India and were received by the PM. I tried to resist the requests for meeting him and he agreed, but Rasgotra brought a lot of pressure, and the PM could not say no to the Foreign Secretary all the time. And as it turned out, these meetings did not help in influencing the views of the senators.

Once, US Senator Charles Percy was in Delhi. He was so patronizing I could have hit him on the head. He said, among other things, that he had seen the Sri Lankan President just before meeting the PM; he wanted to come to India. Rajiv told him that he had spoken to J.R. Jayewardene on the phone that very morning and asked him to come over. To this, Percy replied, 'Fine, fantastic, well done.' I found him to be very shallow and patronizing. For him, India was just a profession, a tool to further, to enhance his political career. He really flattered Rajiv: 'America is very excited about you, you would receive a reception which no other head of state has ever received.' He brought up the question of IBM and other big companies and advised him to talk to those companies. After Percy left, the PM told me we must follow up on IBM. No one was giving us the computers except the Soviets, and one knew what their computers were like.

About an hour later, Barnes rang me up. He said that Percy was prepared to modify his travel plans and go to Pakistan to talk to Zia on India's behalf, if the PM so wished. I was quite shocked and wanted to decline the offer straight away, but I had to ask the PM. I first wanted to check with Alexander, Rasgotra and Parthasarathi. They all said that there was no question of accepting Percy's mediation. I conveyed this to the PM and asked him whether I could convey this to Barnes. His reaction was, 'What do we lose? If Percy goes to Pakistan with our list of complaints, won't it amount to a prominent American senator accepting the rightness of our claims?' He suggested I talk to PV in his new office of defence minister. Rao's reaction was the same as ours. The PM appeared a bit disappointed and reluctantly agreed that I might convey our reaction to Barnes. Barnes said that Percy would have a few days before returning to the US from Rome and his plan would not be affected by a visit to Pakistan. I said he need not take the trouble, but if the senator still decided to go to Pakistan, he may speak to Zia, but on his own and certainly not on our behalf. Barnes got the message but that did not help. A few days later, he brought another senator and told the PM that Percy's flight at Karachi had been delayed and he had conveyed 'your message' to Zia. The PM thanked him.

Percy claimed that he was responsible for the release of

90,000 Pakistan prisoners of war after the 1971 war. He told Rajiv that Zia had written to him in 1972, seeking his help in the matter. He had flown to Delhi, met Indira Gandhi, told her how the continued detention of the prisoners of war inflicted so much human misery and violated Geneva Conventions. 'Within two weeks, they were released.' Rubbish. Or, was he right?

Diplomacy at Top Speed!

The PM met ministers and secretaries to discuss problems and programmes of each ministry. He sent a note to all the officers in his office for follow-up reports of decisions taken or instructions given. He succeeded in creating an impression all around that he was a young man in a hurry to take the country into the twenty-first century.

He headed a meeting of the MEA on 9 January. He did not have in-depth acquaintance with all the issues, but he displayed a sound approach. Rasgotra suggested sending someone to China to make discreet soundings on the boundary question. Parthasarathi kind of supported him; the two of them would have discussed this before coming to the meeting.

'Do you seriously believe that you can solve a problem like this in matter of even a couple of years? And what is in it for us? What do we get in return? How do we sell it to the people?' was Rajiv's response. Rasgotra agreed that it was a complex problem, and that the Opposition would get a handle to beat the government with. 'But the Opposition is not relevant to this; we have to consider what is good for the country,' Rajiv said.

I pointed out that before we embarked on such secret diplomacy, we had to be clear in our minds on the terms on which we were prepared to settle. Alexander was strongly opposed to the proposal, asking what the hurry was about. We had to first build up trade links, he said, since the whole world was trying to cash in on the Chinese market.

There was a telegram from Ambassador A.P. Venkateswaran in Beijing. During his farewell call on Zhao Ziyang, the Ambassador expressed hope that in the next round of talks, we would start a discussion on the substantive issues of the boundary question. The PM noted on the cable, 'The Ministry of External Affairs is bombing at such top speed. Do we really need another discussion?' He was clearly not in a hurry to settle with China.

For the first few weeks after Rajiv took over, we had assumed that to get the PM to agree to something, all we needed to do was say the previous PM had agreed. We soon found out that that was ineffective.

For example, on Sri Lanka, the PM simply refused to agree to what the government and the previous PM had said. He took a hard line on Tamil militants and sent a clear signal to that effect to the Sri Lankans. When Lalith Athulathmudali, the leader of the Sri Lankan Tamils, was in Delhi, the PM met him alone for over an hour. Athulathmudali went back extremely pleased because Parthasarathi, who had a hardliner stance and was most concerned about the situation in Tamil Nadu, was kept out of the talks.

The Sri Lanka High Commissioner, Bernard Tilakaratne, came to see the PM on 16 January. The situation in Sri Lanka was bad. The multiparty talks had broken down and there appeared to be no hope whatsoever for its resumption. The PM's attitude probably left a deep impression on Tilakaratne. The PM said, 'We are not interested at all in destabilizing President Jayewardene, or his government. I sympathize with him, he must be in a difficult situation. We want to help within our constraints. I am speaking to you from my heart. It would be nice if he were to come over here even for a couple of hours. If he can't come, I can go down to Madras or Trivandrum and we can meet there.' I could see that he really wanted to go more than halfway in making up with our neighbours.

I believed that I had gradually acquired a fair idea of the PM's style of functioning. He wanted immediate decisions and expected us to follow up without any delay. I enjoyed his style, but was sceptical whether this change in mentality would filter down to lower levels of bureaucracy.

16

THE ESPIONAGE SCANDAL

The month of January 1985 turned out to be momentous. P.C. Alexander, principal secretary to the PM, was out; the French ambassador was being withdrawn at our request; diplomats from Soviet, Poland and German Democratic Republic embassies were expelled. And all this was a fallout of a spy network that was cracked. It was functioning right from the absolute nerve centre of the Indian government—Principal Secretary Alexander's office itself! His entire personal staff was involved—private secretary N.T. Kher, personal assistant (PA) Malhotra, the clerk, even the peon. On the night of 16–17 January, the counterintelligence arrested Kher and, by morning, the others were nabbed. They were passing on the most sensitive documents to foreign governments through an Indian businessman named Coomar Narain, who was himself a PA once.

All the ramifications were still not clear, for they were still being explored. The key man was the deputy military attaché of the French embassy named Bolley. He had been thrown out, of course. Alexander resigned, accepting moral responsibility for the security lapse in his office. I saw him at about 2.30 p.m. the same day the case was cracked; I obviously had no clue by then. I asked him something and he said he would check with the PM. Had he not submitted his resignation by that time? Possibly not. Sharada told me about the espionage scandal at 4.00 p.m., adding that Alexander was under great pressure. We realized the enormity of the situation.

Vincent George, who had replaced Dhawan in the front office, called me the following day in the morning and said that the PM would meet us all at 10.30 a.m. to talk about what had happened the previous day. The PM had made short statements in both Houses without naming anyone, confining himself to saying that some officers had been functioning against the interests of the country and had been arrested.

In the meeting with the PM, Alexander was naturally not present. The PM said, 'We are without a principal secretary now.' He tried to sound calm, but it was clear that he was stressed. We discussed how to run the work of the office and how to tighten up security. In the afternoon, Sharada asked him about what should be told to the press. The PM asked whether the press could be fobbed off for some time, but Sharada said that doing so would be difficult. The PM said that he had accepted Alexander's resignation, so he can tell them so.

Sharada asked, 'Can we say "accepted regretfully"?' Both he and I pressed for 'accepted with regret'. The PM agreed.

The Fall-Out

The investigations led to the arrest of the PAs in the president's secretariat, finance ministry, defence ministry and commerce ministry. It seemed that all of them had a weakness for the bottle. They had sold secrets for a bottle of scotch and for ludicrously low sums. The businessman Coomar had organized parties for them at his farm and made copies of the documents at his Hailey Road office. No senior officer was arrested.

The French connection received the maximum publicity. A cable was sent to Narendra Singh, our ambassador in Paris, instructing him to call on the French foreign minister to ask for the French ambassador's recall and to reduce the size of the French embassy to the size of our embassy in Paris. Narendra sent back a cable, not objecting to the substance but suggesting a redraft.

Polish, Czech and German Democratic Republic embassies were also involved. Parthasarathi wondered what to do. The Polish PM was due for an official visit on 11 February. Should we call it off? Should we ask for the recall of these three ambassadors, too? It was a very embarrassing situation for us. That was the first day of Bhandari as the foreign secretary. Parthasarathi, Bhandari and I went to the PM's house. He showed a lot of cool. We had acted precipitately in asking for the recall of the French ambassador, he said.

The PM decided to ask for an emergency meeting of the CCPA. Hari Anand Bhandari, director, IB, was also summoned. The PM announced the decision: We ask the three embassies to send back the offending staff. Ought we to go further? His instinct was we should be even handed. Parthasarathi asked whether there was any way in which we could make a distinction between the crimes of the French and others. PV was clear, 'We cannot afford to throw out the Soviets, we have to treat them differently. We have too much at stake with them.' He said we would have to give out an official version soon, but our interests with the Soviets were far too serious for us to take a hasty action against them. The PM saw the wisdom in PV's advice and that was that. Bhandari was asked to tell the three ambassadors to send back their offending staff.

Later, the PM said that we had dealt too harshly with the French. Bhandari told the PM he would try to retrieve the situation. I suggested that one thing we could do was to give an immediate agrément to the new French ambassador. The PM agreed. Bhandari suggested that we could ask the French to send a special emissary to talk things over. The PM agreed to that.

We had thought that the expulsion of the staff of the three embassies would be a quiet affair. But two days after the CCPA meeting, G.K. Reddy of *The Hindu* broke the story. Two days later, the Delhi newspapers got it from the confessional of one of the arrested officials. It was supposed to be an in-camera confession, so we were all concerned about the leak. Later, Sharada found the answer to the source of the leak. The magistrate was pounced upon by the media—AP, Reuters, AFP, *The Times*?, and others. He was so overwhelmed that he blurted out the whole story.

PV was most concerned with the whole thing, especially about the Soviet connection. He told Bhandari, 'I can't tell you how important and crucial were the negotiations that we were having with the Soviets. Why did the PM not consult me before taking the action against the French? He consults me on all kinds of petty things.'

We asked IB director whether there was any difference between the guilt of the French and the others. Barari turned out to be of no help. He said the socialists also got everything. Were the Americans involved at all? Again, we drew a blank. I found it hard to believe that the Central Intelligence Agency (CIA) missed out on the action.

On 22 January 1985, French President François Mitterrand's brother came to Delhi. It was essentially a gesture to say, 'We are sorry', though, of course, these words were not used. Mitterand was bowled over by the PM's straightforwardness. He assured the PM that what had happened was behind us and would not be allowed to come in the way of the friendship between the two countries.

The case against all the 13 accused dragged on for 17 years. They were found guilty of passing on state secrets to foreign agents. They were all government servants, including four from the PMO and four from the Ministry of Defence. They were sentenced to 10 years in prison. Coomar Narain, the chief accused, had died of natural causes by then.

17

TESTING TIME FOR RAJIV

An East African Gujarati newspaper had predicted way back in 1981 that Indira Gandhi would not see November of 1984, that Rajiv would succeed her and rule for 30 years and turn India into a real 'Ram Rajya'! Rajiv himself wished to create such an image of himself that any country that came to India looking for something would not go back disappointed. He could afford to have this generous attitude because of our very comfortable agrarian situation and reasonably comfortable foreign exchange reserves, thanks to his mother's policies. However, there was a tendency in the immediate entourage of the PM (I did not include myself in it) of not acknowledging any good in Indira Gandhi's stewardship of the country, of letting it be felt that the praise of her policies would not be welcome. One hardly ever heard her name even in governmental pronouncements. She was completely forgotten. I had realized, in the limited area of my work, that a case would be weakened if I were to say that it was so decided by her. So, I hardly ever referred to her. True, I did not come across a case where the PM deliberately ruled against his mother's decision, but he was anxious to make a clean break from the past.

Konstantin Chernenko, the general secretary of the Communist Party of the Soviet Union, breathed his last on 10 March 1985. The PM went to Moscow in March 1985 for Chernenko's funeral. (That made me Azharuddin of Soviet funerals. Azharuddin had scored centuries in three successive test matches; I attended three back-to-back Soviet funerals). One of the persons who met the PM in Moscow was the PM of Morocco. His king wished to send an emissary to India to explain the Western Sahara problem. The PM readily agreed. I told the Moroccan PM that we would let them know the dates for the visit immediately on our return to Delhi. Rajiv said, 'Why not suggest the dates straight away?'

On the way back from Moscow, he spent a lot of time in the cockpit—that was his way of relaxing. He was not fond of reading like his mother was. He was more practical. A friend of mine who was an artist told me they missed Indira Gandhi because she always found the time to meet them.

We were all together in the PM's cabin. As the plane was taxiing to take off, he was identifying all the aircraft parked there. He noted that there were four American air force planes, obviously Roland Reagan's party. I narrated a few political jokes, which Rajiv seemed to enjoy. He suddenly asked, 'Who shall we send to Moscow as ambassador in place of Nurul Hasan? How would the Russians react to Parthasarathi?'

I said that Russians would welcome him, but I was not sure how Parthasarathi would react.

He said, 'I know Parthasarathi would think we were getting rid of him, but that is not the case. But what good is policy planning doing anyway? The previous ambassador, what was his name, something Ahuja?' I told him that the name was Vishnu Ahuja. 'The Russians told me he spoke Russian but did not speak our language at all.'

I know the PM was a bit upset with Ahuja. When Rajiv had gone to Moscow a couple of years ago, before he became the PM, Ahuja had kept telling him, 'You must write to your mummy,' and nearly embraced Sonia.

I asked the PM what he thought of Mikhail Gorbachev. He said, 'A positive, straightforward person full of self-confidence.' Both Gorbachev and Rajiv were young and looked forward to a long association.

Between East and West

Sometime in early 1985, the Soviet embassy in Delhi had a couple of unfortunate incidents. One of their officials was killed in his car by two people on a motorcycle and another defected to the US. The PM sent a message to Gorbachev and PV went to Moscow. Defence minister of state, Arun Singh, said, 'Look at it from his point of view—he [Rajiv] is Cambridge educated, has an Italian wife, is trained pilot, has a natural western orientation and a penchant for technology. The Russians were bound to look at all his actions with the greatest suspicion. All the more reason for Rajiv to be extra sensitive to the Soviet angle.'

The Americans, however, saw in Rajiv their opportunity to wean India away from the Russians. They seemed to have selected the Afghan issue for the purpose. Every important visitor from the US took the same well-orchestrated line: 'India is the only country that can talk to the Soviets frankly. India as the Chair of the NAM has an important role to play in finding a solution to the Afghan problem, so please do something.'

Regarding this, the PM had asked us in Moscow, 'Why are the Americans taking this line?' Bhandari's response was that they were really interested in a peaceful solution. The PM said that that did not make sense. I suggested that the Americans had concluded that now was the best chance to ruin our relations with the Soviets through the Afghan issue. He said that made sense. He then asked, 'Do they really think that we are so naïve that we would fall for their flattery?' I said maybe they were naïve enough to believe that we were.

Rajiv had inherited the complex about the British from his mother. Thatcher came on a brief visit and the PM made a special gesture by taking Sonia to the airport to receive her. Perhaps this was his way of softening the blow of the helicopters. The Brits wanted to palm off the helicopters made by Westland company to us. No other country, including Britain, wanted them. The machine was evidently so bad that the Brits were prepared to fully finance our purchase by a grant. The deal was very important for Thatcher because thousands of jobs were on the line. The PM was satisfied that we should not acquire these choppers even if we got them free because the operational costs would be heavy. But Thatcher did not take no for an answer. She wrote letters to him, and her High Commissioner in Delhi pestered everyone. She had only one item on her agenda during her visit to India and the PM knew it. They met for an hour. I had placed myself in a position where I could watch the PM. It was clear to me that he was sticking to his ground. I had to interrupt them once with an urgent message from Fotedar and I could see that the atmosphere was tense.

After the meeting, the PM told Minister of State, External Affairs, Khurshid Alam Khan, Bhandari and me,

> I have told her 'no' almost categorically, but I was thinking about something. She had a real problem because she says she had said in Parliament that India had agreed to buy the machines. Perhaps, we could use her predicament to make Reagan compel Pakistan to give up its nuclear weapon programme. If she could deliver on this, we could offer to buy the copters. The loss for us would be ₹20 crore in 15 years, but it might be worthwhile if we could get Pakistan's nuclear ambitions stymied.

Khurshid felt that the idea might be worth considering. Bhandari also murmured words of encouragement. I was aghast. Perhaps, the PM was looking for a way to say yes to the deal. I said that Thatcher could never deliver on a thing like that. In any case, Pakistan had already got all they needed to make the bomb. Also, on the nuclear issue, we were the ones on the defensive because Pakistan had made many proposals—nuclear weapon-free zone and the like—which we were not prepared to accept. In fact, we could not even discuss the nuclear problem with Pakistan directly because we would not be able to react positively about any of those ideas. My reservations probably made some sense as the PM dropped this idea.

But Thatcher did not. The morning before leaving Delhi, she spoke with the PM for a few minutes at the airport, 'batting for Britain'. The High Commissioner told me that the previous night Thatcher worked till 1.00 a.m., collecting all the arguments.

One morning, there was a cable from our High Commissioner in Colombo. The PM read it very carefully and asked, 'Does this mean that the Sri Lankan government is saying we support the Sinhalese?' I said they were definitely saying that the new government in Delhi had changed its policy. Khurshid said that even in our Parliament, there was the same sentiment. The PM appeared to take this very seriously. Perhaps he was a bit naïve. He might have thought that his transparent sincerity would make the Sri Lankans more reasonable in dealing with us. He was so pleased with his talk with Athulathmudali a few months ago that he thought he had cracked the Sri Lanka problem. He had been telling Arun Nehru that he would settle the problem in three months. He said in the Lok Sabha, 'There is light at the end of the tunnel.' He was in touch with Jayewardene through some channel, perhaps the R&AW. He told me that he had received a letter from Jayewardene but asked me not to tell 'those chaps in the ministry'. He asked, 'Who should we send to Sri Lanka to talk to Jayewardene? It should be a non-Tamil, no doubt, to rule out Parthasarathi.' He asked, 'What about Karunakaran?' I said he would be fine, but we should think of someone who was not from the South at all. 'How about Arun Nehru? I should send someone who had my complete confidence and whose selection would give a clear signal to Jayewardene that he had sent someone who enjoyed his confidence.' He asked Bhandari and me to think about it. We suggested two names: K.C. Pant (a senior Congress leader and son of the legendary Govind Ballabh Pant, former CM of Uttar Pradesh) and Arun Nehru in that order. It was Romesh Bhandari who finally ended up going, as the PM decided on the name.

Meanwhile, on 12 May 1985, I completed five years in Delhi following my return from Geneva.

Inheriting a Difficult Legacy

Ever since Rajiv Gandhi became the PM, he had not had a single day of relaxation. He had inherited so many and such difficult problems from his mother. He made sincere efforts to solve the Punjab problem, offered several concessions to the Sikhs, such that the Hindus accused him of appeasing the Sikhs. The problem only kept on becoming more and more intractable. The so-called moderates among the Akalis had thrown in their towel. The Akali Dal was taken over by Baba Joginder Singh, father of Bhindranwale, without even an iota of resistance from Harchand Singh Longowal, Gurcharan Singh Tohra and Prakash Singh Badal—all three had immediately handed over their resignations.

Two days in May 1985—10 and 11—witnessed one of the worst kinds of terrorist acts ever seen in India. The whole of North India was rocked by transistor explosives in buses and trains. Nearly 100 people died and several hundreds suffered injuries. The maximum casualties were reported to be in Delhi. The Sikh terrorists operated methodically and with a lot of planning. Their objective was transparent: They wanted to spread terror among the population and provoke the government into taking retaliatory action. But apart from asking the army to patrol the areas, the government did not take any other step.

The question now facing the government was how to solve the Punjab problem. The extremists enjoyed their power of terrorizing. No one was even talking about the original demand regarding Chandigarh and the river water distribution.* The Akal Takht, which the government got rebuilt through karseva at the cost of crores of rupees, was going to be demolished and built again by the Akalis. It was believed that every gurdwara had become the centre of terrorism.

---

*The Akalis wanted Chandigarh to be a capital city of Punjab alone and demanded a disproportionate share of the rivers flowing through Punjab and Haryana.

During the course of three months of May, June and July, the PM delivered the most important of his election campaign promises—signing of the Rajiv–Longowal Accord on 24 July 1985. The Punjab problem wasn't solved yet, but there was a big change in the situation on the ground. People started discussing the possibility of holding elections in Punjab in October. The credit went entirely to Rajiv and, of course, Longowal who had taken immense personal risk, even greater than Rajiv.

The Sikh radicals were opposed to the accord and it resulted in the assassination of Longowal. According to the accord, the government agreed to the demands of the Shiromani Akali Dal in return for which the Akalis agreed to withdraw the agitation. Under the terms of the accord, Chandigarh would be transferred to Punjab; a commission would be set up to resolve the border dispute between Punjab and Haryana; and a tribunal would be established to decide the sharing of the waters of Ravi and Beas between Punjab, Haryana and Rajasthan. However, establishing peace was not easy. Violence continued for many years.

A question came up whether foreign journalists should be allowed to go to Punjab. All the top officials present—home secretary, cabinet secretary, director of R&AW, foreign secretary—were against the idea. The PM asked P.K. Kaul, cabinet secretary, what the premise of his objection was. Kaul said that the journalists would report all the disturbances that would undoubtedly occur. To that, the PM said that we could live with that so long as the journalists themselves did not instigate the people. Kaul suggested that the PM might consult the governor. The PM said he already did, and the governor had agreed with the PM. The ban on foreign press was lifted.

Upward and Forward

On the economic side, there was an atmosphere of optimism and enthusiasm. The PM got very good support from Vishwanath Pratap Singh, his minister of commerce. The share market was bullish. Investment was growing, though the national saving rate had come down from 24 to 22 per cent. The inflation scenario was not good and the curse of corruption had not been tackled either. However, other indicators were encouraging.

On the foreign affairs side, the PM had grown into a seasoned statesman. In a course of two months, he had visited the USSR, the US, France, Algeria and Egypt. His main assets were that he was utterly sincere, did not have any hang ups and was willing to listen. He had no pretension of being an intellectual and his instincts were excellent.

He succeeded in bringing the warring Tamils and Sinhalese to the conference table in Sri Lanka. This was entirely his achievement, though Bhandari had been an effective and credible instrument in executing his policy. The PM decided very early in his premiership that the Tamil militants must not be allowed to hold veto power over our policy. He recognized that the Tamils had genuine grievances, but he was clear that the Tamils could not have more powers than what the states in the Indian Union enjoyed. He was also categorical in not encouraging Tamil terrorism from operating within the Indian territory. He assessed the situation correctly and concluded that both sides in Sri Lanka had had enough and were ready to talk.

There was one thing that worried me about the PM's style of functioning: Decisions were taken more or less off the cuff and by instinct. He hardly had the time or the inclination to read anything, even brief notes. He preferred to discuss with a few people and take decisions on the spot. Since the time for meetings was always limited, all the viewpoints did not get properly expressed or understood. Once we were talking about Pakistan nuclear programme and what we should do to counter Pakistan public relations advantage. We had only 15 minutes for discussion. So, when Subbu K. Subramaniam, widely recognized as the guru of strategic thinking in India, made a couple of suggestions, he gave his nod.

In this situation, the role of advisors became crucial. He hardly ever made changes in drafts, letters or speeches—though the same could not be said of his speeches in Washington. The speech in the Joint Session of the Congress was an interesting experience. Sharada had prepared a draft in Delhi. We had one meeting with the PM in Delhi. Then Mani Shankar had prepared another draft with Montek Singh Ahluwalia's help. On the flight from Algiers to Washington, we all sat with the PM for four hours going over the speech. After the PM came back from the White House banquet, we again sat till 3.00 a.m.

We had a free and argumentative discussion at times. I had suggested that there should be no reference in the speech to Pakistan. 'Why should we give any importance to Pakistan? Are we so obsessed with Pakistan? Is Pakistan the sole content of our foreign policy?' Everyone disagreed with me.

Ambassador Bajpai said the PM could not afford not to mention Pakistan in the speech because he had to think of his constituency back home.

'What constituency?' the PM had asked. The PM had told everyone not to worry about his constituency. 'I can take care of that.' I was in minority at this point, but the PM agreed with me. The ambassador suggested consulting PV, but the PM saw no need for that. So, perhaps for the first time, there was no reference to Pakistan in such an important speech.

PM Becoming Popular

On 15 August 1985, Rajiv addressed the nation from the ramparts of the Red Fort for the first time. Rita and I went to the Red Fort for the historic occasion. He spoke in his usual flat, monotone style, never showing any emotion, always in control of himself. He did not disappoint the people. Everyone was expecting him to announce the settlement of the Assam problem. He said the agreement had been signed only at 2.30 in the morning of 15 August. He might have deliberately arranged for the negotiations to last in such a way that he did not have to announce the deal in Parliament.

People, including foreign leaders, were surprised at Rajiv's air of self-assurance. Facing Gorbachev, Mitterand or Reagan did not make him conscious at all.

I learnt soon that quoting the previous PM did not influence him at all. In as early as February 1985, when we were going over Parliament questions on Sri Lanka, he had made it very clear that we would not say anything that would amount to interference in Sri Lanka's internal affairs.

When we went to Moscow in March 1985, the PM called on a few leaders— Thatcher, Helmut Kohl, chancellor of Germany, Yasuhiro Nakasone, PM of Japan, as well as Zia. They all sang the same song that the PM was the only leader who could talk to the Soviets about Afghanistan.

At that time, the PM was very sceptical of all these people and of the Americans. He shared my feeling that they were only interested in spoiling our relations with the Soviets. But when we went to Moscow in May, the PM spoke to Gorbachev about Afghanistan. A change had come over him since then and it was further strengthened during his visit to Washington afterwards. He sent Bhandari to Moscow directly from Washington on an Afghanistan mission. He was convinced that the Soviets would like to leave Afghanistan, provided they could get adequate guarantee against interference. He seemed to be equally satisfied that the Americans were sincere when they said that they were not interested in bleeding the Russians in Afghanistan and that they preferred a political settlement, which would recognize Soviet interests in that country. Rajiv undertook what he had rejected two months ago, to actively offer our good offices, almost mediation, to solve the Afghan problem so much so that Diego Cordovez, UN special envoy for Afghanistan, was getting nervous and jealous that the Indian diplomacy would deprive him of the credit

Bhandari was very keen on this diplomacy. He was studying the Austrian state treaty and Finland's friendship treaty with the Soviet Union in search of models for Afghanistan. I sent a note to the PM, pointing out the ground realities as to why the Soviets could not leave Afghanistan and counselled caution. My main point was that unlike the Americans in Vietnam, the Soviets had a common border with Afghanistan. Hence, they did not have the logistical problem of supplying everything that their troops might need. Also, the Soviets were genuinely concerned about the threat that a Muslim state next door to them might pose, given the large Muslim population in their country. Arun Singh agreed with me. The PM merely initialled the note. Eventually, his instinct proved right.

Our neighbours were excited at the PM's transparent sincerity. Pakistan was banking everything on him and had expressed so openly. Jayewardene repeatedly said and wrote that he had placed himself in Rajiv Gandhi's hands. Even Ranasinghe Premadasa, PM and later Jayewardene's successor, wrote fairly civil letters to the PM. Bangladeshi military strongman, Hussain Mohammad Ershad, was convinced that

Rajiv would see merit in Bangladesh's case of Farakka waters.* The PM had agreed to the extension of the water sharing agreement for three more years.

Even the King of Nepal, Birendra Bir Bikram Shah Dev, who was the most hostile of our neighbours, came to meet the PM in the hope of bringing about a change in our posture. In our internal discussions on Nepal, the PM showed great annoyance with the country. All in all, the atmosphere in the sub-continent was more relaxed and tension-free than it was in Indira Gandhi's time.

In contrast to his approach to the neighbouring countries, the PM enjoyed giving 'hell' to officers who did not have satisfactory answers to his questions. He always wanted to find out who did the wrong things or did not do the right thing. Time and again, he used the briefing sessions for parliamentary questions to issue on-the-spot decisions to sack or suspend officers, giving rise to the impression that he derived a sadistic pleasure in doing so. I should add that he was willing to listen to evidence in defense of a conflicting view, but remained unconvinced most of the time.

*India's decision to build a barrage at Farakka to divert the water to Calcutta port, which was getting heavily silted, was objected by Bangladesh, as it would have deprived them of the water supply.

18

A DIFFERENT PRIME MINISTER

On 31 October 1985, Rajiv Gandhi completed one year as the PM. Both at home and abroad, he had been a great success. Punjab seemed quiet; Assam was going to election in a month's time; Gujarat had settled down; and Mizoram, too, was peaceful. His biggest achievement was that he had restored credibility in the government. When he said something, people believed him. And that was equally true in foreign affairs. All the neighbouring countries looked up to him. Pakistan seemed to be genuinely convinced of his sincerity. That was why when he criticized Pakistan's nuclear programme, it had more impact than similar statements issued by Indira Gandhi.

Of Carpets, Curtains and Microphones

He, however, had his own eccentricities. The PM was even more finicky than his mother about sending messages and replies. He loved to talk to foreign leaders on the phone. The moment he heard that Andrei A. Gromyko had been made the president of the Soviet Union, he booked a call to the Kremlin; he was the first non-socialist leader to congratulate him.

He surpassed his mother in observing and taking note of small details. Within two minutes of entering a room, he knew that a picture was hanging crooked, that one corner of the carpet was dirty, that the curtains did not match the carpet, that there were too many switches in the room, etc. He told me once that we must have cordless microphones for his banquets in Hyderabad House because all the wires seemed very messy. I had told the chief of protocol about it, but he forgot. So, when we had a visitor from Trinidad and Tobago, the PM asked me about it. I told him that the microphone had to be imported. 'I know it has to be imported, but what about the dinner tomorrow? Why has the microphone not been imported so far?' Luckily, we found that the Press Information Bureau had a cordless one and I reported this to him. 'Do you know what frequency they use?'

Gaining Global Popularity

The Commonwealth summit in Nassau, capital city of the Bahamas, was about to begin in September 1985, and I accompanied the PM. Without even trying to, he emerged as a leader there. Rajiv Gandhi became the star of the show, whom everyone wanted to meet. *The New York Times* carried his photo on the front page on two successive days in coverage of the CHOGM. At the PM's initiative, a group was organized consisting of the PM of Canada, Brian Mulroney; PM of Australia, Bob Hawke; President of Zambia, Kenneth Kaunda; President of Zimbabwe, Robert Mugabe; and he himself. They met in the PM's suite on the first day after dinner. The only topic discussed was apartheid and sanctions against South Africa. All the leaders were in unison except that there was one problem—Thatcher had to be tackled. We worked for five days, working till late at night, at the Indian residence. Finally, a draft was prepared but the question arose as to who would take the draft to Thatcher. She, along with the Americans, was opposed to the sanctions. South Africa was a racially segregated state with a white supremacist government, but because of close relations between the UK and South Africa and because of economic and commercial factors, Thatcher was opposed to the idea of sanctions. She also felt that the sanctions would hurt only Britain and other developed countries since all the others who demanded sanctions did not have much economic stake in South Africa.

Mulroney suggested that he and Rajiv should talk to Thatcher about the sanctions since she was somewhat allergic to Bob Hawke. The two of them saw Thatcher. She said she would not budge. She stood up, put her feet together, moved her left foot six inches to the left and said, 'I would not move even this much.' The two of them came back and reported to the others, who, by now also included Ramphal. Kaunda said we should not make any more compromises. A draft was prepared, clearly stating that 45 heads of states supported sanctions and only the British PM did not. But Rajiv said, and others agreed, that sanctions would not make much sense unless the Brits joined in. More discussions followed. We obtained the text of what Reagan had agreed to. 'Surely Margaret cannot do less than Reagan', and as such more negotiations followed. Thatcher came over to Rajiv's residence, but no deal could be brokered. The conference met in the plenary session and Thatcher lashed out at some of the

Africans. Her constant refrain was that only Britain was asked to make sacrifices, whereas the frontline states merrily carried on trading with South Africa.

To cut a long story short, Thatcher eventually agreed to some sanctions. But more importantly, she agreed that a group of five to six PMs would meet in London in six months to review the implementation and effectiveness of the sanctions and decide upon further action. This time frame was Rajiv's idea. He argued that in case South Africa cooperated, we might even think of unwinding some of the sanctions. His transparent sincerity convinced everyone. My worry was that his reasonableness might affect his as well as India's image among the Africans and I told him so. But I was wrong. After the conference, his reputation among the Africans and the Brits soared higher. He came back from the conference with his reputation high amongst the Africans as well as the Americans.

Mulroney, Hawke, Kaunda, Mugabe and Rajiv got along with one another. Mulroney said, 'I think Margaret is a racist, it came out clearly in her approach to the sanctions issue.' Hawke agreed, as did Sonny Ramphal, secretary general of Commonwealth, and Rajiv.

The only reservation I had was that the PM got carried away with his own enthusiasm in support of a cause, be it apartheid or disarmament. He was almost prepared to spoil relations with the British on the apartheid issue. We had other more important reasons to be unhappy about with the British, and we did not need to make apartheid a bilateral Indo-British issue.

Media Savvy but Sometimes Blunt

Talking of disarmament, the PM was a keen proponent of nuclear disarmament, so much so that he worked out, all by himself on a computer, a detailed blueprint for nuclear disarmament, to be achieved over a 15-year period in three phases. He received expert help from Dubey, who was highly knowledgeable on matters of disarmament. The PM presented his plan to the special session of the General Assembly devoted to disarmament in 1988.

It was, therefore, logical that he should be enthusiastic about the Six-Nation Five-Continent Peace Initiative, which was started during the period of the prime ministership of his mother. In 1983, a group calling itself Parliamentarians for Global Action, called on Indira Gandhi in her office and laid the foundation for the initiative, led by Ólafur Ragnar Grímsson of Iceland (he went on to get elected as the president of Iceland for four consecutive terms). Their idea was that a select group of leaders should join in appealing to the two superpowers, the US and the USSR, to halt further development of nuclear weapons and agree to reduce their stockpiles. In addition to the Indian PM, the group of leaders included Olof Palme of Sweden, Julius Nyerere of Tanzania, Geórgios Papadopoulos of Greece, Raul Alfonso of Argentina and Alfonso García Robles of Mexico. García Robles was not the leader of Mexico but had won a Nobel Peace Prize for his pioneering work, which had resulted in the whole of South America being declared a nuclear-free zone under the Treaty of Tlatelolco. Indira Gandhi had readily agreed and named me as her sherpa. When I had come back after attending a meeting of the sherpas in London, she had asked me, 'How was the meeting?' I had told her the meeting was successful;

we had agreed to meet again in Stockholm.

It was Rajiv who was helming the affairs now and was emerging as a leader who exhibited great self-confidence. We organized a summit in India in February 1986 of presidents and prime ministers of Sweden, Mexico, Greece, Argentina, Tanzania and India to discuss nuclear disarmament as a follow-up of the Six-Nation Five-Continent Peace Initiative, but our main interest was to project the new PM on the international scene. And boy, did he exceed our expectations! He conducted himself extremely well, was very polite to the other leaders who were older and senior to him. His interviews with American news networks were telecast live through satellite and left an excellent impression on viewers. He became a media hit in the US.

But sometimes, he talked too frankly, even bluntly, with the media. In New York, where we went from Nassau for the fortieth anniversary of the UN, the press asked him what he thought of Reagan's address. He said that the only comment he had was that he would not like to make any comment. A few minutes later, he was again asked the same question, to which he said, 'I have already said I do not wish to make any comment. Isn't that enough of a comment?'

In Nassau, a draft declaration was prepared on the fortieth anniversary of the UN. The PM asked me to go through it, and I did. He asked whether it read alright. I said yes, except for one word—it should be 'collective' security and not 'common' security as mentioned in the draft. The PM was so impressed that he seriously suggested I should stay behind (I was supposed to accompany the PM on a visit to Cuba from Nassau) because nobody else in the delegation would have such expertise to correct the various drafts. I persuaded him that this was not so: Natarajan Krishnan, our permanent representative, was an expert on the UN; there was the Foreign Secretary and a couple of excellent officers from the MEA who could take care of the drafts.

When we arrived in New York, the PM saw the programme booklet. Until Indira Gandhi's time, the booklet containing the programme for each visit used to be somewhat big. Rajiv had the booklet shortened, so that it could be carried in one's pocket. By the time we reached Waldorf Astoria Hotel in New York, everybody was looking for me. Natwar told me that the PM was hopping mad because the programme was filled up with too many appointments and calls, leaving very little time for him to spend in the General Assembly. As soon as Rajiv saw me, he asked, 'Didn't I tell you that I wanted to spend maximum time in the UN building? I said, yes sir and the instructions were duly conveyed. He said, 'They have made a complete mess of it... I am not going to sit in the hotel, meeting all those people.' Well, we did sort out the issue at hand and the PM did spend a lot of time in the UN and was seen by many, many people.

The draft declaration on the fortieth anniversary of the UN was prepared after a lot of negotiations over several months. Ambassador Krishnan was the chairman of a small negotiating group. The Americans had agreed to everything except for a paragraph on Palestine. They went back on everything, including the paragraphs on which they had earlier agreed. Krishnan briefed the PM about it, and the latter was not happy. He said that had Krishnan told him about this earlier, he would have spoken to Reagan and Thatcher. He asked Bhandari to speak to Michael Armacost, the US undersecretary of State, about it, but it was too late. I told the PM that there was no need to worry if the General Assembly did not adopt a declaration; it would only demonstrate

America's unreasonableness and rigidity. He agreed, not that we could have done anything if he hadn't. As things stood out, the General Assembly did not adopt any declaration.

In New York, I was riding with Rajiv and his wife when she told him, 'You better read your speech well, you made too many mistakes in Nassau.'

He said, 'I must have been nervous. It was the first time for me in an international conference.' Like a good sycophant, I said that he was just too tired. He agreed with me.

A Generous Third-World Leader?

The PM talked much too freely to people with whom he needed to be rather circumspect. He found his meeting with Reagan in New York in October 1985 to be very disappointing. The day after this meeting, he told a correspondent of *The New York Times* that he was worried because he was not sure who was incharge or in control in Washington. 'One thing is clear, Reagan is not incharge,' he added by way of clarification. Since then, he had said the same thing to several people. He told Palme that he had a 'very bad' meeting with Reagan, that Reagan's aides did not brief him properly. He said the same thing to Vasili Kuznetsov, deputy PM of the Soviet Union, and would no doubt repeat himself to George Papandreou, the Greek politician. This was probably the PM's way of winning the confidence of other leaders. Perhaps, I was influenced by my stint with Indira Gandhi, who used to say very little and did not feel embarrassed by awkward pauses. Rajiv was probably anxious to impress his interlocutors with his sincerity, but things did not work like that in international relations.

During the same visit to the US, he was taken to Houston, Texas. There was a dinner in honour of the PM. Vice President

Bush had made a special gesture and had accompanied him in the plane to Houston. In his reply to the toast, the PM thanked everyone but did not even mention Bush's name. Next day, we told him he could have thanked Bush for his special gesture. He said, 'But he is such a clout!'

The PM was also anxious to be acknowledged as a generous Third-World leader. He found it difficult to say 'no' whenever other heads of states would ask him for anything. Tanzania asked for a loan of $15 million. Everyone advised against it. Our own foreign exchange position was rather precarious and there was no hope of getting the money back. We succeeded in persuading the PM and conveyed our regrets to the Tanzanians. But a few weeks later, Salim Ahmed Salim, Tanzania's foreign minister, asked for the loan again, and the PM could not refuse. Sure enough, Salim came with another list of requested 'gifts'. It was not easy to say no, especially when the request was made personally by fellow heads, but he would have to learn. Indira Gandhi never committed herself on the spot.

I was working fine with Rajiv, who didn't have a negative opinion about me. But the same PM, on the eve of his departure to Bhutan towards the end of September 1985, said, 'I don't want Gharekhan in my office for one more day, he must be replaced immediately. Find someone else to come with me to Bhutan.' All this happened because he, or rather Sonia Gandhi, was very upset about the gifts selected for Bhutan. I was aghast since I had absolutely nothing to do with the gifts. The PM was returning from somewhere in the evening. I went to the airport, so that I could take a ride with him and utilize the time to explain everything to him. When I saw him at the airport, he said he was being accompanied by Romi Chopra, a friend of his, and suggested I talk to him the following morning.

I asked, 'On the plane, Sir?'

He paused for a moment, smiled and said, 'Alright, on the plane.'

He was under the impression that I was responsible for the selection of gifts when I wasn't. There was another officer who had been entrusted with the job to select the gifts. But, the PM did not care to find out. He simply assumed that it was my job. On the plane, I explained my side of the story. I think he realized his mistake and said, 'Yes, yes, but other things were also moving too slowly, including the replies to letters from Reagan...'. I told him I had already sent him the drafts. Anyway, I knew that he knew, that he had acted precipitously and without following the principles of natural justice.

Rajiv Gandhi and the Neighbours

On 27 December 1985, I got a written order of my posting to New York as permanent representative. This posting was of my choice.

However, there was a feeling of insecurity among civil servants that they could be transferred any time, with no explanations offered. This had happened a few times. We had gone to Dhaka in December 1985 for the founding summit meeting of the South Asian Association for Regional Cooperation. The newly arrived high commissioner had organized a reception. The PM was such a draw that every single person invited came to the reception. The women went gaga over him. Some of them came again and again to shake hands with him, some were heard saying that they would not wash the hand with which they had shaken Rajiv's hand! All this naturally pleased our PM, but then there was a near stampede, which made him angry. He sent for me and asked to manage the crowds. I did what I could, but the following day, he told Bali Ram Bhagat, the external affairs minister, 'Bhagatji, what kind of ambassadors have you got? I have been seeing them for the past one year. You better send a strong letter of censure to your high commissioner here and I want you to organize a crash course for all your ambassadors on how to dress, how to talk, how to entertain, etc.' I did what I could to protect the high commissioner and even concocted a lie in the process.

More drama was to follow us on our Dhaka visit in December 1985. One of the events organized there was an exhibition of stamps to be brought out by all the members, especially for the occasion. Our postal department had brought out nice stamps. Just an hour before the exhibition was to be inaugurated by all the leaders, our postal department official came running to me and showed me two stamps brought out by Pakistan. One stamp showed the whole of J&K as part of Pakistan and the other showed our entire boundary with China as undetermined. This was a serious issue. I rushed to the PM who had just returned from the retreat. I explained the situation to him. He asked what could be done—the exhibition was due to open at 3.00 p.m. and it was already past two. Fortunately, I thought of an idea. I told him he should speak to Lt Gen. Hussain Muhammad Ershad, the host president, as a matter of urgency and ask to see him before three o'clock. Further, he should tell Ershad that if the offending stamps were not withdrawn, he would have to leave for India. The PM did so. He first talked to Ershad and told him that not only would he not attend the exhibition, he would be obliged to return to Delhi straight away if he did not do the needful. Ershad called all the leaders for a talk. When they came out, Zia told me in Urdu, '*Gharekhan Sahab, humne apki baat maan li* (Mr Gharekhan, we have accepted your request).' The offending stamps were withdrawn, and everything went on smoothly.

Perhaps, this incident was still fresh in Rajiv's mind when he gave an unexpected compliment to me during the flight back home. On 9 December, on the way home from Dhaka, he told me, 'I am very happy with your work, I get very good inputs from you. This is why I want someone to come and understudy you for a few months.'

With Pakistan, Rajiv gave the impression that he was keen to normalize the relations. His line of contention was that though Zia was alright to work with and meant whatever he said, his officers did not implement his policies. He wanted to give Zia the benefit of the doubt even for what had happened in Dhaka regarding the special postal stamps. Later, in December 1985, Pakistan's finance minister, Mahboobul Haq, came to India. He said that his PM Mohammad Khan Junejo had not had the privilege of meeting Rajiv Gandhi and would be very happy if he could visit Pakistan. Rajiv readily agreed and said he would go to Pakistan the very next month, telling me, in Haq's presence, not to fill up the January calendar and to keep a few days for the visit to Pakistan. A few days later, he asked Bhandari and me whether we were overdoing the meetings with Zia. He was referring to a meeting to which he had already agreed in Muscat, where they had both gone for the Emir's fifteenth anniversary of coronation.

I told Rajiv, 'This is not too much, but a visit to Pakistan would be.'

'Why? I don't think so,' he reacted.

The next day, I sent him a note giving reasons why he

should not go to Pakistan in such a hurry. Since then, for whatever reason, he started soft pedalling his promise to go to Pakistan. In fact, he started telling people, including Kuznetsov, that we did not trust Pakistan at all and it was only a matter of diplomacy. The feeling in some quarters in India, especially in the Left, was that we were being 'boy scoutish' in our approach towards Zia. Gradually, Rajiv became more sceptical about Zia, but his instinct for dramatic gestures remained. Aiyar, media advisor, pushed the PM in this direction. Arun Singh was also talking in these terms at one time. But when he became the minister of state for defence, he became more realistic and wise, and no longer trusted Pakistan. Sometime in late 1985, Arun Singh, PV, Natwar and I had a meeting with the PM about Pakistan. At that meeting, Arun Singh made a serious and startling statement; at least, it startled PV, who was also the former defence minister. Arun Singh said that if we were to have a war with Pakistan, it would thrash us at least in the short term. Apart from our weakness due to the Sikh problem, he said Pakistan enjoyed distinct superiority over us in certain aspects, especially in electronic warfare and the F-16s. Therefore, he said, we must keep talking to Pakistan and ensure that it did not attack us at least for a couple of years.

The PM said that Arun had thrown up a completely new dimension of Indo-Pak relations because our chiefs had been assuring us that we could thrash Pakistan if they started something. If what Arun explained was true, the PM said, then we would have to readjust our foreign policy. Arun said what he had told the PM was present in the defence ministry files. The PM clarified that what Arun had said was only his assessment and that the government and the PM did not share it. At a subsequent meeting, too, Arun told me that we had to buy time as far as Pakistan was concerned. When I told Natwar about all this later, he said that these people, meaning Arun, had to learn the hard way that foreign policy was not the same thing as selling Cherry Blossom shoe polish! (Before joining politics, Arun was with Reckitt and Colman, the manufacturers of Cherry Blossom).

19

A TENURE OF TRIALS AND TRIUMPHS

The year 1986 wasn't the best for Rajiv Gandhi. The Punjab situation was, in fact, heading towards another Blue Star scenario—back to square one, as many people said. Then there was the crisis of increasing prices of essential commodities, such as wheat, cooking gas, kerosene, petrol, etc. This provided a very good handle to the Opposition, which was busy organizing bandhs in various cities. What was worse was that it generated an internal revolt in the Congress. Many party leaders urged the PM to review the price hike. When the oil prices in the world had tumbled so drastically, how could the government increase the petrol prices in India? Finally, the PM convened a meeting and had the party direct the government to reduce the prices. This entire incident did not go down well with the PM.

Rajiv's honeymoon period with the media ended by March 1986; it had lasted longer than the traditional 100 days.

Girilal Jain of *The Times of India* was spitting venom against Rajiv. He carried on a personal campaign against him, and all for one simple reason—Rajiv did not grant him an exclusive interview. Nikhil Chakravarty, a senior journalist and editor of a magazine called *Seminar*, also wrote 'anti' articles, but unlike Girilal's, his editorials were not personal. The main grievance of the media was the lack of access to the PM. Indira Gandhi used to meet these major-domos from time to time. Hence, Girilal was very pro-Indira Gandhi. Rajiv had not met him, and this explained his ire. There was also a widely shared perception that Aiyar was promoting M.J. Akbar, a senior and serious journalist, granting him all kinds of favour at the cost of alienating almost the entire corps of senior editors and correspondents. Attempts were being made to remedy the situation. The PM met some of these journalists in groups of four to five, including Arun Shourie, a respected journalist and editor of several papers, but the resentment against Akbar was strong.

Arun Singh would have liked to post Aiyar, media advisor, out somewhere as an ambassador. He felt that the latter was not helping the PM. The January issue of *The Probe* magazine quoted Aiyar, without naming him, as saying, in reply to a question about the PM's reading habits: 'I don't go to bed with him, so I don't know what he reads at bedtime.' Arun said that the PM had personally read this out to him. The PM did not react to Arun's suggestion that Aiyar be posted out. The PM liked him.

On our return flight from Dhaka, the PM asked me, 'Shall we send Mani out somewhere?

'Maybe,' I said.

After a few moments, he replied, 'I have no problem with Mani, I like him but you chaps in the office seem to be fed up with him.' I told him that was not true, people liked him, but they thought that he had overdone the PM's exposure to the media and that the impact had been largely negative.

'When the Cat Is Away'

During our visit to Male in February 1986, I asked Rajiv about the Punjab problem, which had started rearing its ugly head again. I told him there was speculation that we were heading for another Operation Blue Star. The PM said there was a significant difference this time, as now the Akalis would have to deal with it. I asked what would happen if Surjit Singh Barnala, the Punjab CM, was not able to or did not take any action as and when needed. To this, Rajiv replied, 'If he does not, he would be finished politically.'

'What if Barnala joined hands with the extremists?'

'Then we would have a problem,' the PM said.

But he was relaxed, even complacent, about the whole thing. I asked whether there would ever be an end to extremism, at least in India. He said it would be all over in two years, by the end of 1987. However, he had spoken too soon. The Panthic Committee declared Khalistan on 29 April 1986. Initially, I thought there shouldn't be any panic, but I was wrong. I happened to be at 7, Race Course Road in the evening, and Vincent George, the private secretary to Rajiv Gandhi who had replaced Dhawan in the front office, was frantically trying to contact several ministers. The PM wanted to speak to all the CMs on the phone. Barnala had not been traceable for a long time. Ministers and secretaries were summoned and panic ensued. The PM, however, didn't panic. He used the opportunity to flush out the extremists from the Golden Temple. He consulted a large number of people and, most importantly, Barnala, whose support was critical. If Barnala had not shown guts and courage and dithered instead, it could have resulted in the formation of an extremely serious situation. The Central Reserve Police Force and Border Security Force went into the Temple complex on 30 April at about 5.00 p.m., and the operation was completed in 12 hours with the loss of only one life. This incident went a long way in restoring Rajiv's image as a decisive leader.

Finance Minister V.P. Singh was with us on the Male visit. Girilal had told me if there was one person who the PM distrusted, it was V.P. Singh. 'He would destroy Rajiv Gandhi, you mark my words.' I found V.P. Singh to be a man with a sense of humour and one who was reasonably informal. When the PM went off for rest and recreation at the Maldives President's retreat island, I said aloud that now that the cat was away, the mice would play and have fun. I realized that V.P. Singh was present. So, I added, 'This was only in respect to bureaucrats.' To that, he added that we were all mice, the only difference was that some were bigger and others smaller.

Some Wrong Turns

Then there was the famous Shah Bano case. Shah Bano, a Muslim woman, had been divorced by her husband after a marriage of 40 years. She had filed a suit for maintenance. The case had gone right up to the Supreme Court, where the judges decreed in 1985 that her husband had to give her maintenance. The judgement had been hailed by progressive Muslims and by others, but bitterly opposed by conservative and fundamentalist Muslims. My friend Shahabuddin won his election on the strength of the backlash created by the Shah Bano judgement, though he swore he never mentioned the

Shah Bano judgement even once in his campaign. The PM himself told me there was no way in which Muslim women's rights would not be protected.

But the government decided to introduce a bill in Parliament, which, according to popular perception, nullified the Supreme Court judgement. The PM mentioned that we would protect Muslim women's rights under the Indian Penal Code. But the specific right to maintenance from the divorced husband was not mentioned in the Bill. People in his own party were very upset. One of his ministers, Arif Mohammed Khan, even resigned.

I was disappointed that Rajiv had allowed himself, against his own convictions, to be guided by some who had no secular credentials and who were only interested in remaining in power. This brought communalism into the political landscape, which was also evidenced in the opening of the lock in the Ayodhya temple to enable Hindus to worship Lord Rama, even though the entire matter was pending before the courts.

The PM had to go to Ixtapa, a resort in Mexico, for a summit meeting of the Six-Nation Five-Continent Peace Initiative. The previous summit had been held in Stockholm. The PM's idea was that I should go with him to Mexico and, on the return journey, I should be dropped off at Bermuda in the middle of the night, where the plane would make a stop for refuelling. I would proceed to New York from Bermuda to take charge of my assignment as permanent representative. So, I spent one night in Bermuda. 'Baby' R.K. Thadani, a popular and senior executive of Air India, arranged a game of golf for me there and then flew me to New York the next day. I was literally airdropped on to my next assignment!

PART II

Diplomacy during the First Gulf War

2 August 1990–28 February 1991

The collapse of the Berlin Wall on 9 November 1989 triggered an irreversible trend that eventually led to the dissolution of the USSR on 26 December 1991, and the emergence of new Eastern European nation states. The new state of the Russian Federation contrived to retain all the privileges of the Soviet Union, including permanent membership of the UNSC. Ukraine and Byelorussia were already founding members of the UN; the other units applied and became the UN members during the ensuing months. The dissolution of the USSR, in turn, caused the Socialist Federative Republic of Yugoslavia to break up into different sovereign states, albeit with armed, internecine and bloody conflicts. With the collapse of the Soviet Union, the US emerged as the sole superpower and the consequent Pax Americana.

It was under these circumstances that the President of Iraq, Saddam Hussain, decided in August 1990 to invade Kuwait and incorporate it as the nineteenth province of Iraq. The timing of his decision could not have come at a worse possible moment for him. With the end of the Cold War, the former Soviet Union had been reduced to a middling power, with only the possession of a huge nuclear weapon stockpile to claim to be a superpower. The new regime in the Kremlin, with Boris Yeltsin as President, was anxious to remain in the good books of the US and the West in general. The Russian Federation was not prepared to use its privileged position as veto-wielding permanent member of the UNSC to come to the aid of its former 'friends'. Saddam might have believed that Russia would continue to be friendly and protective towards Iraq as it was in the 'good old days' of the Cold War; he could not have made a more disastrous miscalculation as the following narrative would show.

As the record of Saddam's meeting with April Glaspie, the American ambassador in Baghdad, a few days before he invaded Kuwait, made it clear, he was most concerned about the fall in the price of oil, which was the principal source of income for Iraq. The Iran–Iraq War had just ended after eight years. Iraq was heavily in debt. Saddam claimed that he had, in fact, 'saved' other Arab states by weakening Iran and, for that, they should at least forgive its debts and not allow the price of oil to fall any further. He blamed Kuwait for it and negotiated with the oil producing Arab states, but did not get any satisfactory response. It was only when the negotiations did not yield the desired outcome that he decided to invade Kuwait. That was his story.

1

A STAND FOR PRINCIPLES OR FRIENDS?

On 2 August 1990, Iraqi troops marched into Kuwait and occupied the country within a few hours. The Emir of Kuwait fled to Saudi Arabia and Saddam Hussain, the President of Iraq, installed a nine-member transitional government. The Americans came to know about Iraq's invasion of Kuwait at about 9.00 p.m. and went into immediate action. Their Permanent Representative to the UN, Thomas R. Pickering, traced the Permanent Representative of Kuwait to the Russian Tea Room, where he was enjoying dinner with some friends, blissfully unaware of what had happened to his country. Pickering galvanized other members of the UNSC into holding all-night consultations, prepared a draft resolution, got eight other members to co-sponsor it and had it adopted almost unanimously by 6.05 a.m. on 2 August.

Resolution 660 strongly condemned the Iraqi invasion of Kuwait. It called for immediate and unconditional withdrawal of the Iraqi troops and threatened further measures under Chapter VII of the UN Charter. It was adopted under Articles 39 and 40 of the UN Charter.

While the UNSC was meeting in crisis mode, I was watching a movie on the television with my family in my apartment at Park Avenue. I fell asleep soon after that. Local news media did not carry anything on this development at least until 11.00 p.m. My successor, Ronen Sen, joint secretary in the PMO, called me from Delhi at about 7.00 a.m. on the morning of 2 August and asked me about what was going on in the UNSC. I had no idea what he was talking about. He asked, 'Don't you know? Saddam has invaded Kuwait.' I made inquiries soon afterwards and sent reports to the MEA. I spoke to Dubey, the foreign secretary, on the phone at about 9.00 a.m. and asked him if India had made any statement. He said it was a very difficult situation for India since (1) Iraq was the only country to have objected to the inscription of the Kashmir issue on the agenda of the ministerial meeting of Organization of Islamic Countries (OIC) then in session in Cairo, (2) India had millions of dollars' worth of projects in Iraq, and (3) there were roughly 175,000 Indians in Kuwait. Dubey explained that this was the reason behind us not wanting to say anything, which may come across as too strong, about Iraq. We might, he added, appeal to the countries to resume their talks.

I told him that Iraq and Kuwait could not be placed at par under any circumstances, since it was our firm position that the victim of aggression could not be treated at par with the aggressor. I added that we could make a statement that would take care of our interests and still reflect a principled position. I also advised him that we did not have to be in a hurry to say anything; we could wait until the following morning in Delhi, instead of issuing a wishy-washy statement right away. This was a faux pas on my part. Dubey said that we had already made a statement to the effect that we were still receiving reports about the situation and that the Indians in Kuwait were reported to be safe. He thanked me for my 'very useful' suggestions. He was not aware of the UNSC action and was surprised at the swiftness with which it had acted.

Later that morning when I went to the UN, there was an atmosphere of great excitement about Iraq. Pele Pejic, the permanent representative of Yugoslavia, had given me a call in my office, and we met in the coffee shop of the Delegates' Lounge. He had been approached by Abul Hassan, the permanent representative of Kuwait, for a meeting of the NAM bureau. I told him that the NAM had to meet; it could not keep quiet. The Yugoslav foreign minister, Budimir Lončar, had already issued a statement. I suggested to Pejic that he should just read out his statement at the bureau meeting. Others strongly suggested that the bureau should endorse Lončar's statement and should also issue a communiqué of its own. Since I already knew my ministry's mind by this time, I asked Pejic how he could subject his minister's statement to endorsement by mere ambassadors. The argument went home. But the meeting itself could not be avoided. Pejic said that he would convene it on the following day.

I came back to the office and called Sen. He said the PM himself had decided that we must tilt in favour of Iraq because of its support for us in the OIC as well as on earlier occasions, especially during the Bangladesh War. I told him bluntly that any support to Iraq would be interpreted by others as one regional bully supporting another and that our credibility would come to be at stake. I said that I would have to make a statement at the NAM meeting, to which he replied that he would get back to me the next day.

Sensing the ministry's mood, I drafted a statement and sent it to Delhi. I avoided using the word 'condemns', but proposed expressing our shock and deep concern at the developments, without even mentioning Iraq. I did, however, suggest calling for immediate withdrawal of Iraqi troops. I deliberately made the draft under the impression that the ministry would dilute it in any case.

It was 3 August and I had still not received any response from the ministry. Fortunately, or rather unfortunately, the bureau meeting got postponed until that afternoon. Chandrashekhar Dasgupta, additional secretary in the MEA, who had been my colleague in the Indian mission to the UN as deputy permanent representative until September 1989, called me to say that he had faxed the text to me. He read it out over the phone. It bore no resemblance to my draft. I had no difficulty with that, but I had several problems with the actual wording. I called him when I got the fax and suggested a few changes. He ruled out all of them, saying that I.K. Gujral, the foreign minister, had personally worked on the draft and that it was the result of all of them pondering together. In the meantime, I had received the text of the official spokesman's statement. It was not a 'tilt' but a surrender. What he said shocked me. He said the situation was not quite clear and that there were reports to the effect that Iraq was in fact invited by some Kuwaitis to send troops. He was reflecting the collective view of the ministry.

I was aghast. I told Dasgupta, 'For heaven's sake, don't talk about this in public.' The similarity with our statement on Afghanistan back in January 1980 at once came to my mind. When the Soviet Union had invaded Afghanistan in 1979, India had stated that it had been invited by the government in Kabul; it was a puppet government.

The spokesman's statement equated Kuwait and Iraq, 'We regret that it had not been possible for Iraq and Kuwait to resolve their differences', hoped for Iraqi withdrawals (instead of calling for them) and, in the same sentence, noted Iraqi statements in this connection. There was not a word of disapproval of Iraqi action.

On 6 August, the UNSC adopted Resolution 661, imposing mandatory economic sanctions under Chapter VII against Iraq. On 8 August, T.P. Sreenivasan, the joint secretary in charge of the UN Division in the ministry, called me early in the morning and asked me if the sanctions would have to be implemented by us. I replied in the affirmative and said, of course, they were mandatory under Chapter VII. He said the foreign minister would like me to find out if any country would try to circumvent the sanctions, and if so, which ones. It was incredible. We were looking for accomplices to violate the sanctions. I refused to participate in such a ridiculous exercise.

On the same day, Saddam declared that Kuwait had returned to Iraq. In one stroke, Iraq had obliterated and wiped out Kuwait from the map.

The UNSC met in an informal session the same evening to consider a draft resolution which would declare Kuwait's annexation null and void. Thirteen members were ready to adopt it immediately, but China and the Soviet Union asked for time. The UNSC convened on the morning of 9 August and adopted Resolution 662 unanimously, declaring the annexation null and void. In the afternoon, Kuwait asked for an NAM bureau meeting to condemn the annexation. Yugoslavia fixed the meeting for 10.30 a.m. the next day. I had a problem whether I should say anything; if yes, what. I sent a message to Delhi, suggesting that I could make a brief intervention to the effect that India opposed annexation of one state by another and hoped that the efforts of Arab League meeting in Cairo would help reduce the tension in the Gulf and find some solution. Sreenivasan called and said that he had consulted both Dubey and Gujral and they had agreed with what I had suggested. But they would like me to say that India opposed the annexation in principle. I objected to the words 'in principle' because they implied that there could be exceptional circumstances that could justify an annexation. Sreenivasan explained that the ministry definitely wanted me to use those words. I replied that in that case, I would prefer not to make any statement. He said Foreign Minister wanted me to intervene. I repeated my strong objection to the words 'in principle'. There was a back and forth between us regarding this, after which he promised to consult and get back to me. He called me a few minutes later and much to my relief, and to his credit, said that 'they' had agreed to delete 'in principle'. As it happened, the meeting got cancelled because Kuwait felt that it might not be possible to avoid a reference to 'outside intervention' in the communiqué and would prefer, in that case, not to have one at all.

The UN and American Posturing

The situation on the ground, volatile as it was, appeared to be heading for a standoff. The Americans, whose presence in Saudi Arabia could reach 50,000 men before the end of the month, were already talking of 225,000 men in case hostilities broke out. Who was miscalculating? President Bush or Saddam? Both had taken extreme positions, leaving them hardly any room for retreat or face-saving. Bush demanded that Iraq must withdraw and the Sabah family—Kuwait's ruling family—be restored in Kuwait. Saddam's position was that Kuwait had become an integral part of Iraq. He called upon all states to close their embassies in Kuwait within two weeks, by 24 August, and shift to Baghdad.

The US was sending its mighty force to Saudi Arabia at their request to defend it against possible Iraqi attack. Nobody gave any credence to this 'request'. King Fahd of Saudi Arabia was personally prevailed upon by Bush, on telephone, and by Secretary of Defense, Dick Cheney, to make the request. King Fahd did not want to invite upon himself the odium of asking the US for protection and insisted that the US troops should form part of a multinational force, which would include some Arab contingents. Americans gave him the assurance and he made his request.

Cheney had gone to Cairo and the Americans had announced that Egyptian President Hosni Mubarak had agreed to send two divisions. However, it soon transpired that Egypt had not agreed to any such thing after all. It was possible that Mubarak might have given some encouraging but vague response to Cheney and the latter might have read too much into it; they might also have wanted to force Mubarak's hand. This was a faux pas by the Americans; they should have at least let Egypt make the announcement.

The US was in an embarrassing situation. So far, only Britain (which, under PM Thatcher, was considered by many as the fifty-first state of the US) had promised to send Royal Air Force squadrons, but no ground troops. By now, Australia and Canada had announced to send some token force. The Americans were feeling let down by their allies. One American observer said that on a scale of 1 to 10, non-participation by allies would rank eight for unfriendly response; Arabs would rank 12 for no participation.

The Americans did not consult their allies before the event. They had also put King Fahd in a humiliating situation and boosted Saddam's image in the Arab world. All my Arab friends were unanimous regarding the belief that Saddam had become very popular and was perceived as the new Nasser (which was the ambition of every Arab leader starting with Muammar Gaddafi). Saddam called on all the Arabs to revolt against the American presence that had defiled the holy places—Mecca and Medina—as well as for the overthrow of the Saudi monarchy. He also asked Mubarak to not permit foreign naval vessels to pass through Suez Canal.

On 8 August, Mubarak had called for an emergency meeting of the Arab leaders within 24 hours. He got immediate response. Twenty leaders reached Cairo by the next day. Only Tunisia was absent. To the surprise and dismay of many, Saddam sent his vice president. The Emir of Kuwait was also there.

The meeting planned for 7.00 p.m. did not take place; instead, Mubarak hosted his guests to a banquet. They finally met on 10 August, with the summit being regarded as the last opportunity to find a peaceful solution. The Arabs had been saying they should be given time to find some face-saving formula among themselves. They would, most likely, fail and claim that it was too late since the Americans had precipitated matters beyond the point of no return.

Most people, including myself, believed that the Americans had moved too fast. They did not give time for sanctions to bite. I felt sanctions would have definitely hurt Iraq. Hardly anyone thought it was likely that Saddam would have attacked Saudi Arabia, with many Americans even saying that if Saddam had wanted to attack Saudis, he would have done that before American deployment in the region. He had managed to direct the Arab attention away from his invasion of Kuwait to the American presence and called for jihad against non-Arab presence in Saudi Arabia.

Meanwhile, the American investment in Egypt paid off handsomely. The way Mubarak called the meeting of the Arab League and pushed through a resolution condemning the invasion of Kuwait had made him a hero in the US. (The Libyan ambassador Ali Treki told me that this was the first time ever that the Arab League had adopted a resolution by vote.) The Americans could now claim that they had the support of their allies, with the Arabs backing their actions. The naval armada consisted of 40 American ships and also ships from Britain, Australia, Canada, the Netherlands and France. Pakistan was reported to have agreed to send ground forces at the request of the Emir of Kuwait. This gave strong support to the theory that the recent constitutional coup in Pakistan, which led to the dismissal of the Benazir Bhutto government, was in some way connected to the Americans and the crisis in the Gulf. This would also suggest that Pakistan had concluded that Saddam was finished.

On 11 August, Saddam announced a three-point initiative: (1) withdrawal of all the countries from the territories occupied by them in the Middle East. As far as Iraq was concerned, the historic rights of Iraq to its territory and the choice of the people of Kuwait should be taken into account. This plan would be implemented in the order in which the occupations occurred; (2) withdrawal of American forces from Saudi Arabia to be replaced by Arab forces whose composition would be decided by the UNSC; Iraq and Saudi Arabia would agree on the nationalities of the forces to be deployed; exclusion of Egypt's troops, and; (3) freezing of economic sanctions against Iraq.

By linking the situation to Israeli occupation, Saddam was

hoping to embarrass the Arab governments and incite the Arab people. He seemed to be hoping for some offensive action by Israel in which case it would become an Arab–Israeli war. What would the Arab governments do in that case? Could Saudi Arabia afford to keep American troops on its soil?

The Americans claimed that they had the legal right to use force to compel compliance with the UNSC resolutions on sanctions. The legitimate government of Kuwait, the one in exile in Saudi Arabia, made a formal request to the US to that effect. The US felt that they needed something that could provide a legal justification, however dubious, to enforce a blockade or quarantine. They carefully refrained from the use of these terms in view of their implications in international law. Instead, they used the term 'interdictions'.

There was a big debate in the UN circles. Did the US have the right to impose a blockade or interdiction to implement the UN sanctions? The US and its allies maintained that they had, whereas Cuba and others argued that the US could perhaps claim the right to take action under Article 51 of the Charter—right of individual and collective self-defence—but they did not have the right to use force to implement sanctions, unless the UNSC specifically authorized them to do so. This would mean that Secretary General Javier Pérez de Cuéllar had to first give his report as directed by Resolution 661 on compliance with the sanctions. Only thereafter, the UNSC could consider other measures. But the Americans did not want to wait for that. Also, they were not confident that the UNSC would agree to authorize any measures under Article 42, first, because the Secretary General was most likely to report near-universal compliance with Resolution 661 and second because they were not sure of the Soviet Union and China going along with them.

There was a lot of speculation about real American motives. *The New York Times* carried an interesting article by Thomas Friedman, wherein he analysed the vital interests to protect which the US had ostensibly dealt with in Saudi Arabia. He pointed out that the administration had not defined those interests. His conclusion was that the troops were sent to shift the control of oil supply in the hands of pro-American Saudi Arabia, so that the prices remained low.

Friedman referred to a cartoon in *The Boston Globe* in which Bush could be seen in Oval Office, addressing the American people: 'I have sent our troops to the Middle East to defend the security…the value…the principle we hold dear…18 miles per gallon.'

Ambassador Pierre Louis Blanc of France had told me a few days before that Pickering's treatment of the Soviet's acting permanent representative was incredible. He treated him as if he was the ambassador of Trinidad and Tobago, and the Soviet attitude was pathetic. Blanc said there was simply no one now—after the political demise of Gorbachev—with the guts to contradict the Americans. Blanc was very unhappy with his own government; he felt that President Mitterrand was the only one who could restrain Bush but refused to use his influence. Even France seemed to miss the countervailing influence which the Soviets brought to bear on such issues in the pre-Gorbachev days.

True, the crisis was not initiated by the US, but it could not have come at a better time for the Pentagon and defence ministers in the Western world. Especially in the US, there was heavy pressure to reduce the defence budget. It would be unpatriotic to talk about a cut in defence budget when brave American men and women had been sent to faraway places to defend vital US interests.

Pakistan's decision to send troops to Saudi Arabia was based on the considerations to back the winning side (during the Iran–Iraq War, it had sided with Iran, the losing side), to express gratitude to Saudi Arabia for its support in the OIC (Saudis led the campaign, along with Iran and Turkey, to push through a resolution against India on Kashmir) and to clinch Saudi and other Muslim support in case Pakistan decided to raise the Kashmir issue at the next General Assembly session. It would reap dividends from the US by this one act—the US was desperate to get concrete support from Muslim countries.

Pakistan was lucky. In 1980, the Soviets had come to Zia's rescue with their invasion of Afghanistan. Zia had received political, military and economic support on a massive scale from the Americans, Saudis and most Western and Muslim countries. This time, the caretaker government of Ghulam Mustafa Jatoi, which was really a front for the army, had been bailed out by Saddam. Why did India have friends who turned out to be more helpful to Pakistan than to it?

2

THE JET-SETTING MINISTER: GUJRAL IN A BIND

King Hussein of Jordan met Saddam on 13 August in Baghdad. He was to go to Washington on the next day with a message from Saddam.

The same day, on Cuba's initiative, the UNSC met in an informal session to discuss the US claim to enforce sanctions on behalf of the UN. Not a single member supported the US—even the Brits kept silent. Others, Malaysia in particular, took the line that the UNSC must first wait for the Secretary General's report before even considering military action under Article 42.

India's stand on the situation in Kuwait reminded me of our approach to Vietnam's invasion of Cambodia. Friendship with Vietnam appeared to be very important for India, to the extent that it was almost a determining factor in our policy towards the Cambodian problem. It became obvious to me at the Paris Conference on Cambodia in August 1989 that India did not have an independent policy for Cambodia. But what did or could Vietnam do for us? What clout did they have in the region or in international relations? We kept opposing the UN role in Cambodia because we thought Vietnam was opposed to it when I kept telling Natwar, who led our delegation to the conference on Cambodia, and others that Vietnam would agree to UN involvement.

On 15 August, Saddam conceded all of Iran's demands, including joint sovereignty over the river Shatt al-Arab, return of Iranian territory and exchange of prisoners of war. On the same day, Gujral went to Washington, via New York.

Saddam's letter to Iranian President Akbar Hashemi Rafsanjani came as a surprise to everyone, including even to Iran. He had taken this step in desperation to release his forces from the border with Iran for deployment on the Saudi border. He also probably hoped that Iran would join him in his effort to preserve the Persian Gulf as a lake of peace, one free from evil forces from outside. He must have hoped that Iran could act as a conduit, albeit a clandestine one, for much needed supplies of food and other essentials. Iran welcomed Saddam's initiative. However, it maintained that it did not support Iraq's annexation of Kuwait, that Iraq must withdraw and that Iran would abide by the UN sanctions. Iran could have the best of both worlds: get everything from Iraq as well as please the Americans by at least making noises about respecting the sanctions.

King Hussein of Jordan met Bush for two hours in Kennebunkport. He did not bring any message from Saddam, written or oral. He obviously wanted to talk to Bush about his own problems. He was perhaps the shrewdest Arab leader, but he also knew that 60 per cent of his population was Palestinian, all of whom were fervently pro-Saddam, 90 per cent of the oil came from Iraq and 50 per cent of his exports went to Iraq. The Port of Aqaba was the lifeline, not only for Saddam but also, even more so, for Jordan. Bush wanted him to close this port. But how could he? How could he take this step knowing it would be immensely unpopular with his own people? Furthermore, his own supplies came through Aqaba. He would surely have explained all this to Bush, but the latter showed no sympathy for his friend's predicament. Bush said Jordan would be compensated for its sacrifices but must close the port. The King said he would not permit supplies for Iraq to go through Aqaba, but pointed out that even under Resolution 661, food supplies were permitted. Bush was not impressed. The King said that he would approach the UNSC for clarification.

Meanwhile, Mubarak claimed that Saddam had promised him that he would not attack Kuwait; Saddam clarified that he had said that he would not attack Kuwait only so long as Kuwait continued negotiations in Jeddah. He added that there were at least eight Egyptians and Iraqis 'who are still alive' and witness to what he had told Mubarak.

Gujral's Grand Tour

The US Secretary of State, Jim Baker, told Gujral on 15 August that one more misadventure and Saddam would feel the full force of the US. Saddam was hoping that Israel would oblige him by attacking him, which would act as a distraction from his own invasion, but Israel was not saying or doing anything.

Gujral had gone on a trip to Moscow and Washington earlier in the week. I had received a message on 14 August that he would come to New York from Moscow the next day and leave for Washington by the first available flight. I met him at the airport, and he asked me to go with him. We went directly from the airport to meet Baker for an hour. Gujral did not have anything specific to tell him. Gujral asked him whether there was any possibility or hope for a diplomatic solution. He told Baker of the difficulties India was facing in reassuring Indian people about the welfare of the Indian community in Kuwait, Baghdad and elsewhere in the Gulf. When Gujral said that the Indians were panic-stricken, Baker responded that the feeling of panic should disappear once the US forces are deployed in full strength! All in all, Baker was understanding and appreciative of our concerns. He, and later, National Security Advisor Brent Scowcroft, promised help in the matter of oil supplies to India. Baker clarified that there should be no objection if India wanted to send ships to evacuate its nationals or to take food for them, but asked, 'But how can you be sure that your people will get the food and that it won't be taken away by Iraqi soldiers?'

Gujral told Baker that he was planning to go to Baghdad to talk to the Iraqis about the safety and possible evacuation of the Indian community and not to offer any mediation. Baker said that it was the duty of every government to ensure the safety of its people; if India felt that the only way to ensure this was to go to Baghdad, he could understand. I thought Baker could not care less what India did or said. His only concern was, and he said this more than once, that India should implement the sanctions fully. Gujral assured him that India was with the international community. Baker was aggressively confident about Saddam. He said, 'Very soon, we shall be in a position to protect the remaining Gulf states and to annihilate Saddam. At that time, there may be scope for diplomacy, but not before that. Saddam must realize that he has to withdraw.' Even though Baker made no such request,

Gujral said he would convey this to Saddam. All in all, I felt sorry for Gujral; he cut such a pathetic figure.

It was obvious that Saddam was determined to use the American and British nationals in Iraq as hostages, and as human shields in case of US strikes. He made them 'restrictees' and ordered them to move into two separate hotels in Kuwait.

In spite of the Government of India's placatory attitude, Iraq did not show any particular favour to us. Gujral told me that our embassy in Baghdad was not allowed to meet the 500 Indians who had gone to Baghdad from Kuwait. The Iraqi treatment of Gujral was particularly shocking. He spoke to Tariq Aziz, Iraq's foreign minister, from Moscow on phone. Aziz invited him to come to Baghdad and offered to send a plane to bring him from Amman, but added that he would confirm the arrangements later. On the morning of 16 August, I.P. Khosla, additional secretary in the MEA, who had come with Gujral, was told by Prem Badhwar, minister-counselor at our Moscow embassy, that all was arranged. Gujral was happy and proudly announced it to the press. Two hours later, the Iraqi embassy in Washington told us that it would not be convenient at this time to send a plane for Gujral. It was embarrassing. Gujral said he would go to Amman anyway and asked this to be conveyed to the Iraqis. He wanted to speak to Aziz on phone, but it was not possible. He said we would arrange our own aircraft, but Kamal Bakshi, our ambassador in Baghdad, said it was doubtful whether the Iraqis would give clearance.

I told Gujral that if he went all the way to Amman and then was not allowed or invited by the Iraqis to go to Baghdad, it would be interpreted as a serious rebuff to him and to India by Iraq. He saw the point, but said he had to take the risk, otherwise people back home would say he was keen on going to comfortable places but not to Baghdad. Poor man. He was a very decent and courteous person. It was obvious that his predicament was a reflection of the extreme weakness of the V.P. Singh government. The other aspect was that India was going out of the way not to annoy Iraq, but the latter could not care less.

The Security Council in Action

The Americans issued instructions on 16 August to their navy to use proportionate force to interdict ships suspected of carrying cargo for Iraq, despite the controversy regarding the legality of such action. The Secretary General said that a blockade could be put into effect only by a resolution of the UNSC and that unilateral interception, outside of the council's authorization, would be a violation of the Charter. (Later, the UN issued a clarification that the Secretary General had said nothing about violation of the Charter. The US mission had acted fast and furious!) The Americans knew that they did not have the necessary votes, so they had to act on their own. The CNN announced at 5.00 pm on 17 August that *USS England* and *USS Bradley* had challenged Iraqi vessels exactly four hours ago, but did not board them; they were empty. Gujral asked Baker about all this. The latter said they had started consultations with the other permanent members, which were limited to discussing a possible vote in the naval field. He made it clear that the UN had nothing to do as far as ground forces were concerned.

Eduard Shevardnadze, the Soviet foreign minister, announced on 17 August that the Soviet Union would be prepared to send troops if the UNSC set up a UN force.

The other members, even some permanent members of

the UNSC, were beginning to express their resentment at the extreme pressure the US was exerting to push through resolutions at short notice. The US had realized that it could not get away with unilateral action to blockade Iraq, justifying it as an action on behalf of the UNSC. As *The New York Times* correspondent Paul Lewis said, the US wanted to have a fig leaf from the UN. The P-5 had been consulting all day long at the French mission and called the other 10 members of the UNSC to the council at 10.30 p.m. The US desperately wanted a resolution before the morning because an Iraqi tanker was expected to reach Yemen. But the other 10 were not ready to oblige this time. They asked for time to study the draft and to ask for instructions from their governments. Eventually, a face-saving was found. Yemen's Permanent Representative, Al Ashtal, announced that Yemen would turn the tanker back. So, the UNSC did not meet and the resolution was postponed.

On 18 August, the US fired nine warning shells across the bow of two Iraqi tankers laden with oil, without hitting them.

The next day, Saddam announced a five-point initiative. The media oversimplified it by saying that Saddam had promised to let the foreigners leave in return for withdrawal of the US troops from the region. This was rejected outright by the Americans. But a careful reading of the five points indicated that they did contain some opening, however small, for talks. Saddam had said in effect that the US troops would be replaced by the UN presence, which would guarantee Saudi security; Bush would give a solemn promise to withdraw, and the foreigners would be freed. He said Kuwait could be discussed within the Arab framework.

The consensus in the Delegates' Lounge was that the Americans had built up such an enormous power in the region and Bush's public posture was so tough that the Americans would do something serious in the next few days, that the US was not interested in any talks because the talks would drag on and on, and that time was not on American side, as American people would not support a long-drawn out affair. Two to three American soldiers were collapsing every day in the Saudi desert and so the logistics of the situation suggested that the US must move fast. They must provoke Saddam to take the first foolish step and then launch devastating air strikes, even if it might kill a few American hostages.

Meanwhile, Syria moved a few troops to Saudi Arabia, Egypt sent more troops and tanks, the UAE agreed to give base facilities to the US cargo planes, the Federal Republic of Germany decided to send ships to Eastern Mediterranean, Spain announced decision to send four ships, France started interrogating vessels about their cargos and destinations and, very interestingly, Gaddafi condemned Iraq for treating foreigners as hostages and offered to send troops if asked by the UNSC.

Gujral turned out to be fully justified in his decision to go to Amman; he went to Baghdad and even Kuwait. Iraq received him warmly. He went to Kuwait on 21 August, becoming the first foreign minister from any country to go there after the 2 August events. I was too cautious, though right, in cautioning him of a possible rebuff, but his political instinct was sound.

As of 23 August, the UNSC could not meet to act on the US draft. While having lunch with Yves Fortier, the permanent representative of Canada, Pickering said that they had the text of the resolution and that he would ask for a formal meeting on the same day. But Li Daoyu, the Chinese permanent representative, told me that there was no such agreement. However, the five members met again and arrived at an agreement: China would abstain; there would be 10 votes in favour, two against and three abstentions.

Bush ordered a recall of reservists for the first time since the Tet Offensive of 1968. The build-up in the desert had surpassed the Berlin Airlift of 1948.

Jordan had closed its border with Iraq on 22 August; it simply could not cope with the flood of refugees from Kuwait and Iraq. King Hussein seemed to have managed to get Saddam to agree to pull out of Kuwait and go to Saudi Arabia for a mini summit, along with the Emir of Kuwait.

India, like other nations, was exposed to closing its embassy in Kuwait but could strengthen its consulate general in Basra.

Talking to the Foreign Minister and Foreign Secretary, it was clear to me that the welfare of the Indian community was dominating the thoughts and actions of Government of India; it had paralysed us, like the hostage crisis in Tehran had paralysed the Jimmy Carter administration in 1979. This explained why we had not said anything about Kuwait's annexation.

Dubey told me we needed Iraq's help and cooperation at every stage. Perhaps, I felt strongly because I was in New York, and constantly met with permanent representatives of other countries in the Delegates' Lounge. Abul Hassan got hold of me and asked, 'Brother Chinmaya, we are simply shocked at India's position. How can India, which has always upheld all the principles, take such a position? The Emir told me he was simply shocked.'

The US, Japan and the 12 countries of European Communities (EC) declared they would not close their embassies in Kuwait. The deadline for the closure was 23 August. Soviets said they had not closed their embassy but had withdrawn everyone. Iraqi forces had surrounded these embassies.

Jordan reopened its border with Iraq; it would allow 20,000 refugees to enter every day. King Hussein told Gujral that Bush did not have a clear idea about how the crisis began. King Hussein was convinced that a solution could have been possible before the Arab League action; Saddam would have agreed to withdraw, followed by election or plebiscite. The American intervention had greatly complicated the situation.

What the US Wanted

What were the American objectives? The rhetoric about upholding principles convinced no one. Kuwait's future was only a side show. Even if Saddam were to withdraw, would the American troops pull out? Even if Saddam was eliminated, what would the US achieve? They said that they had gone to Saudi Arabia to defend the American way of life, to protect the lifeline of the industrialized world. This would mean they must physically stay in the region forever. Israel, of course, was another explanation. A powerful Saddam would be a serious threat to Israel and thus had to be finished off before that. In another five years, Saddam would have nuclear weapons and would not hesitate to use them. But the irony was, the moment Israel would come into the equation, all the Arabs would join Saddam.

Even some conservatives, such as Pat Buchanan and Jeanne Kirkpatrick, were critical of Bush's involvement in the Middle East. The argument was that during the Cold War era, it was essential for the US to get involved everywhere to defeat communism. But now that communism had been defeated and the US had won, it was not America's role to act as the global policeman. Situations such as the one in the Gulf were best left to the UN, which, for the first time, was United Nations in the true sense.

Action in the UNSC was postponed once again. The Soviets were engaged in crucial talks with Saddam and preferred more time. In the meantime, Columbia and Malaysia produced a draft. Enrique Peñalosa Camargo, the permanent representative of Columbia, spoke to Pickering about it and the Americans moved fast. Baker immediately contacted Columbian foreign minister and urged him to instruct his ambassador in New York to support the current draft, which had the approval of the P-5.

The Soviet effort at moderating Saddam failed; they were ready for the vote. Gorbachev spoke for over an hour with Saddam on 24 August and warned him that the Soviets would support strong measures in the UNSC unless Iraq accepted its resolutions. The P-5 reached an agreement on the draft at 9.30 p.m. on 26 August. The 10 non-permanent members were summoned to the UN, where the Brits, Soviets and Americans explained the draft to them. The non-aligned were very unhappy because not a single element from the Columbian–Malaysian draft had been accepted. They asked for time for consultations among themselves; they prepared a set of amendments that they, after checking with Kuwait and Iraq, presented to the P-5. Agreement was finally reached at 1.30 a.m. and the council met in a formal session at 3.30 a.m., which ended at 6.00 a.m. on 27 August. I was there with Dinesh Jain, my counsellor, from 10.30 p.m. till 5.00 a.m.

The UNSC adopted Resolution 665 with 13 in favour and two abstentions (Cuba and Yemen). Ricardo Alarcón, the Cuban permanent respresentative, made an excellent speech on how the Resolution violated several provisions of Chapter VII. The Americans' decisive success was a demonstration of their clout. The Resolution denied any role for the UN or the Secretary General. At the same time, even some non-aligned members felt that it was incumbent on the UNSC to send an unequivocal signal to Saddam.

Li Daoyu told me that his personal preference was to abstain, 'but Beijing decided to vote in favour, so what could I do?' As several ambassadors there, he too did not have high opinion of his bosses back home, and said, 'They don't understand all the implications.'

The Secretary General fixed a meeting with Aziz in Amman on 30 August. He insisted that the initiative for the meeting was his; he was very sensitive to any remark suggesting that he should check with the P-5 first.

Since the announcement of the Secretary General's visit to Amman, there was a glimmer of hope that the tensions in the Gulf would abate. Cuéllar made it clear that his talks with Aziz would be strictly within the framework of the UNSC's resolutions. The Americans were not too happy with Cuéllar's initiative, but they did not oppose it.

This tiny glimmer of hope vanished within 24 hours. Saddam, unpredictable as he was, announced that from now on, Kuwait formed the nineteenth province of Iraq, and that Kuwait would henceforth be known by its ancient name of Al Qadima. This was a rebuff to the Secretary General. Even the Yemeni ambassador said that Saddam had made it difficult for anyone to remain neutral in this crisis.

Saddam told a group of hostages that he was ready to talk to Bush and Thatcher, even to have a television debate with them. Was this what he really wanted? Was it all a question of ego?

The US expelled 36 Iraqi diplomats from Washington on 28 August following this move, to which Iraq reciprocated.

Saddam was not insane. He did not want to do anything that would provide a legitimate or reasonable casus belli to the US. Hence, Iraqi ships were ordered to not resist if American or other ships demanded the right of inspection and verification of the cargo. Perhaps, he was counting on the Soviet veto.

Israeli PM Yitzhak Shamir accused Jordan and Yemen of continuing to violate the sanctions and publicly warned King Hussein that his position was contrary to Israel's interests. Saddam would be most happy if Israel joined the diplomatic war against him, since it would compel the Arabs to support him.

US senator Frank Lautenberg said that Mubarak had told him that Saddam had offered $15 billion to Mubarak if he went along with Iraq's annexation of Kuwait.

Saddam Sweats, Americans Flex

The UN sanctions and the US arms build-up seemed to be working. On 29 August, there were unconfirmed reports that a senior US official brought an offer from Saddam, delivered through back channels to the effect that he would be prepared to concede limited self-rule to Kuwait and might even consider pulling out, except for the oil wells of Rumaila, provided the sanctions were lifted and the US gave an assurance that it would pull out of Saudi Arabia. It was further announced that foreign male 'guests' would also be allowed to leave along with women and children if the US gave assurance that it would not strike Iraq.

There was a lot of discussion in America about what the US objectives should be in this whole operation. Expulsion of Iraq from Kuwait was the bottom line on which there was complete agreement. But that would not be enough. Iraq would have to be eliminated as a threat to the stability of the region (meaning the assured availability of cheap oil) and to the security of Israel. That meant that the war-making potential of Iraq must be destroyed—all its tanks, chemical weapons, missiles, aircraft, etc. But for this, Saddam must provide a pretext. So far, he had acted sensibly. Henry Kissinger, a respected analyst, advocated a surgical strike because he felt that the American people would not tolerate a long-drawn-out stalemate like Vietnam.

The temperature was cooler on 29 August, in comparison to a few days ago. The Americans had demonstrated that they alone were the true superpower of the day; no other country could have deployed such a large force in the Arabian desert in a span of three weeks, nor could any other country have mobilized the UNSC so effectively to the extent of coaxing it into adopting resolutions that were, at best, of doubtful constitutionality (the US could have its way, even if others had doubt about it). This was perhaps a US-centric view. The Soviet Union continued to be important. It would not encourage the US to embark on any military adventure and would do everything to promote a political solution. But all said and done, its clout was limited. China, for its part, was anxious to end its isolation. It needed the US technology and markets.

We were witnessing the emergence of Pax Americana.

The atmosphere in the last week of August was less pessimistic because of the impending talks between Secretary General and Aziz on 1 September in Amman. However, Cuéllar announced the failure of his mission. On a televised address, he said, 'I am not playing any diplomacy with you, but I can tell you that I am disappointed.' His blunt admission of failure no doubt pleased some people in Washington. On the other hand, one got the feeling that the US administration would welcome some 'out', some way of achieving their objectives without having to go to war. The initial US rhetoric of wanting to eliminate Saddam gave way to more guarded 'hopes' that he would somehow be overthrown. At the same time, a report started doing the rounds that Bush had signed an executive order asking the CIA to work towards Saddam's demise, at least politically, and that Saudi Arabia had offered to fund this supposedly covert operation.

On 2 September, Bush made the surprise announcement that he would meet with Gorbachev in Helsinki on 9 September. I wondered what Gorbachev expected to get out of the meeting. He would welcome this public reaffirmation of the status and importance of the Soviet Union as an equal partner. Bush would hope to align the Soviets even more firmly with his side and get them to join him in issuing a joint warning of tough action against Saddam if he did not comply with the UN resolutions. The Soviet spokesman Gennadi Gerasimov defended the military build-up in the Gulf and rebuked Soviet media for suggesting that the American deployment threatened superpower relations. We were living in strange times.

The naval blockade was in full swing. Close to 75 ships were stopped initially. Gradually, the traffic diminished. The US ships boarded two Iraqi vessels, but without any untoward incident.

The US announced that the $7 billion owed by Egypt for military sales would be written off in appreciation of its help in the Gulf crisis. Israel lost no time in demanding the same. Baker and US treasury secretary, Nicholas F. Brady, set off on separate missions to persuade Federal Republic of Germany, Japan and other countries to finance the Gulf operations. They were particularly unhappy with Japan, which had pledged only $1 billion and had been very tardy in fulfilling even that commitment.

Foreign ministers of India, Yugoslavia and Algeria agreed to meet in Belgrade on 11 September at India's initiative.

Baker told the House Committee on Foreign Affairs on 3 September that even if Saddam were to pull out of Kuwait, the US presence in the Gulf would remain. He said, 'We are not there to keep the price of gasoline low; it is about a dictator who acting alone and unchallenged could strangle the global economic order.' He proposed that a new regional security structure should be put in place; just as the North Atlantic Treaty Organization (NATO) successfully contained communism, another security pact or system must be found to contain Saddam.

Everyone agreed that the political and social map of the region would be transformed by the time the crisis was over. The seven families ruling the sheikhdoms and Saudi Arabia would be extremely shaky, and some of them might lose their kingdoms. King Fahd issued a decree calling upon all young men to join the armed forces and, for the first time, women were permitted, even invited, to take up jobs which would bring them in contact with men. The region was playing with fire. Islamic fundamentalism, unfortunately, turned out to be the biggest winner.

Baker perhaps realized that he went too far in asserting that the US presence would be maintained for a long time in the region. He later clarified that the presence would be maintained only if the Arabs wanted the US to do so.

Aziz, Saddam's well-groomed spokesperson, read out a message on TV that Iraqi children were dying because of sanctions and called upon Arabs to rise against the American conspiracy. Saddam also called for jihad and overthrow of the Saudi regime.

3

OF OIL, TRUCE AND A SHIP OF FOOD

The problem of food supplies for the Indian community in Kuwait occupied all my time and effort for several days in early September. The situation was grave and rapidly deteriorating. We approached the UNSC for permission to send food to our people. I contacted ambassadors of the Philippines, Sri Lanka, Bangladesh, Pakistan and Thailand to see if they would join in making a joint démarche to the UNSC. The Philippines joined and signed the letter. Sri Lanka sent a separate letter. Pakistan and Bangladesh refused; they were firmly in the US camp.

After imposing sanctions under Resolution 660, the UNSC established the sanctions committee to monitor the implementation of the sanctions by member states of the UN. The committee also had the authority to allow exceptions to the sanctions in some cases of extreme hardships experienced by some State.

I made a 20-minute presentation to the sanctions committee on 10 September. I was quite emotional because I had been deeply affected by the plight of the Indians. I demanded, and not just requested, that the UNSC should display at least the same urgency that it did while adopting the five resolutions, 'Why can't you meet at night as you did then?' When some members giggled, I said that this was not a matter to laugh about.

My intervention had some effect. The P-5 met the same evening. The sanctions committee met for the whole day and almost took a favourable decision. But the US and the Brits came in the way, saying they needed more time to obtain instructions. Later, they presented a paper on general guidelines for such humanitarian circumstances. They said they would agree to India's request only if their paper was accepted. Cuba and Yemen strongly argued to delink the two issues, but the US clout and arrogance was so strong that they had to agree to the link. The Americans succeeded in blackmailing. The committee met and first approved the US paper and then approved the Indian request. We had a ship ready in Cochin (now Kochi) with 10,000 tonnes of food.

Whether Iraq would let us send the food was another matter. The Iraqi government told our ambassador in Baghdad that they could no longer give our people food, and that we had to make our own arrangements for it from now on. Not only that, but they also said that any food that was brought to Iraq must be for all the people living in Iraq and Kuwait, and not just for Indians. They had told Gujral in Baghdad that India could arrange evacuation of Indians directly from Baghdad and even Basra. Later, they said that any plane that came to evacuate Indians must also carry food and medicines for Iraqis. Even Gujral had to admit in Parliament that there had been delay and distortions in Iraqi government's fulfillment of the promises made to him.

On 13 September, I spent 24 hours at the UN. The UNSC and the sanctions committee met several times, and the permanent members got their draft approved as Resolution 666 at about midnight. India's request was approved by the committee at about 1.00 a.m. next morning. I had to indulge in a lot of negotiations with several members. The main concern was that the UNSC should not bind us down by declaring that the International Committee of the Red Cross (ICRC) would be the only agency to supervise the distribution of food. Iraq was strongly opposed to it and we in India did not like it either. By its recent behaviour, the ICRC was rightly perceived as favouring the Western nations. I told the Brits and others that restricting the choice to the ICRC would render the whole exercise meaningless.

I gave Dubey the good news. He was gracious and said some nice things about me and added that the whole country had been waiting for this news. I requested that we should launch the ship as soon as possible and that Delhi should not say anything to criticize the ICRC.

But then the struggle with Iraqis started. Al-Anbari, the Iraqi permanent representative, called me and conveyed his government's official position—the distribution of food should be negotiated bilaterally with Iraq. I suggested to Dubey that either he or someone senior should fly to Baghdad to reason with the Iraqis. The Western nations were banking on Iraq not permitting the food to reach the Indians. If that happened, they would obtain a big propaganda coup.

Saddam's Appeasement

Out of the blue, a most significant development took place during this time, namely, the establishment of diplomatic relations between Iran and Iraq after the particularly bloody Iran–Iraq War. Ali Hosseini Khamenei, the Supreme Leader of Iran, called upon his people and Muslims everywhere for a jihad against the American presence in the Gulf—highly inflammatory stuff. It was a new ball game. The Iranians were exceptionally clever people and certainly had no intention to go to war with the US.

By the middle of September, the US had deployed close to 150,000 men together with impressive naval armada and airpower. Nearly two dozen countries had joined the US.

The Helsinki Summit on 9 September had turned out to be as I had expected it would. Gorbachev's statement had language that was almost the same as I had anticipated in a wire to Delhi. There was a great show of solidarity between the two leaders. However, there were also some differences. Gorbachev had refused to endorse any military option and insisted all further moves be made in the UN. He had argued for an international conference where all the issues would be taken up. Bush could not reject it outright but had said that the first issue was to get Iraq out of Kuwait. Gorbachev was happy that he had got Bush to publicly admit that the Soviet Union had a role to play in the Middle East. When Bush had said in the press conference that he would reward Gorbachev in dollars, the latter had immediately retorted that the Soviet policy cannot be bought for dollars.

The Indian cargo vessel *Vishva Siddhi* left Cochin for Kuwait on 16 September, carrying 10,000 tonnes of food. As usual, there was considerable wrangling among ministers.

K.P. Unnikrishnan, the minister for shipping and surface transport, wanted to flag off the ship, but the PM had asked Hari Kishore Singh, Union minister of state for external affairs, to do it. In the end, they both did the honours.

In mid-September, Iraq announced that it was offering free oil to developing countries. Because of the blockade, countries concerned would have to send their own ships to pick up the oil, but apart from that, there were no strings attached. Saddam, in effect, was using oil as a weapon to win the sympathy and support of developing and non-aligned countries. He was not likely to get much mileage from this move.

One of Bush's grievances was that Saddam had all the access to American TV without corresponding access to him in Iraq. 'Fair enough,' said Saddam, 'We shall send a team to interview you for our TV.' Bush understandably was not enthusiastic about the idea. So, Voice of America taped an eight-minute statement, subtitled in Arabic, and sent it to Baghdad with a courier. It was shown on Iraqi TV. Sure enough, it was followed by a 20-minute reply by an Iraqi spokesperson.

There was fear in the US about a recession. The price of oil had already reached $31–32. Whatever marginal benefits accrued from the war would be more than offset by inflation, loss of jobs, less consumption, etc. Unemployment had already reached 5.6 per cent.

Doubts and opposition to the American policy in Gulf were being aired openly and frequently in America. One Congressman said the policy was a mixture of 'fiction and fantasy'.

Around this time, Iraq released the minutes of a meeting between Saddam and the US ambassador April Glaspie on 26 July in which the ambassador clearly conveyed Bush's desire for better relations with Iraq. In that same meeting, Saddam had clearly stated that the entire problem was about the price of oil; he was against lowering the price of oil, something he believed Kuwait was doing. He indicated, unambiguously, that if Kuwait did not agree to Iraq's reasonable demand, Iraq would be obliged to protect its interests. There was a demand in the Congress for sanctions against Iraq, but the State Department vehemently opposed it. It was suggested that the US had followed a policy of appeasement, had helped Iraq in many ways to build its defence capability and was, in fact, responsible for indirectly leading Saddam to believe that US would not go to the defence of Kuwait. Some Congressmen were unhappy that the State Department sought to make a scapegoat of Glaspie who had left Baghdad the day before the invasion.

Uneasy Allies

Grumbling in Saudi Arabia became more audible. The regime felt it necessary to organize a gathering of 350 Islamic scholars who opined, after bitter controversies, that Saudi Arabia was justified in asking a non-Muslim country for help. This showed that Saddam's propaganda about the infidels defiling holy places was having an impact. The Saudis were beginning to realize that the Americans intended to stay on for an extended period in the region.

The Soviets were the beneficiary of the crisis. They received public acknowledgement of their role in the Middle East, established diplomatic relations with the Saudis, which was broken off in 1938, and the Saudis even declared they would welcome Soviet military participation on Saudi soil.

The US administration tried to push through the US Congress a huge arms sale for Saudi Arabia, totaling to

$21 billion. But they had not reckoned with the Israeli lobby, which lost no time in countering the sale. In the end, only about 10 per cent of the deal was approved.

The Arab League, for all intents and purposes, formally split. Twelve out of 21 members met in Cairo. Clovis Maksoud, the League observer in Washington and the most articulate exponent of the Arab cause, resigned.

Yasser Arafat, chairman of Palestine Liberation Organization (PLO), went to Baghdad and came back with a message from Saddam saying that he was prepared to discuss withdrawal from Kuwait with the Secretary General, who said that if Arafat had such a message, he would like to get it directly from Saddam. There was no truth in this report.

Meanwhile, *Vishva Siddhi* was en route Um Qasr and expected to arrive on 23 September. The sanctions committee was putting pressure on India to ensure physical presence of the UN on the ship. I told them this was a non-starter, as Iraq would never agree to that. Then they suggested that the ICRC should be invited on to the ship. I said that if Iraq was willing to let the ICRC associate itself with the distribution, we could arrange for it to meet the ship on arrival at the port, but not while the ship was still out at sea. I offered to send a full report once the operation was successfully completed. We were told by the Iraqis that they would let the Indian Red Cross, together with Iraqi Red Crescent Society, arrange and supervise the distribution.

Iraqis systematically removed everything of value from Kuwait. They started depopulating Kuwait of Kuwaitis in an attempt to change the demographics of the country.

The Saudis announced that they were cutting off oil supplies to Jordan. The ostensible reason was late or non-payment of bills, but the real reason was extreme annoyance with King Hussein for his pro-Saddam stance and because of his shuttling around looking for an Arab solution. They expelled 20 Jordanian and 30 Yemeni diplomats. The Saudis perhaps realized that there was no such thing as an Arab nation and they did not owe anything to anyone, be it free oil to Jordan or several billions to the Palestinians.

When Gujral was in Kuwait in August, he had advised the Indians to stand in solidarity with their Iraqi brothers. No wonder we were facing difficulties on the food front.

The sanctions were hurting Iraq. They declared they would not allow the sanctions to strangle Iraqi people and that they would strike at the oil installations in Saudi Arabia and other Gulf states. For the first time, Saddam threatened to attack without waiting for the US to attack first.

Iran turned out to be the most intriguing. The Iranians were trying to extract the maximum, not only from Iraq but also from others. They condemned Iraq's actions in Kuwait, but connived at small-scale violations of the sanctions across the border. They equally condemned the American presence in the region, but hinted that they would not make a big issue of it if the presence was not long term. They played host to President Bashar al-Assad of Syria, who flew to Tehran with a message from the Americans, urging Iran to abide by the sanctions. Imagine, Assad, the arch terrorist in the eyes of the Americans, goes to Tehran, another terrorist country for the Americans, with a message from the US to enforce sanctions against Iraq whom they helped during the Iran–Iraq war!

The Sanctions Begin

On 25 September, the UNSC adopted Resolution 670, imposing an air embargo against Iraq. The vote was 14 in favour, with Cuba alone voting against. The meeting was attended at ministerial level except for Cuba and Ivory Coast. Shevardnadze, as the Soviet president, welcomed all the ministers, whereas Baker referred only to ministers of the P-5, pointedly ignoring the others. It was being speculated in the UN corridors that Resolution 670 was in the nature of preparing the ground for expelling Iraq from the General Assembly.

Mitterand's statement in the General Assembly attracted a lot of attention. He proposed a four-phase approach. In the first phase, Iraq would declare its intention to withdraw and release the hostages; everything would become possible after that. In the second phase, the withdrawal would be supervised by the international community, Kuwait's sovereignty would be restored, and Kuwaiti people would express their will democratically. In the third phase, other regional problems would be resolved, Lebanon would regain full sovereignty and Palestinians would have their own homeland. In the final phase, there would be reduction of armaments and the whole region would become an area of peace and cooperation. The significant element in this plan was that implementation would start only with the intention to withdraw and not actual withdrawal. There was also total and, no doubt, deliberate omission of any reference to return of the legitimate ruler of Kuwait. Shortly after Mitterrand's speech, Bush declared the US would not concede even an inch to Saddam. On the other hand, Saddam said on 30 September that Mitterrand's speech contained a lot of positive elements.

The sanctions were expected to bite the Iraqi regime to the extent of forcing it to leave Kuwait. In the meantime, Iraq was systematically denuding Kuwait of all valuable things. There was an unbroken traffic of trucks on the

Kuwait–Baghdad Road. There were stories of infants being deprived of incubators in hospitals. Faucets, bulbs, pipes, etc., not to talk of bigger equipment, were being shipped to Iraq.

Saddam talked of a 1,000-year war. He said that the next war would be the 'mother of all wars'. The oil wells in the Gulf would stay aflame for several years. (American oil experts pointed out that this was not possible because of lack of oxygen underground.) At the same time, he was careful in not giving any pretext to the Americans to launch an attack.

During this time, *Vishva Siddhi* lay off the port of Um Qasr. I understood that only 1,000 tonnes could be unloaded a day; thus, it would take 10 days to unload the entire cargo and several days more after that to distribute the food. People in the UN were asking me about the food situation. I had painted a picture of desperation. I had asked Gujral that if the entire community was going to be evacuated by 10 October, why did we need to send the food. His unconvincing reply was that we would still have 30,000 people left behind in Kuwait. I had this uneasy feeling that the whole thing about shortage of food and sending the ship was a political stunt, staged for domestic political reasons by the government. If the situation was really bad, we would have heard of starvation deaths by now. I hoped I was wrong.

My doubts about the Indian ship proved right. The UN Joint Secretary told me over the phone that the Indian community had told the government that they did not need the food and that they had enough stocks for at least two months. How ridiculous and dishonest of the government! The Indians added that in any case, there was no space to store so much food. The embassy was trying to persuade the community to accept the food. Other Asian communities were also being offered the food, as much as they wanted.

Gujral maintained that the Indians needed the food but were afraid to accept it for fear of enraging the Kuwaitis. Ratan Sehgal, the officer in charge of security and vigilance in the ministry, who had been deputed to Kuwait to help in the evacuation, sent a message to the ministry that there was not only enough food in Kuwait but the Indians had even offered to send some food to Baghdad for the Indians living in Iraq.

4

WHO BLINKS FIRST?

In his address on 1 October in the General Assembly, Bush repeated his line on the Gulf. But he also said that once Iraq left Kuwait, other issues, including the relations between the Arabs and Israel, would also have to be attended to. He had said similar things in Helsinki, but it attracted more notice this time because he had said it in the UN. The UN was like a stock market in those days. The mood changed from day to day. On 1 October, the mood was bearish. The foreign minister of Jordan told his Indian counterpart that there were preliminary positive signals from Iraq in response to Mitterrand's speech. Saddam said he needed some clarifications and elaborations. He also released nine French hostages on 1 October. The Americans were not happy with the French.

Qian Qichen, the foreign minister of China, told Gujral that China did not favour war as a means of solving the conflict. He said that China was opposed to big power presence in the Gulf, especially if it was going to be on a long-term basis. The Soviets, on the other hand, maintained that while they preferred a political solution, they would, if everything else failed, be ready to support military action, provided it was carried out under the aegis of the UNSC. The Americans definitely wanted to act on their own, should the use of force become unavoidable for whatever reasons. They would not tolerate their forces to come under the command of the UN. Jeanne Kirkpatrick, US ambassador during the Reagan administration, the arch enemy of UN, stated that the President did not have the authority under the Constitution to place American forces under anyone else's command.

The question for others, including India, was whether war, if it became unavoidable, should be authorized and carried out by the UN or by the US unilaterally. Which was the less attractive alternative? If the UNSC was involved, the US would be justified in claiming that it was acting on behalf of the international community. If it acted on its own, we all would be able to disassociate ourselves from it, would be under no obligation to take part in it and even be able to deplore or denounce it.

The saga of our food shipment was becoming more embarrassing by the day. I received a cable from Dubey relaying that no more than 1,000 tonnes could be used, and that the government planned to give away the rest to Iraqi and Kuwaiti schools and hospitals. He asked me to 'discreetly' sound out sanctions committee. My own reaction was almost violent. Any such move or even intention on our part would be vehemently opposed by the committee, most of whose members would impute mala fides to our decision to send the ship. I discussed with Gujral and he fortunately agreed with me. I conveyed his decision to Dubey that no action of the type contemplated in the cable should be undertaken.

Dubey's own feelings were very much like mine, but additional secretary Khosla, who, I understood, was apparently convinced that India's future lay with Saddam, strongly believed that we should give away the food to Iraq. Perhaps he had access to information from several sources, something I obviously did not. I told Dubey that the humanitarian exception could only be decided by the UN and not by individual countries. The whole idea of sending the ship turned out to be a big fiasco and an embarrassment.

The key passage in Bush's televised address on 1 October was as follows: 'In the aftermath of Iraqi unconditional departure from Kuwait, I truly believe that there may be opportunities—for Iraq and Kuwait to settle their differences permanently; for the states of the Gulf to build new arrangements for stability; and for all states and people of the region to settle the conflict that divides the Arabs from Israel.'

The Jewish lobby in America protested this perceived shift in Bush's position, linking the Kuwait situation to the Palestinian problem. Bush tried to reassure them to not read too much into it. But the fact remained that he had moved somewhat from his erstwhile rigid position. The Secretary General told Gujral on 2 October that Mitterrand's and Bush's statements offered an 'opening'. This seemed to be Iraq's interpretation, too. Iraq's permanent representative postponed his statement in the General Assembly perhaps because he expected fresh instructions. Diplomacy seemed to have received a shot in the arm following Mitterrand's speech. He was in the UAE on 3 October and was scheduled to be going to Saudi Arabia the next day. Japan's foreign minister, Toshiki Kaifu, went to Amman, where he would also meet Iraqi officials. Gorbachev sent Yevgeni Primakov to Baghdad. As if to compensate for these moves, Saddam went to Kuwait.

After Saddam's visit, the Kuwaiti dinar was demonetized, and all Kuwaitis were asked to obtain Iraqi citizenship before 31 October.

Gujral had to rush home because of political developments. The last person he met in the UN was the foreign minister of Kuwait. The two ministers met in the UN along with their permanent representatives. The Kuwaiti representative told Gujral, as politely as he could, but unambiguously, that he was disappointed with India for not condemning Iraq.

Gujral tried to tell him that India never used the word 'condemn', 'but we are 100 per cent with you, we do not recognize annexation', and so on.

The Kuwaiti foreign minister was, however, interested only in one thing, 'You went to Kuwait for your nationals, but you did not utter a word of sympathy for the people of Kuwait who have lost their country.'

Gujral reiterated, 'We are 120 per cent with you!'

The Kuwaiti foreign minister replied that a 100 per cent was enough, and as for the balance of 20 per cent, it could be used to condemn Iraq. Hearing this, Gujral asked, 'Is this word so important to you?'

'Yes' was the simple response of the Kuwaiti foreign minister. So, Gujral promised to think about the matter as soon as he returned to Delhi. His exposure in New York should have convinced him that our reaction to the Kuwait crisis had certainly not won many friends for us in the Gulf region. He told me that we would have to do something to regain the trust of the Gulf nations.

The mood became bullish again. A study by the London-based International Institute for Strategic Studies stated that Iraq would not last more than two weeks if war broke out. Primakov's visit to Baghdad failed to persuade Saddam to modify his position. On the other hand, the several thousand Soviet experts and advisers in Iraq were finding obstructions in their return to their country.

Saddam had been speaking before the 2 August events, that in the new international situation, the US would play the dominating role, that the Soviet Union was finished as a global power and that the developing countries would be left completely at the mercy of the Americans and their allies.

I asked Abdul Amir Al-Anbari, the permanent representative of Iraq, at a dinner whether there was any way for any country to do anything. His prompt reply was 'yes'. He said his President had clearly indicated desire for peaceful solution. I told him that the starting point would have to be withdrawal from Kuwait. He referred me to Saddam's proposal of 12 August and his more recent message of 1 October on the occasion of Prophet's birthday, in which he had not referred to Kuwait as an inseparable part of Iraq. Al-Anbari told me that this omission was deliberate but unfortunately had not received any attention. I reminded him that Saddam had linked the withdrawal with other issues in the region. Al-Anbari said that these were negotiating positions. He suggested that India and Algeria, together with perhaps France or Sweden could try to offer their good offices or mediation. I was not sure if Al-Anbari spoke on instructions from his government, but I passed on what he said to Dubey. The Saudis recalled their ambassador from Jordan.

Israel–Palestine in the Mix

Early in the morning of 8 October, Israeli forces killed 22 Palestinians and wounded more than 300. The exact circumstances were not yet known. It seemed that some

Jews had announced plans to build a Jewish temple in the compound of Al-Aqsa Mosque, which the Muslims regarded as the third holiest place for them. Riots followed. The UNSC met in the afternoon. Speaker after speaker stated that the UNSC could not adopt double standards and that the Israeli repression and denial of fundamental rights to the Palestinians must be condemned, just as Iraqi aggression on Kuwait had been rightly condemned. How could anyone be opposed to Iraq's occupation of Kuwait and still not speak up against Israel's annexation of Golan Heights and Jerusalem? The US was conspicuous by its silence. It no doubt felt embarrassed, and so was Pickering.

Pickering kept getting up from his seat, perhaps to ask for instructions. He even came up to where the Israeli acting permanent representative was sitting and sat down on the floor of the aisle to talk to him, something unseen in the UNSC chamber. The non-aligned members prepared a draft resolution, condemning Israel and proposing a three-member mission of the UNSC to go to the occupied territories. The US was in a fix. Would the US use veto? If they did, their action would be in stark contrast to their newly discovered and asserted moral leadership role in the Gulf crisis. They might agree to a presidential statement including the proposal to send a mission. I did not think the US should be let off so lightly, but I suspected the PLO might agree to it.

Li Daoyu was lamenting to me about the weakness in Soviet position. He said that the Soviets were always anxious to please the Americans. 'But I hope Yuli Vorontsov will take a firm position at least on this issue.' Even the Chinese regretted the loss of real Soviet influence.

The UNSC did not act on the Israeli–Palestinian issue. For the US, a veto would severely erode the Arab coalition, which they believed they had built up against Saddam, whereas a vote in favour or even an abstention would greatly anger Israel and the Jewish lobby. For the PLO, it was tempting to force the US to veto since it would turn Arab public opinion against the US. At the same time, they did not want to alienate the Americans too much, since they knew that ultimately it was only America that could work out a settlement for them. The main difficulty was about sending the mission. Americans, together with other permanent members, would have not liked to send the mission on behalf of the UNSC, whereas the PLO and others would have liked the mission to go on behalf of the UNSC, or at least at the request of the UNSC. This development came at a good time for Saddam. He could project himself as the great champion of the Palestinian cause. He claimed to possess a missile with which he could destroy Israel; he called it 'the stone' based on the stones that the Palestinian youth used during the Intifada of 1987. To make the Gulf crisis more complicated, Iran publicly warned Kuwait not to make any deal that would transfer effective control of the two islands to Iraq. According to a report emanating from the Egyptians, Saudis and Kuwaitis, there was a secret understanding among Iraq, Yemen and Jordan, permitting them to carve out portions of Saudi territory and incorporate them into their respective countries.

Resolution 672, following the events of Al-Aqsa Mosque in Jerusalem, was finally adopted the night of 12 October 1990. It took five days of sustained negotiations to reach agreement. It was adopted unanimously. It was the first time since 1982 that the US had joined in condemning Israel. The resolution 'especially' condemned Israeli violence. The word 'especially' was an acknowledgement, to some extent, that there was implied criticism of violence on the Palestinian side, too.

The other bone of contention was related to the proposal to send a mission. In addition to the point of who should send the mission, the PLO also wanted the mission to propose recommendations on how to extend protection and safety to the Palestinians, something that was totally unacceptable to Israel, since they interpreted it as the installation of a permanent presence of the UN in the occupied territories. The resolution was a victory for the US. The Africans could not withstand American pressure.

Israel rejected Resolution 672. It permitted the Secretary General's mission into the country but refused to cooperate with it. The mission could go as tourists, said Israel, but it would not have diplomatic status and would not be received by the government. Bush demanded the UNSC to prosecute Iraqi regime for war crimes and Thatcher wanted reparations.

In an interview with Judith Miller of *The New York Times*, King Hussein once again lamented the fact that diplomacy was not given an opportunity to find an answer during the crucial 48 hours following the 2 August invasion of Kuwait. He said that when he saw Saddam on 3 September, a month after the invasion, the latter had appeared very relaxed and confident. Saddam had assured the King that Iraq would begin to withdraw within two to three days and complete the withdrawal within a week. But he had demanded that the Arab League must not issue any condemnation and must give time for a political solution. King Hussein had spoken to King Fahd who, according to the former, put all the blame on Kuwait. King Hussein had also spoken to Mubarak and conveyed Saddam's message to him. When the Arab League's foreign ministers were to meet in Cairo on 4 September, King Hussein had again called Fahd and Mubarak, but the latter did not return his call for six hours. In the meantime, Egypt had rushed through a very condemnatory resolution. King Hussein knew and had said so to others that Saddam would not submit to humiliation. He had asked Bush to give him 48 hours and Bush had agreed. Unfortunately, Mubarak had precipitated matters. King Hussein also said that Thatcher had told him that the US forces were already more than halfway to Saudi Arabia by the time the Saudis made their formal request to the US for help.

Even after a month and a half from 2 August, diplomatic activity in search for a political solution was not very visible. Primakov planned to go to Italy, France and the US. Arafat kept jumping from one Arab capital to another. King Hussein received Aziz in Amman. But the US position remained that it would not give any sort of victory to Saddam to save his face; he must be made an example to all would-be aggressors that aggression did not and would not pay in this post–Cold War era wherein the US wanted to establish a new world order.

The Opinions of the American Public

The US Senate Committee on Foreign Relations, during a two-and-a-half-hour hearing on 17 October with Baker, made it clear that it would not support any unilateral military action against Iraq. Senator Claiborne Pell was unambiguous: Any military activity should be undertaken only within the UN. The committee also insisted that the administration must seek authorization from the Senate before using force. All that Baker was willing to commit himself to was 'consultations' with the Congress. He would not agree to anything that would curtail the maneuverability of the commander-in-chief.

The New York Times reported that there was plenty of food in Iraq. (Though I had not heard anything from the ministry,

I understood that the Iraqis were refusing permission to our ship to return to India without unloading all the food. So much for Saddam's friendship for India…)

The American soldiers in Saudi Arabia would have liked Bush to visit them and 'drink hot water' with them.

The US and the UK prepared a lengthy resolution, affirming Iraq's responsibility to compensate other states and individuals for losses suffered as a result of the invasion and subsequent annexation, plundering, murdering, etc.

Senator Bob Dole confirmed that what had been well understood by most people, namely, the US forces, were sent to the Gulf for one and one reason only: oil.

An influential body of opinion in the academia in the US was warning the administration against contemplating unilateral action. Some in the government argued that going to the UN and the Congress would destroy the element of surprise. Saddam, in any case, had got all the advance notice that he might care to have. He had only two choices: withdraw and surrender or perish. Washington would, of course, have liked to follow a policy which would lead to withdrawal and perish of Saddam's forces.

There were two reasons for the fall in oil prices. One was a dream. It seems that the Prophet appeared to Saddam in a dream and told him that his missiles were facing in the wrong direction and advised him to pull out of Kuwait. The other was a statement by Prince Sultan, Saudi defence minister, indicating that Saudi Arabia would not oppose legitimate Iraqi claims, even if they involved territorial concessions by Kuwait. He said, 'Arab countries were ready to grant Iraq all its rights' and that Saudi Arabia 'sees no harm in any country giving a site or a position on the sea to its Arab sister land'. He added the Arab states' claims against one another should be resolved by understanding and not by force.

Prince Sultan's remarks caused concerns and worry in Washington. His son, Prince Bandar, who was Saudi ambassador in Washington, said that his father had not said what he was reported to have said, and that he was being quoted out of context. Sultan himself later clarified that he favoured complete and unconditional Iraqi withdrawal.

But Sultan's press remarks and Saddam's dream perhaps pointed towards a possible scenario. What better face-saving was there for Saddam other than claiming that he was acting under and obeying Allah's orders? Primakov was again setting off on a tour of Saudi Arabia, Egypt and other Arab countries. He believed that he got a hint from Saddam that he might be prepared for a partial withdrawal under certain circumstances. Two other signs of such a possibility were that all organizations were asked to complete the stripping of Kuwait by 24 October and the latest Iraqi maps showed southern two-thirds of Kuwait as the nineteenth province and northern one-third regions, together with Warba and Bumiyan islands, as part of Basra province.

By the fourth week of October, the US had deployed 240,000 troops in the Operation Desert Shield. Pentagon estimated that this number, wholly adequate for defensive role, would have to be augmented by at least 50,000 if the US would go on the offensive.

The UNSC unanimously adopted Resolution 673 on the Jerusalem incident on 25 October. The word 'deplores' was retained, but 'demands' was replaced by 'insists'; 'demands' contained an element of threat that if Israel did not cooperate, the UNSC would consider sanctions under Chapter VII. The US went along with the draft even though abstention would have been enough for the resolution to be adopted.

Secretary of Defense Dick Cheney announced on 25 October that the US would send an additional 100,000 troops to Desert Shield in addition to the 240,000 already deployed. There were also between 150,000 and 200,000 troops from Saudi Arabia, Kuwait, Egypt, Morocco, Syria, the UK, France, etc. David Hannay, the British permanent representative and current president of the UNSC, thought that war could be a possibility by January or February the following year, 1991. Weather was an important factor. Another factor was the Haj season in April 1991.

Saddam went to northern Iraq and told the Kurds that they would be free to resume their struggle if he failed to provide them prosperity. He wanted to secure his northern flank.

The UNSC had been considering the P-5 draft on reparations and compensation for over a week. On 27 October, the UNSC was on the point of adopting the resolution when the Russian diplomat Vorontsov suddenly demanded postponement on the ground that Primakov was going to Baghdad. If a permanent member, especially a close ally of the US, gave such a weighty reason for postponing the vote, the UNSC had no choice in the matter. Vorontsov even stated in the formal meeting that he had great hopes for the success of the Primakov mission.

Primakov left Baghdad on 29 October for Saudi Arabia, without realizing the 'great hopes'. The UNSC adopted resolution demanding compensation and repatriations the same day as Resolution 674, with 13 in favour, and Cuba and Yemen abstaining.

Saudi Arabia and Kuwait were pressing for early military action. One assessment in Washington was that the war would last 10 days if Saddam did not fight and 14 days if he did. Iraq's casualties would run into thousands, but American casualties would be much less because of their tremendous technological superiority.

Bush and Baker made tough statements to the effect that there was a limit to their patience. The rhetoric was being jacked up. The plight of the hostages was at the centre of their rhetoric. Baker said that Saddam was carrying on an economic and political war on the hostages. Public opinion was being prepared for a possible military strike. Saddam was making his own contribution to add to the tension. He told his top military commanders to put the armed forces on 'extreme alert' against the US attacks and told them to prepare for 'urban warfare' in the 'province' of Kuwait. However, all this bravado on Saddam's part could not hide the fact that he feared American strike. That was why he repeatedly sought assurances that the US would not attack.

Gorbachev continued to state that war was not an option. He said, even after Primakov's mission failed, that there were signs that Iraqi leadership might be heeding the will of the UN. He called for Arab efforts under Saudi sponsorship to 'deal with this man'. As if to counter Gorbachev, Mubarak declared that he was opposed to an emergency meeting of the Arab League which, he said, would merely become an occasion to trade insults. However, the foreign ministers of Egypt, Syria and Saudi Arabia were meeting in Riyadh. All these meetings were held only to show to their people that the governments were actively engaged in finding an Arab solution to the crisis, but the people could not be fooled so easily.

5

THE UN MOVES ASIDE, THE US TAKES OVER

India got elected to the UNSC on 1 November 1990 for a two-year term beginning 1 January 1991. We got 141 votes out of a possible 154. Austria got 150. Our vote share was very satisfactory considering several Arabs did not vote for us because of their displeasure with India's position on the Gulf crisis. Membership in the UNSC in the 1990s was a responsibility, more so than in previous decades. The positions taken in the council were very much under the scrutiny of public opinion and even of heads of government in most countries. This was, of course, due to the Gulf crisis and the renewed, and resultant, fears regarding the Palestinian crisis. India feared pressure from all sides. I hoped we would acquit ourselves creditably. I had decided to use our membership in the council to try and at least reduce the damage done to us by our policy on the Kuwaiti issue.

Gen. Norman Schwarzkopf, commander of the US forces

in Operation Desert Shield, said in an interview to *The New York Times* that his troops could obliterate Iraq, but cautioned that total destruction of Iraq might not be in the interests of long-term balance of power in the region. He spoke like a statesman. He said there were alternatives to 'having to drive up to Baghdad and literally dig out the entire Baathist regime and destroy them all in order to restore peace and stability in the area'. He thought Iraqi missiles would have only a modest effect because of their high degree of inaccuracy. The General also played down the ability of Iraq to mount chemical warheads on its missiles. He further opined that the continued operation of Saudi oil fields and production of oil is substantially immune to Iraqi attacks, though Kuwait oil fields would be damaged severely. He said he had made a deep study of Saddam's character and described him as 'megalomaniac' and 'ruthless' but 'not stupid'; he wanted to be the leader of the Arab world no matter what the cost—'an island of a man who has really both isolated and insulated himself from the rest of the world'.

Bush was to go on an eight-day trip to Prague, Bonn, Paris, Cairo and Riyadh, starting 17 November 1990. He was to spend thanksgiving with the men and women in the Saudi desert.

Saddam made many proposals or initiatives, all of which had one thing in common: an assurance of non-attack on Iraq. This suggested that all the talk of American soldiers going back in coffins was empty bravado. The Arab mind worked in such devious ways that it was impossible, even for fellow Arabs, let alone non-Arabs, to fathom the true intentions.

Bush's almost casual announcement in the second week of November of his decision to nearly double the troop strength in the Gulf—200,000 additional troops, 1,200 tanks to be diverted from Europe and one more aircraft carrier—created a storm in his country. This was interpreted as announcing that Operation Desert Shield was not only to defend Saudi Arabia but also to invade Iraq. Baker's mission apparently was quite successful. Shevardnadze said on 8 November that the Soviet Union could no longer rule out the use of force. Gorbachev declared in Bonn that Saddam's efforts to divide international resolve failed and would continue to be doomed. Thatcher was, of course, the most belligerent. The French, however, continued to be cautious.

What had upped the ante even more was the US decision that there would not be a rotation of the troops in the Gulf. This was an unambiguous signal that there would be war before March or April the following year. Saddam was left with two alternatives: utter humiliation or utter destruction. He deserved to be humiliated, but not for the sake of satisfying the American ego. Nearly everyone was convinced that Saddam would prefer to go down fighting like a martyr and be remembered as a great hero, a modern-day Saladin.

The heartless cynicism of the American administration was laid bare by Baker. He thought that the efforts to convince the people about the correctness of the policy had failed. The people did not favour the sacrifice of the lives of their boys and girls for the sake of saving the corrupt, feudal ruling families of Kuwait, Saudi Arabia and other sheikhdoms. So, Baker said to his people,

> Let me put it in terms that you will understand; if I have to put it in one word, it is jobs. Jobs! That is what it is all about—to hell with principles, with not rewarding aggression, with restoring the legitimate government of Kuwait. It is jobs, American jobs which are at stake. To hell with the rest of the world, with the shattering impact which a war will have on the economies of the

> third world. To hell with the hundreds of broken homes, including American homes. So long as American jobs can be saved, anything and everything is worth it.

What about diplomatic efforts? King Hassan II of Morocco called for an urgent meeting of the Arab League. Saddam was willing, given the agenda, date and venue were acceptable to him. Soviet Emissary Grigory Petrovsky had gone to Rabat. Qian Qichen went to Baghdad after visiting Cairo and Paris. The Egyptian, Syrian and Saudi foreign ministers met and were scheduled to meet again.

The Americans intensified efforts to gain the support of the UNSC members for a resolution authorizing use of force. Baker personally met with the foreign ministers of Zaire, Ethiopia and Ivory Coast. Baker travelled to Bogotá since Columbia was not on board yet. He asked the foreign minister of Malaysia to meet him in Muscat, but the latter refused to oblige. Baker met the Soviet foreign minister in Moscow and Paris. Bush had private dinner with Gorbachev in Paris. China's position was not clear. There was a report that China would not veto such a resolution, but Li Daoyu maintained that it was not correct. When the chips were down, I doubted if China would use a veto. Both Saddam and Bush were victims of their rhetoric, and both needed face-saving. How could Bush back down now? Perhaps, he might welcome Soviet or/and Chinese veto?

Saddam offered to release all the hostages during a three-month period, starting 25 December, provided there was no war. It was precisely during those months that the allied powers were most prepared to launch hostilities. The Americans and Saudis had planned an exercise called 'Operation Imminent Thunder' in mid-November as a part of Operation Desert Shield. It had to be called off because of choppy sea.

Bush on the Ground

From Paris, Bush went to Riyadh on 22 November, where he spent Thanksgiving with the troops and met with King Fahd and Emir Al-Sabah of Kuwait. Thence he went to Cairo, where Mubarak made an important change in his position. Previously, he had said that his troops were sent only to defend Saudi Arabia and would not take part in any offensive operations. After Bush's visit, he said that his forces would take part in liberating Kuwait.

On 23 November, Bush went to Geneva for talks with President Assad of Syria. This meeting attracted a lot of adverse criticism in the US, but the ends (of preserving the coalition) justified the means. Baker went to Sana'a, capital of Yemen, where the Yemeni President told him that all foreign forces should be withdrawn from the region, so that the Arabs could solve the problem among themselves. He also made it clear that Yemen would not support any resolution authorizing the use of force. Baker certainly would have anticipated Yemeni reaction, but it was a good diplomatic move on his part to have taken the trouble of consulting the Yemenis.

Bush and Baker had invested enormous energy and prestige in getting a resolution on the use of force. Moscow would fall in line, but they wanted to avoid giving the impression that they were giving in to the American pressure. The US had at least nine votes, possibly more. Baker was keen on presiding over the UNSC just as his Soviet colleague did in September. He probably discussed a draft text with the Soviets, but in New York nobody had seen any draft, not even Pickering, it seemed. The four non-aligned members had their own draft.

The general expectation was that the next resolution would have a two-stage approach. To start with, it would give 60 days to Saddam to comply with all the resolutions, failing which member states would be authorized to take all appropriate measures to enforce compliance. The words 'use of force' would not be specifically mentioned.

Senator Daniel Patrick Moynihan said in a TV interview that he was pessimistic about avoiding a war. He felt that logistics were determining the US policy. The month of Ramadan would start on 17 March 1991. The administration would be compelled to exploit the eight-week window in January to February to launch the offensive. Asked about Bush's reference to Iraq's alleged imminent nuclear capability, he said Pakistan had 'machined' six nuclear warheads last summer. He further hoped that the UN will not ask the US to finish off Saddam. He told viewers that Kuwaitis were sitting comfortably in a hotel in Taif and were ready to fight Saddam to the last American!

Bush's decision to meet Assad, which American officials said was recommended by Mubarak, drew huge flak in the Congress and the media. Bush ought to have known that Assad was in this game for his own calculations and not out of love for Bush or Fahd. Giving Assad his personal seal of approval betrayed Bush's nervousness and revived the unhappy memories of the 10 years of Reagan-and-Bush administration's courting of Saddam during the Iran–Iraq war.

The bottom line was that most Americans were not yet convinced that their sons and daughters, brothers and sisters, ought to put their lives online either to protect jobs or to control oil supplies or to restore the dictatorial and corrupt ruling family of Kuwait to its throne or to destroy Saddam's military machine. Only Israel was keen on this.

6

RESOLUTION 678: A NEW HOPE

The moment of reckoning would arrive at 3.00 p.m. on 29 November. At that time, the UNSC would begin a formal meeting, chaired by Baker, to adopt a resolution that would authorize member states 'cooperating with the government of Kuwait, unless Iraq on or before 15 January 1991 fully implements' Resolution 660 and all subsequent resolutions to 'use all appropriate measures' and to restore international peace and stability in the area. The resolution would 'allow Iraq one final opportunity, as a pause of goodwill,' to implement the resolutions. Thus, the US would get what it had always wanted: a carte blanche from the UN to do as it pleased, unilaterally without any constraints of Article 42 or any other article of the Charter—no UN command, no military staff committee, no nothing.

It must be acknowledged that the US acted in a competent and professional manner. Baker consulted foreign ministers of the other permanent members. Even Cuba was sort of consulted at the level of undersecretary of state, Robert Kimmitt, with the result that Cuba's foreign minister Isidoro Malmierca Peoli would be attending the meeting on 29 November. All other countries would be represented by their foreign ministers. If that was what the US wanted, so it had to be.

But what about China? China's position would be influenced by the result of the visit of its vice minister of foreign trade to Washington in early December. If China did not cooperate enough, the visit might not be very successful. The Soviets, in any case, were being more American than the Americans. They even suggested proposing a Nuremberg-style war crimes tribunal. The phrase 'final opportunity' in the resolution hinted at Soviet contribution.

The President of the UNSC sent a note to all members about the date and time of the meeting at Kuwait's request. The only snag was that there was no request from Kuwait! This was remedied on 26 November when Kuwait handed over a letter requesting the meeting.

Cuba demanded that the four-power resolution on occupied territories be taken up as an additional item on the agenda for the meeting. Pickering effectively silenced him and did not agree, only promising informal consultations.

The Soviet Union was desperately short of food. Germany agreed to help. The Soviet ambassador in Tokyo asked Japan too for help with food supplies. The Soviets were as vulnerable to the US and Western pressure as the worst-hit African countries. How could it be expected to take an independent stand?

The six weeks leading up to 15 January witnessed heightened diplomatic activity. Vorontsov speculated that Primakov or even Shevardnadze might travel to Baghdad.

Morocco, Algeria and Syria might try their hand once again.

A striking aspect of the whole episode was the total side-lining of the Secretary General; he was a sad man those days.

Vishva Siddhi managed to offload about 4,300 tonnes of food for Thai, Vietnamese, Bulgarians and Filipinos, apart from Indians. The crew was getting restless and was on the verge of mutiny (according to the Foreign Secretary). So, we got the sanctions committee to agree for the ship to return to India. But Iraq refused to let the ship set sail, unless all the remaining food on board was offloaded and handed over to Iraq. Fortunately, the PLO came to our help, unexpectedly. There were 400,000 Palestinians in Kuwait, in need of food. The PLO approached us in New York for help. We told them to approach the sanctions committee for its approval. They said, 'no problem', but I knew better. Sure enough, the US and the UK objected. But the chairman of the sanctions committee wrote to us, requesting us to leave the food behind in Iraq. Naturally, we lost no time in acceding to this request. So, *Vishva Siddhi* was now on its journey back to India, after fulfilling an internationalist duty.

Malaysia said that it would vote in favour of Resolution 678 on 29 November. The question remained about China. Abstention would indicate China was not totally for sale. On the other hand, Qian Qichen had been extended the honour of being invited to pay an official visit to Washington on Friday, the day after the voting was to take place. Qian had said in Beijing, before leaving for New York, that China would not vote for the resolution.

Iraq declared it would ignore any deadline set by the UNSC. Iraq's deputy PM called for direct talks between Iraq and the US. Saddam's ego was perhaps the key to the whole crisis. He felt humiliated that the US ignored his 'offer' of direct talks. Even if at that stage, had the US agreed to it, Saddam's vanity or pride would have been salved and he might have taken a more realistic view of the situation Iraq was in. The Americans refused this offer before Saddam could withdraw from Kuwait.

The International Atomic Energy Agency (IAEA) gave a clean chit to Iraq—the uranium was still where it was, without any diversion.

Saudi Arabia announced a credit of $1 billion to the Soviet Union. Other Gulf countries were working out a package for the Soviets, the total value being at $6 billion.

The UNSC convened on 29 November. Its chamber might not have witnessed anything like it across the last 45 years. The meeting was scheduled for 3.00 p.m. By 2.30 p.m., every single seat in the chamber and visitors' gallery was occupied. By the time Baker banged the gavel at 3.30 p.m. to call the meeting to order, delegates were sitting in the aisles, on the floor and standing all over the place. For the first time, permanent representatives could sit only in the seats reserved for each delegation in the chamber; there were no other seats.

The international community recognized the significance of the moment. The UNSC was convened to authorize the US and its allies to use force, unilaterally, to compel Iraq to comply with the UN resolutions and to issue an ultimatum to Iraq to comply by 15 January 1991.

There was a lot of speculation about the number of votes in favour of the resolution. The single and the most talked about vote was that of China—would it vote in favour or abstain? Despite its foreign minister's comment in Beijing, most people, including myself, expected China to vote in favour.

In the end, China abstained. The vote was 12 in favour, two against (Cuba and Yemen) and one abstention. China's abstention would earn it respect from Third-World countries. (It certainly earned respect in my eyes!) The US projected China's abstention as success for their diplomacy, but they were in for disappointment. China might have asked to be treated as the most favoured nation for a yes vote, but Baker could not promise it even if he might have wanted to, because the decision making-power rested with the Congress.

Malaysia would have dearly liked to abstain. When its foreign minister met Baker in Los Angeles earlier in the week, he had told him that it would help if the other resolution on occupied territories was allowed to be voted upon first. According to one story, just before the start of the meeting, Baker sent for the Malaysian foreign minister alone, without the permanent representative.

Colombia had surrendered a few days ago. There was speculation about Cuba, too. It was being alleged that Baker had held a 75-minute meeting with Rodrigo Malmierca Díaz, the foreign minister of Cuba, the previous night and had offered to discontinue radio and TV Marti broadcasts if Cuba abstained (as they were anti-Cuba), but there was no substance in this story.

Ambassador Abdullah Saleh Al-Ashtal of Yemen made a moving and sincere statement before the vote. He described the resolution as 'a war resolution'.

The US was, and had good reason to be, highly pleased with the outcome. As many as 12 foreign ministers 'accepted' Baker's 'invitation' and attended the meeting, including Díaz. Only Yemen and Ivory Coast did not send ministers. The US bullied, badgered and bribed to get the votes. They flouted rules of procedure and traditions of the UNSC to ensure nothing would detract from their show. They did not permit the four-power draft on occupied territories for consideration. They deliberately delayed granting visa to Farouk Kaddoumi, the 'foreign minister' of the PLO, to prevent him from going to New York in time for the Palestinian debate.

Resolution 678 was promptly denounced by Saddam. He said Iraq would not kneel before such ultimatums and if war was inevitable, Iraq would fight in such a way that Arabs and Muslims would be proud.

With the adoption of Resolution 678, the clock started ticking and the countdown to 15 January begun. The next 47 days ought to witness intensified diplomatic efforts to avoid war that nobody really wanted. The Secretary General told me he was going to try very hard to find a peaceful solution.

The day after the adoption of Resolution 678, Bush announced a major initiative, which might have defused the Gulf situation. Aziz was invited to Washington for a meeting with Bush, along with ambassadors of several coalition partners in the Gulf, during the second week of December. Baker was scheduled to go to Baghdad before 15 January for a direct meeting with Saddam. The announcement came as a surprise. It was believed that the US must have told the other four permanent members on 29 November about Baker going to Baghdad in general terms before the vote, so as to bring them on board. *The Washington Post* of 1 December suggested that King Fahd had been told about the announcement in advance and had approved, but Kuwait had no inkling and was worried. Bush took pains to emphasize that Baker was not going to Baghdad to negotiate and repeated his usual demand for unconditional withdrawal, etc. He said Saddam had not yet understood the strength of the US commitment. So, Baker would look Saddam in the eye and tell him that

Bush meant business. Bush said he was not even sure Saddam would agree to the meeting.

One of the reasons for this turn in the US position could be that Bush wanted to convince his people that he had tried everything and gone the extra mile in search of peace. If Saddam did not respond, Bush's support in the Congress would increase.

I expected Saddam to accept Bush's initiative. He asked for clarification about the ambassadors who would be present at the meeting with Tariq. Naturally, he would not agree to the presence of the Kuwaiti ambassador. Many details had to be discussed.

Saddam Softens?

There was an air of cautious optimism on 30 November. Bush's initiative might turn out to be the beginning of the end of the Gulf crisis. I hoped I was right because that is what I had dared to convey to the ministry in my telegram.

On 1 December, the Iraqis took some fruit and cigarettes to the US embassy in Kuwait and would take more the next day. Should it be seen as a significant development? It should be, even though it seemed to have happened before Baker's press conference. Did this suggest that the Iraqis had prior knowledge of Bush's initiative?

Iraq accepted the offer made by the US regarding Baker's travels. Aziz would go to Washington and Baker would travel to Baghdad, but the dates were not specified. Saddam's acceptance of this offer already brought down the oil price.

The flurry of diplomatic activity had started. Arab leaders from Yemen, Jordan and the PLO were in Baghdad. The mood was upbeat and there was hope for a peaceful solution to the crisis.

But Bush and Baker were repeatedly emphasizing that the talks were only about the implementation of the UNSC resolutions. Still, Baker said on 2 December that if Iraq implemented the resolutions, the US would not attack Iraq. In other words, the consistent demand of Iraq, vis-à-vis guarantee of no attack, had now been conceded. It also meant the US had given up on its objective of toppling Saddam or destroying his military potential and capability.

All this made Israel nervous. Some Israeli leaders said that Israel could not accept a situation whereby Iraq's war machine remained intact.

Iraq declared that all 3,232 Soviet nationals were free to leave, but the Soviet government must pay compensation for the unexpired contracts.

On 6 December, in a surprise move, Saddam announced that all the hostages would be released immediately. He explained that the Iraqi troops had completed deployment, so there was no need for human shields. He said he was taking this humanitarian step in deference to the appeals made by Arab leaders from Jordan, Yemen and Palestine, and from European parliamentarians as also in recognition of the anti-war resolution passed in the Democratic Caucus of the US Congress. The timing of this decision was determined by the need for a public relations impact before Tariq Aziz's visit to Washington. One report suggested that the meeting would be held on 17 December.

The same day, the BBC announced that the previous night, the Americans had proposed to the other four permanent members the early convening of an international peace conference on Middle East. This was certainly big news, if true, since the US and Israel had been strongly opposed to any such idea and it would undoubtedly be perceived as a victory for Saddam. Later during the day, it became clear that the news was not quite correct. What had happened was that the draft resolution on occupied territories contained a paragraph on the international conference to which the Americans had proposed some changes. Israel became very agitated at this news. Israeli PM Yitzhak Shamir scheduled a visit to Washington for the next week.

Israel was most concerned about the Bush initiative, particularly at the prospect of Iraq's military capability remaining intact. It warned the US against allowing the Iraqi military to remain unimpaired and hinted that it might take preemptive action on its own against Iraq. Israeli foreign minister David Levy summoned American ambassador William Brown.

A peaceful solution would have left Iran unhappy because a war-devastated Iraq would ensure Iran's supremacy in the region. By the same token, Syria and Egypt also preferred a military solution. Egypt had proposed to Syria and Saudi Arabia that the three of them should form some kind of political and security union. It was obvious that they were not consulted or even informed in advance by the US about the initiative. A war, on the other hand, would have left Iran as the undisputed leader in the region, a prospect that the US and Saudis would not have relished. Kuwait should have preferred a peaceful solution since it would have left its oil fields intact.

Were we definitely moving in the direction of a peaceful solution? It seemed so. But B and B (Bush and Baker) continued to make tough statements. A public opinion poll printed in *The Washington Post* suggested that an overwhelming majority would support Bush's initiative, but many would also support use of force if diplomacy were to fail. Hassan agreed that the beginning of the end of the crisis had already begun. He couldn't have been more wrong.

The US and Iraq started negotiating the dates of the two meetings. Iraq proposed December for the meeting in Washington and 12 January for the Baghdad meeting. The US was extremely unhappy about the 12 January date; it wanted the meeting in Baghdad to be held on 20, 21 or 22 December or 3 January. What could have been a more serious difficulty was handled quietly. Bush had said that a group of ambassadors from concerned countries would be invited to the meeting in Washington. Baghdad said, in that case, it would invite the PLO too to join the meeting. The US promptly dropped its plan to invite ambassadors.

Al-Anbari felt more optimistic about a peaceful solution. He told me that Baker, who was more ambitious and more determined than the former Secretary of State, Shultz, was good at making deals.

I held a private meeting with the Secretary General on 11 December for about 45 minutes to exchange views on the Gulf crisis and other issues. He was a sad and worried man. He was sad at the way the US was misusing the UNSC. He was worried at the intransigence and arrogance of the Americans, at the emergence of the 'unipolar' world. He was, of course, unhappy that his own role had been completely marginalized. He told me he was preparing himself to 'step in' at an appropriate time. He was not enthusiastic about Bush's decision to send Baker to Baghdad. He felt that if Baker's mission was to fail, that would be the end of the road. He added he would not be surprised if Saddam was to announce withdrawal before 14 January, with a stipulation that the issue of the islands should be referred to the international court.

Al-Anbari agreed that Iraq would have to withdraw from

all of Kuwait, but Iraq desperately needed control over the islands, not for strategic but economic reasons. He also felt that Saddam would insist on some alternative to the Emir.

A Failing Resolution

The main drama in the UNSC since the adoption of Resolution 678 revolved around the draft resolution by the four other members of the UNSC regarding occupied territories. The US had managed to postpone voting on the draft. The co-sponsors made several changes, but the US was simply not ready to support the paragraph on the international peace conference. The Colombian permanent representative told me that the paragraph was written by Pickering in his own hand!

The US might have gone along, but *The New York Times* published the text of the draft resolution, no doubt an inspired leak, with the result that the Jewish lobby lost no time in mobilizing itself against it. Consequently, the US could not afford to support that paragraph, the ostensible reason being that it would be tantamount to acknowledging linkage between the Gulf crisis and the Palestinian question, which in effect would be tantamount to rewarding Saddam's aggression. On the other hand, a veto would weaken the so-called coalition and Arab support for the US. The latter were just stalling. They were going through the motion of negotiating, proposing amendments, and so on. Given the composition of the UNSC, it was simply not possible for non-permanent members to not agree to negotiate. When the countries proposing the resolution got really impatient, the US put up the Soviets to make a formal move to propose postponement of the vote. The Soviets did this twice. The Americans believed in humiliating their erstwhile foe. Or was it possible that the Soviets were anxious to do anything to ingratiate themselves with the US? Their acting permanent representative commented that he could not understand why the Soviets had to behave like a satellite of the US for the sake of getting some food aid.

Algerian President Chadli Bendjedid embarked on what appeared to be a well-prepared peace effort: He was in Amman on 11 January, in Baghdad the next day and was scheduled to leave for Saudi Arabia on 13 January. His principal objective was to broker a meeting between Saddam and King Fahd.

The dates for the two meetings—Aziz's in Washington and Baker's in Baghdad—continued to be a matter of negotiation. The Iraqis say Saddam simply had no time before 13 January.

During congressional hearings, CIA Director William H. Webster contradicted Cheney's testimony regarding efficacy of the sanctions. He said the sanctions had dealt a serious blow to Iraqi economy and that in about nine months, they would weaken Iraq's war-inciting capacity. Joint Chief of Staff, Gen. Colin Powell, debunked the myth of 'surgical strike' advocated by Kissinger and said that airpower alone cannot do the job and a protracted ground war might become inevitable.

Since Bush's Thanksgiving address to the troops in the Saudi desert, the US had started maintaining that Iraq was quite close to acquiring the bomb, perhaps in as little time as less than a year. Iraq was supposed to have 28 pounds of enriched uranium, which it had managed to rescue from the Osirak reactor destroyed by Israel in 1989 and which would be adequate to make one bomb. But the IAEA inspected the fuel twice a year and had given a clean chit to Iraq very recently for not diverting nuclear material to make nuclear bombs. The explanation for the administration's playing up of the nuclear factor was that *The New York Times* poll had reported that 54 per cent of American people expressed support for the use of force to prevent Iraq from acquiring nuclear capability. The American people were most unhappy about the support or lack of it by the allies. The feeling was that 90 per cent of the casualties would be American, whereas it was Japan and West Europe that depended on the Gulf for 90 per cent of their oil needs.

Shevardnadze was expected to meet Arafat in Turkey on 14 December, but Turkey refused to give Arafat a visa. Just a few days before, there had been a terrorist attack on a synagogue in Turkey, during which several persons, including Jews, were killed. The PLO was suspected to be responsible. In any case, Arafat was reported to be not keen on meeting Shevardnadze. He felt he should have met someone at the level of Gorbachev! And why should he expose himself to pressure from the Soviets? What could they do for him in return, should he agree to moderate his stand on the draft resolution on occupied territories?

7

FROM SHIELD TO SWORD: FAILING DIPLOMACY

The Americans were losing their calm over Saddam's refusal to agree to a date before 13 December 1990 for Baker's mission to Baghdad. Bush said he would not be a party to Saddam's manipulations, that he refused to believe that Saddam was too busy to meet with Baker before 13, while he had received Japanese PM Yasuhiro Nakasone, Austrian PM Kurt Waldheim, Mohammad Ali, the boxing champion, British PM Ted Heath, and others. It was simply not credible that Saddam could not find time even on one of the 15 different dates suggested by the US on an issue of such importance. Saddam said that while he wanted peace, Iraq was prepared to fight and would run over American corpses if need be.

All the Western hostages had left Iraq and Kuwait. W. Nathaniel Howell, the US ambassador in Kuwait, got out on 13 December.

The following day, Bush said that he was putting the talks with Iraq on hold. Iraq, on the other hand, declared that it was calling off the talks because Saddam was simply not free to receive Baker before 13 January.

The atmosphere was becoming tense again. The optimism had dissipated. Perhaps, the mood in the US was changing too and coming around to Bush's support. If Iraq did not adopt a flexible approach regarding the dates, Bush would be the beneficiary. Iraq's information minister said that there was an atmosphere of war in Iraq.

Kissinger pronounced that if Iraq could be so difficult even on a small matter such as dates, how much more difficult it would be when it came to more important issues?

Meanwhile, India joined the UNSC as a non-permanent member on 1 January 1991. After leaving New York on 16 December, I held a day's discussion with the Foreign Office in London the next day and stayed in Delhi from 19 to 27 January for consultations. In Delhi, I met PM Chandra Shekhar, foreign minister V.C. Shukla, deputy minister in the MEA, Digvijay Singh, and, of course, Dubey and other senior colleagues. I found that there was still some reluctance to say or do anything that would upset Saddam. At the same time, our economic situation was so precarious that everyone under the PM was conscious not to upset the Americans. I told them I appreciated this factor but emphasized that we must conduct ourselves in the UNSC with dignity and self-respect. Everyone agreed—could they do otherwise?

Iraq accepted the US's offer for a meeting between Baker and Aziz in Geneva, and 9 January was decided as the date. Bush announced this offer on 3 January, adding that it was the last chance to establish peace. I was pleasantly surprised that Saddam had accepted Bush's proposed date and venue.

Interestingly, Israeli newspaper *Maariv* had published a report as early as 26 December, stating that Tariq and Baker would meet on 9 January but in Baghdad. The EC did not want to miss out on the action. They would meet with Aziz on 10 December.

Ever since Bush's initiative, there was an expectation of increased diplomatic activity. King Hussein was once more on the move. Egypt, Sudan, Syria and Libya were meeting at summit level in Tripoli. Bendjedid was considering new initiatives. Pakistan, Turkey and Iran held the meeting of Regional Cooperation for Development in Islamabad. Nakasone came up with a peace plan and it was decided that a Japanese minister would be sent to Baghdad on 3 January. The one conspicuous name missing in all this was that of the Soviet Union!

There was, of course, no let-up in the rhetoric on either side. Iraq still refused to withdraw and Bush still insisted on no negotiations or total and unconditional withdrawal. At the same time, there were indications that there might be some flexibility on either side. Saddam's information minister said that withdrawal could be discussed along with other issues of the region. Bush, for his part, said that once the meeting took place, everything could be discussed.

On 17 December, the NATO foreign ministers endorsed the use of force and committed their countries to respond under Resolution 678. The NATO countries agreed to send fighter aircraft to Turkey at the latter's request.

On 20 December, the UNSC finally adopted the thrice-postponed resolution on occupied territories, along with a presidential statement, which, for the first time, committed the US to the idea of an international conference, albeit at an appropriate time. There was enough in it for Saddam to claim credit for himself and justify the withdrawal from Kuwait to his people.

The deputy commander of the US forces in Operation Desert Shield said that his troops would not be ready for combat at least till mid-February. Most people took his statement as deliberate misinformation.

On 21 December, one million people were evacuated from Baghdad as part of civil defence exercise. But Iraq kept up all appearances of getting ready for war. Diplomatic missions were being advised to shift to a town 60 miles north of Baghdad before 15 January. Iraq said that the meeting in Geneva would last only five minutes.

Shevardnadze announced his resignation on 26 December. Gorbachev said he was surprised as he had been thinking of making him the vice president.

Desert Sword

As of 4 January, there were 335,000 American troops and 245,000 allied troops in the Gulf as part of the Operation Desert Storm as the mission was now being called. Iraq's troops numbered 530,000.

Vorontsov advocated that the UNSC should meet after 15 January to consider additional sanctions.

Cuéllar was scheduled to meet Bush on 5 January at Camp David. He felt very frustrated and was impatient to do something. Meanwhile, Iraq declined the European Union's invitation to Aziz to meet with them on 10 January in Geneva on the ground that EC had refused to meet with Aziz in Rome since the Baker–Aziz meeting did not take place in Washington.

On 6 January, Saddam made a very belligerent speech on

the occasion of the seventieth Iraqi Army Day. He called on his troops to get ready for the next battle, which he claimed would be the mother of all battles. He added there was no question of giving up Kuwait unless Israel pulled out of West Bank and Gaza.

Notwithstanding all this rhetoric, both sides continued to hope for a breakthrough. Iraq demanded that the Palestinian problem must be taken up soon after the withdrawal, not along with withdrawal. Bush remained firm on being against linkage, but added that the other side was free to bring up any subject for discussion and that the US had always advocated steps to solve the Palestinian problem.

The French thought that the UNSC ought to meet before 15 January. The US was strongly opposed to it. I would not have been surprised had the two of them worked out a compromise whereby the UNSC could meet only to give one more warning to Saddam. But that could be dicey because there might not be even 12 votes in favour the next time.

Bush left on 6 January on yet another eight-day seven-nation tour. He had already rejected Mitterrand's proposal for a UNSC meeting before 15 January as also his suggestion to offer Saddam an international conference in return for withdrawal from Kuwait.

There was a report on 7 January that Saddam and Arafat had approached France, through Michel Vauzelle, chairman of the Foreign Affairs Committee of the French National Assembly and a close friend of Mitterrand, with a request to extend the 15 January deadline. However, Iraqi information minister denied it.

Bush was selected 'Man of the Year' by the *Time* magazine. The cover carried his photograph with two faces. He said in his talk with the editor that his gut feeling was that Saddam would pull out. King Fahd agreed with Bush.

Li Daoyu reacted very negatively when I suggested that the council might meet before 15 January merely to reiterate Resoltuion 678. He said, 'We don't want to vote again, once was enough.' Many of us believed that the Secretary General would go to Baghdad if the Baker–Aziz meeting ended in failure.

Six Iraqi pilots defected to Saudi Arabia with their helicopters. The US attached great significance to this defection. As many as 400 Iraqi soldiers were reported to have defected so far. The question was whether Baker would refuse to go to Baghdad if Aziz extended Saddam's invitation to him. Li Daoyu put forward the possibility of Saddam suggesting a summit meeting between him and Bush to me. Would Bush refuse to meet him in Geneva? Conservatives in the Soviet Union were very critical of Shevardnadze for agreeing to the large-scale American deployment in the Gulf.

Saddam upped the rhetoric. On 7 January, he appeared in the regalia of a field marshal and talked of total war, enveloping Saudi Arabia, Israel and the whole region.

Aziz said on his arrival in Geneva that he was prepared for constructive talks with Baker, provided the latter had similar intentions. But the 'latter' did not hold such intentions—this is what was judged by analysing his public utterances. In Paris, he managed to get Mitterrand on the US side.

Vauzelle held four hours of talks with Saddam. According to a report in *The Washington Post*, Saddam made three requests or demands: assurance that Iraq won't be attacked, stability in the oil price with increased production quota for Iraq and recognition of Iraq's security concerns, balancing them with those of Israel and Iran. In other words, what he meant was that Iraq should be recognized as a regional power. In return for these three things, Iraq would be prepared to 'make sacrifices', which was perhaps a euphemism for withdrawal. Apparently, the Palestine question was not included in this list.

The report of defection by six Iraqi pilots turned out to be incorrect. Iraq denied it and Saudi Arabia also denied it. Pentagon also concurred in this denial. So, the story was nothing but wishful thinking by America.

Talks and More Talks

Bush and Aziz met for six-and-a-half hours on 9 January, at the InterContinental Genève in three sessions. Since the talks lasted so long, there was an air of more than cautious optimism throughout the day. After the first session, the White House reported that Baker had described the talks as 'constructive', which further raised the expectations. The failure of the talks, therefore, came as a big anti-climax and disappointment.

Baker, Aziz and Bush held press conferences. Bush said he had sent Baker to communicate, not to negotiate. Aziz kept spinning the web, arguing for a global, comprehensive solution to all the problems of the region. He never once uttered the word 'Kuwait'. He accused the US of double standards. He said that the Americans had apparently wanted to convey the message to his president about the resolve of the 'coalition' and about the consequences for Iraq in case of war. Baker said he had a letter from Bush for Saddam. Aziz asked for a copy and read it 'slowly and carefully'. Thereafter, he refused to receive the letter. As he told the press later, he had no problem if Bush wished to write a direct, forthright letter, but he could not accept the tone of the letter. 'It is not the kind of letter which a head of state writes to another head of state.' Bush told the press that it was not a rude letter, but it did say in very clear language what he wanted to convey. The Iraqi ambassador in Washington also refused to accept the letter. In my opinion, it was silly of the Americans to write a letter in the first place. But Bush said he wanted to make sure that Saddam understood his position; Aziz did not have the heart or courage to give the full report to his President.

During the six-and-a-half-hour meeting, both Baker and Aziz reiterated their respective positions. By both sides' accounts, it was a civilized encounter. Bush conceded that as far as the atmosphere was concerned, it was alright.

When Baker told Aziz that it was not a case of Iraq against the US, but Iraq against the whole world, Aziz replied, 'What is happening here? It is not with foreign minister of the UK or Saudi Arabia or any other country or the Secretary General of UN that I am talking right now. The foreign minister of Iraq is talking to the Secretary of State of the United States!' A telling argument.

Now that the Baker–Aziz talks had failed, the expectation of war increased sharply.

I called on the Secretary General on 9 January at the end of the Baker–Aziz talks. He was, in fact, watching Aziz's press conference on a small TV set in his office. He asked me to join him, and we watched it together. Every time Bush mentioned his name, the Secretary General looked at Dayal and me (Virendra Dayal was chef de cabinet of the Secretary General). He told us that the American eagerness for his mediation was like the kiss of Judas for him because Saddam would think that the Secretary General was going to Baghdad at American initiative. I conveyed to the Secretary General the full support of India for any effort that he might make to find a peaceful solution. He asked me when he should go and whether he should ask for a mandate from the UNSC.

I told him he should go as soon as possible, and he should not bother about asking for any mandate. He agreed and said he would probably leave the following day. He and I spoke almost simultaneously that his would be 'mission impossible'.

Congressman Leslie Aspin believed that the war, if it started, would be brief. It would be in stages, with airstrikes in the beginning and involvement of ground troops in the final phase. There would be as many as 2,000 sorties by 70–80 aircraft every day for one week. He expected about 3,000–5,000 casualties, with less than 1,000 Americans killed. His assessment was deliberately timed on the eve of the congressional debate starting on 10 January. Bush finally and formally asked the Senate and the House to pass resolutions that would authorize the administration to take all necessary measures to implement the UN resolutions. He would get the resolutions comfortably.

The Deadlock Continues

American diplomats were scheduled to leave Baghdad on 13 January. Iraq was allowed to keep a skeleton staff in Washington. Nearly all the missions were preparing to close before 15 January. Jordan closed its borders to all non-Jordanians.

I sent a message to our embassy in Moscow about whether recent strains in the US–Soviet relations would have any bearing on the Soviet support for the US in the Gulf. Vorontsov told me that Gorbachev could not and would not permit disintegration of the Soviet Union, no matter the cost and the Americans had to understand this. He said the US had told them that the use of force by the Soviets to keep the Central Asian republics in the Union would be permitted, but not in the Baltic republics. He added that Stalin had made a huge mistake by incorporating Baltic states in the Soviet Union to enlarge the Soviet empire, but what was done was done. He said that disintegration of the Soviet Union would have implications even for India. I completely agreed. He said, 'If we use force, please do not criticize us.' I was surprised at this. I told him there was no question of India criticizing Soviet government for doing anything to protect its territorial integrity.

Meanwhile, Saddam's bombastic rhetorics continued: 'In case of war, Americans will swim in rivers of their own blood.'

I believed that if the US decided to use force, they would do so sooner rather than later, around the 15 January deadline. It was obvious that most of the 'coalition' partners were anxious to avoid war, even if it became essential to offer an international conference to Saddam. It was only the American pressure that prevented them from actively pursuing their inclination. Once the 'pause of goodwill' ended, the coalition partners started becoming nervous. Therefore, the longer the delay, the higher the possibility of weakening of the coalition.

Aziz repeatedly said that Iraq would not yield to threats. The Americans claimed to have detailed information about all the Iraqi missile sites through satellite photography. Baker told the French that the US could destroy all the missiles in one night. In reply to a question whether Saddam would get killed in the war, Bush replied, 'I am not going to answer that. I don't know the answer to that question.'

Cuéllar left for Paris and Geneva on 10 January. Bush spoke to him twice on the phone. I gather he reminded the Secretary General about his speech in the General Assembly last September in which he had indicated some flexibility in the US position on activating peace process in the Middle East, following Iraqi withdrawal. This suggested that Bush was eager and hopeful of Cuéllar achieving some breakthrough. Saddam, however, continued to talk tough.

The Secretary General met Mitterrand in Paris and all the 12 EC foreign ministers in Geneva. He was in Amman on 12 January and arrived in Baghdad the same day. The all-important talks were to begin the next day.

The Europeans were getting frantic. They were more than ready to work out and offer a package that would be acceptable to Saddam.

Both houses of the Congress adopted resolutions authorizing the President to use force. Before that, both houses had rejected resolutions calling for more time for sanctions to work. Senator Sam Nunn spoke persuasively and warned Saddam not to confuse dissent for weakness or lack of support for the President; in the event of war, the Congress would not deprive the President of funds. The votes in the House were assured but close in the Senate: 52 against 47. Stephen Solarz, Congressman from Brooklyn, was at his fiery best, authorizing use of force. He hoped to become the Secretary of State in the next Democratic administration if and when the Democrats captured the White House.

The US administration placed order for exactly 16,099 body bags; this was the number of US casualties the computers had arrived at!

Time was ticking away, but most of the world seemed paralysed. So strong was the US influence that countries and leaders were reluctant to take initiatives to break the deadlock.

Both Bush and Baker said on 12 January that force will be used sooner rather than later—exactly what I thought.

8

DESERT STORM: A FARCICAL WAR

The Secretary General reached Baghdad at 5.00 p.m. on 12 January. He was put up in a palatial guest house. Aziz came to see him at 6.00 p.m. and they talked for about two hours. By about 10.30 a.m., the Secretary General was ready to meet Saddam. His plan was to have two rounds of talks with him, the first one to tell him the facts of life and the second to receive his response. But Saddam was in no hurry; he was engaged in a serious meeting with his party's top leadership. It was only at 7.00 p.m. that Saddam received him. The Secretary General was upset and impatient. He found Saddam to be very serene, not in the least worried. It was as if he did not fully comprehend the gravity of the situation. Cuéllar told him of the enormous technological superiority of the Americans, but that did not make much impression on his interlocutor.

Saddam was very polite. He told the Secretary General that he felt ambivalent about his visit. On the one hand, Saddam was glad to receive the Secretary General because he had known Iraq over the years; on the other hand, if the meeting produced 'insufficient' results, he knew that Iraq's enemies would exploit it to wage war against Iraq. As for withdrawal from Kuwait, Saddam said that Kuwait had irrevocably become the nineteenth province of Iraq and his people would not even whisper the word 'withdrawal'. In that case, Cuéllar told him that Saddam's desire for him to use his good offices was a non-starter. To that, Saddam said that was not what he meant, and he did want the Secretary General to try to engage the views of the parties, including Iraq, in order to make proposals that could lead to a solution.

Cuéllar told me that Aziz sat with folded hands, 'like a little lamb' when in the presence of his leader.

He read out his well-drafted report at the informal consultations of the UNSC at about 11.00 p.m. on 14 January. All the members complimented him on his efforts. Of course, the Americans were to use his failed mission as part of justification for launching the war later.

Cuéllar returned to New York from Baghdad on 14 January. He travelled by Concorde from Paris, arriving in New York at nine in the morning, but presented his report to the council only 14 hours later. The reason was that his aides could not travel by Concorde, so the report could not be finalized.

The following day, which was the last day of the 'pause of goodwill', Étienne Blanc, the French permanent representative, surprised everyone by producing a fresh peace initiative. It consisted of six elements, the most difficult of which for the Americans was the convening of an international conference for peace in the Middle East. The French presented their proposal on the evening of 14 January, but it could only be discussed the next day.

On 15 January, the British produced their own initiative,

but it was so clearly in the nature of an ultimatum that it was not favoured by anyone, unlike the French text, which was supported by many, including all seven non-aligned members. The P-5 were clearly divided. We, the non-aligned members, saw a window of opportunity for us to play our traditional role. I suggested for us to propose a statement or an appeal as the only way out, since the British and French texts would cancel each other out. This was what the UNSC eventually decided. Secretary General issued an excellent appeal, which was deafted by Dayal, at 6.00 p.m. But nobody expected Saddam to respond positively. Iraq's initial reaction was that the appeal was addressed only to Saddam, whereas it should have been equally addressed to Bush. Even when Cuéllar had gone to Baghdad, the Iraqis had told him that he had already met Bush four times before coming to Baghdad.

On 16 January, we were all in the UNSC lounge since 4.00 p.m., negotiating a draft resolution on the deportation of four Palestinian civilians. At a meeting of the non-aligned caucus, I suggested we ought to worry about the Gulf situation, and we should go tell the Secretary General that we fully supported his appeal made on 15 January and expected him to continue his efforts. Thereafter, I said, we should call the Iraqi permanent representative and tell him to convey to his president our concern and hope that he would respond positively to the Secretary General's appeal. Cuba and Ivory Coast supported my idea. I said our effort would surely produce nothing, but no harm would be caused. The discussion remained inconclusive because Operation Desert Storm had already started by 16 January.

A Storm Arrives

When the CNN broke the story about the beginning of the war just before 7.00 p.m., there was stunned silence in the lounge. People were shaking their heads in disbelief and despair. I woke up Dubey in Delhi and gave him the news.

By the second day of the war, as many as 617 aircraft of all types, belonging to the US, the UK, Saudi Arabia and Kuwait, had flown as many as 2,100 sorties, dropping 18,000 tonnes of explosives. There was tremendous euphoria in America. Evidently, there was little or no resistance in Baghdad. We got latest news of the war, thanks to continuous telephonic reporting by the CNN's team in Baghdad. They had managed to report till 11.00 a.m. on the morning of 17 January—a total of 16 hours. At that time, the Iraqis broke the communications.

Everyone talked of the complete lack of reprisals by Iraq. Aziz had declared that Israel would be attacked even before the US forces in Saudi Arabia. But the 'allied' aircraft, in the first sortie, knocked out Iraq's scud missiles deployed in western Iraq, thus removing the threat to Israel. There was little doubt that Iraq was caught by surprise.

Bush addressed the nation at 9.00 p.m. on 16 January and said that the liberation of Kuwait had begun. It was a good speech; he had been working on it for three weeks and it had undergone four revisions. It was his moment of glory. He had signed the executive order on the afternoon of 15 January, after which Cheney had given the go ahead. Of course, the operation would be called off in case of any last-minute diplomatic breakthrough. On 16 January, Bush called Prince Bandar, Saudi ambassador, to his office and asked him to get his King's approval. Bandar called King Fahd from Baker's office and the King gave his clearance straightaway. The British and

Kuwait envoys were also informed. Gorbachev said that the Soviet Union was informed one hour in advance, through Baker's telephonic conversation with Alexander Besmertnykh, the new Soviet foreign minister. Cuéllar told me that Bush had called him at about 6.00 p.m. to give him the news.

Iraq claimed to have shot down 55 allied aircraft, but the allied admitted to only three aircraft being lost—one each from America, Britain and Kuwait. Iraq hit one Saudi oil storage in Khafji near Kuwait border. There were reports of five scud missiles having hit Saudi Arabia, but it was refuted by the Saudis. According to the them, 40–50 Iraqi tanks, with crew, had defected and surrendered to the Egyptians. Kuwait's permanent representative told me that large numbers of Iraqi troops in Kuwait had been changing into civilian clothes and surrendering.

There was exultation in the US and all over the West. It was reflected in the economic scene. The Dow Jones index jumped 114 points in hectic trading—biggest jump since October 1987. Similar stock market rises took place in Japan and elsewhere. Oil price in New York dropped by more than $10—steepest decline over a single day. Investments in government securities registered big increase. All this indicated general expectation of quick and decisive victory for the US.

Operation Desert Storm continued relentlessly. The US and other coalition partners' air forces kept pounding Iraq and Iraqi positions in the occupied Kuwait. But the initial euphoria gave way to more sober assessment. Bush and others were now cautioning people against expectations of a quick victory. The big danger was the probable involvement of Israel. For the first 24 hours, the Americans claimed that they had knocked out all of Iraq's scud missiles. But at about 2.10

a.m. on 18 January, Iraq fired scud missiles at Israel. Seven of them hit Tel Aviv, Haifa and other places. There was no loss of life, but seven people were injured and many houses were destroyed.

On the morning of 19 January, three more scud missiles hit Israel, injuring a few more people. Saddam dearly wanted Israel to retaliate, in the hope that it leads to a split in the coalition. Israel was raring to go, but the diplomatic and political work done by Bush and Co. before 16 January succeeded in restraining it. The Israelis said that they reserved the right to retaliate. For the time being, Israel did not take any retaliatory action; they were satisfied with Bush's promise to destroy Saddam's missiles. America claimed to have knocked out three missile launchers in the past 24 hours—not very impressive.

The US admitted to losing 11 aircraft far—seven American, two British, one Italian and one Kuwaiti—in the first 72 hours of the war.

Jordan declared that it would not permit Israeli aircraft to fly over them and if Israel decided to launch an air attack against Iraq, Jordan would try to intercept them. Syria also was under tremendous pressure from its people to go to Jordan and Iraqi side if Israel retaliated. The Americans made tremendous effort to prevent such eventuality. The US started saying that the air strikes might have to go into next month. The ground war had not yet started, but would have to, at some stage. There was just no way to assess the damage caused by the air strikes; the news given out by the media was rigorously censored. Iraq asked all foreign journalists to leave the country. There was no electricity in Baghdad for two days.

I went to see Al-Anbari at his beautiful residence and talk to him about an initiative that India had mooted on 18 January to bring about a 'pause of goodwill', a brief suspension of hostilities to give Saddam another opportunity to commence substantial withdrawal as part of a time-bound programme of complete withdrawal. Al-Anbari was interested and grateful but said he had lost all communications with his government since the war began. He said he would try to send a word through their ambassador in Amman. He was bitter and very depressed. He said what Iraq had done—invade and occupy Kuwait—was wrong.

In any case, Iraq did not need Kuwait. Iraq had everything—oil reserves, second only to Saudi Arabia's, plenty of water that the Saudis did not have, human resources, tradition of history and civilization. So, Kuwait was not essential to Iraq. Further, why was it necessary to send the whole army to Kuwait when 40 Iraqis could have accomplished the task of occupying the islands and the oil fields. At this stage, Al-Anbari said that he was prepared to mention to his government the unmentionable—Iraq should not be allowed to be destroyed for the sake of Kuwait. He was being contacted by Iraqis from all over the world who were angry with Saddam for inviting such havoc on their country. He said that now Saddam had proved his point that he was not scared of American strike by defying the 15 January deadline, and Bush had demonstrated his determination and power.

This was a strange war. It was the first war which the UN had been preparing for by passing a series of resolutions. The US and Iraq were at war with each other, but the Iraqi ambassador was still in Washington. The Americans were engaged in annihilating Iraq, but diplomatic relations were still not ruptured.

American military experts pointed out that this was the first time that the US had been fully prepared for war. The war was being waged in the name of the UN, but it had absolutely no control over it.

At 3.00 p.m. on 19 January, the CNN reported live air raid sirens from Tel Aviv and Jerusalem. So far, Iraqi scud missiles had carried only conventional pay load, but no chemical weapons. If Iraq were to use chemical weapons, the situation would change dramatically, for the worse.

The Americans claimed to have destroyed one scud missile in air, which was supposed to be on its way to Dhahran in Saudi Arabia. Large numbers of Patriots were sent to and deployed in Israel to strengthen Israeli anti-missile defences. The US seemed to have tremendous faith in the Patriots. The Pentagon was no doubt thrilled at this UN-sanctioned opportunity to try out, in actual combat, the high-tech weaponry, which was being prepared for use against the Soviets.

By the time the war entered its fifth day on 20 January, the coalition forces had flown more than 7,000 sorties, during which they had lost 15 aircraft—nine American, three British, one each from Italy, Kuwait and Saudi Arabia. Iraq managed to get seven American pilots as prisoners of war. On 19 January, the Americans captured 12 Iraqi soldiers from an oil platform off Kuwait coast from where they had been firing anti-aircraft guns.

Iraq Refuses to Give In

Saddam was or appeared to be defiant. The day after the war commenced, he had delivered a speech boasting that the 'mother of all battles' had begun. On 20 January, he called for jihad and promised victory to his people. A Beirut newspaper reported that Iraq still had at least 140 scud missiles. Iraq launched several scuds—three in Dhahran and perhaps six in Riyadh—but all of them were claimed to have been shot down by Patriot missiles.

Saddam's game plan seemed to be to absorb the airstrikes, to survive them for as long as possible without losing the support of the army. So as long as the morale of the army held, Saddam would survive. At some point, the Americans would have to start ground operations—that was what Saddam was waiting for. Americans had been pounding the elite Republican guards with B-52s, repeatedly carpet bombing them in the hope that ground attacks might not become necessary.

Baghdad was without water and electricity. Foreign journalists had left, except for the CNN, which had been allowed to stay because of its fair and objective reporting.

People were getting used to the war. They were no longer glued to the TV or radio. American football matches were being played to full stadiums; the National Football Conference and the American Football Conference championship playoffs were played on 20 January and Super Bowl too was scheduled for the weekend. Amidst all this, the first Purple Heart medal winner of the Gulf War was declared on 20 January.

An Iraqi scud missile hit a residential area in Tel Aviv on 22 January, causing 60 casualties and damaging several buildings. Five people died of heart attack caused by the shock of the missile attack.

The question being asked by the Americans and the Israelis was: Were the Patriot missiles fired to intercept the scud? If they were, did they fail? For the Americans, the Patriot had come to acquire near mythical dimensions, like the Brahmastra. How could the Patriot fail? The initial explanation was that whereas the operational control over the Patriots was with the US personnel, the tactical control was with the Israel Defence Force (IDF).

The Americans were getting exasperated with Saddam's inactivity. Why was he not doing anything? Why was he not attacking? Why was he not setting oil fields in Kuwait aflame as he had threatened to do? Why was he not using his chemical weapons?

Well, at last, he set ablaze a couple of oil reserves on 22 January, and it immediately set off the speculation around whether he was preparing to withdraw from Kuwait?

Some Western sources estimated that Iraq might still have as many as 500 scud missiles. A senior Soviet general believed that 90 per cent of American strikes had missed their targets. An Iranian news report claimed that 100 allied troops had died in clashes between American and 'Muslim' contingents near Dhahran. Iraq displayed nine allied prisoners on TV. They were obviously brutalized and made to say unpatriotic things, criticizing their own government for attacking the peaceful Iraqi people. There was outrage in the Western countries at this gross violation of the Geneva conventions relating to the treatment of prisoners of war. Bush was already talking of prosecuting Saddam for war crimes.

Indian envoys in Cairo and Damascus reported that Saddam's prestige and popularity had skyrocketed since the missile strike against Israel. In Egypt, Saddam's supporters were feeling despondent for the first day or so, but when the scud hit Haifa and Tel Aviv, their spirit soared. This was the first time ever that Israel had been hit in this manner.

By siding with Saddam, Palestinians turned out to be the biggest losers, as they lost all support from the US and the Russians were in no position to help them. The way the Palestinians and the PLO identified with Saddam did not make them popular with the West. Israel, by absorbing the missile strikes, without retaliating so far, earned a fat IOU.*

---

*A trade term, meaning 'I owe you'.

The Americans were heavily indebted to Israel because Israeli retaliation would have destroyed or seriously weakened the coalition.

The US could not lose and Saddam could not win the war in any military sense.

More air raid sirens in Israel were heard over the following days, which Israel admirably withstood without much escalation or retaliation. The IDF and the US claimed that two Patriot missiles shot down a scud at about 10.00 p.m. Israel was reported to feel reassured after this demonstration of the Patriot's efficacy. Israel submitted its first bill to the US—a trifling $13 billion! By exercising restraint in the face of Saddam's use of scud missiles, Israel had done a big favour to the US, and of course, they wanted some compensation for that.

The fires in Kuwait kept burning.

A British newspaper reported on 23 January that a coup had been attempted in Baghdad, but had failed, and seven security people had been executed.

Turkey finally permitted the use of its air base for American F-111s. Iraq warned Turkey of serious consequences.

Two PLO leaders, including Abu Iyad, were assassinated in mid-January. Israel denied any role. It was widely believed that the Abu Nidal group, which had moved back to Baghdad, was responsible. This was confirmed by the PLO's silence on the subject. Former American spokesperson, Bill Moyers, said that even the greatest concentration of air power had failed to bring Saddam to his knees.

9

RELIGION: SADDAM'S FINAL GAMBLE

With the outbreak of the war, prospective peacemakers got busy. We, in India, took the lead in the matter. On 17 January, Abderrahmane Bensid, Algerian ambassador in Washington and a friend of many years, came to see me. After he left, I developed some ideas, elements of a possible draft resolution. I sent them off to Dubey in a crash telegram. I had anticipated that Indian ministers, with their penchant for taking initiatives, would be anxious to do 'something'. Sure enough, Dubey called me; he said he was speaking from the PMO and told me that my message had arrived just in time. The PM was under great pressure for an Indian initiative to bring about a ceasefire. My suggestions were approved, and I was authorized to consult with other members of the UNSC. I started with Pickering. As expected, the US and the UK were not at all happy, and the French were non-committal. Vorontsov, who had a peace plan of his own, said, 'Your initiative is emotional, whereas ours is logical.' But there was considerable interest among others; they said they would consult their governments.

The essence of our proposal was a suspension of hostilities for a limited period, together with the beginning of the process of substantial withdrawal as part of a time-bound programme of complete withdrawal. The difficulty with our proposal was that it could not be implemented unless Iraq gave a firm, credible indication that it wanted a way out to withdraw without feeling humiliated. Pickering said that the US will never agree to a pause because it would give military advantage to Saddam.

We knew that the Americans would not agree. Our principal objective was to show to others, our people as well as others in the UN, that we took an independent position and were active. In this, we succeeded much more than I had anticipated. In Delhi, the PM held an all-party meeting at which I later learnt from Dubey that Rajiv was almost rude to Chandra Sekhar. PV demanded that India should activate the NAM. He reminded his successor, V.C. Shukla, how he had organized a group of four NAM countries and made strenuous efforts to end the war between Iran and Iraq (without success, of course, but that was not important.) It was amazing how much support Saddam enjoyed with the Congress party.

The upshot of it was that Shukla embarked on a diplomatic mission in January 1991, starting with Belgrade and then Tehran. In the meantime, Algeria had become very active. At its insistence, the Arab Maghreb Union made a joint approach for an official meeting of the UNSC. (The permanent representative of Morocco told me that his country was most unhappy with the Algerian initiative; Morocco was a part of the coalition.) Iran was busy talking to various countries. Pakistan's PM visited Iran and Turkey; he declared that in case Israel attacked Iraq, Pakistan would withdraw its 10,000 troops from the multinational forces in Saudi Arabia.

The Americans were absolutely opposed to a public or formal meeting of the UNSC since it would divide the council and bring comfort to Saddam. The Gulf Cooperation Council (GCC) was also opposed to the idea. Saudi ambassador Shihabi, who had been a consistent pain in the Asian group, even tried to blackmail me by saying that his country would remember in future what positions different countries were taking at the time of Saudi Arabia's biggest crisis. (I could understand their position. Even after 20 years, the MEA in India had still not forgotten that Iraq was the first Muslim country to recognize Bangladesh; even Bangladesh had forgotten that!) Now that Yemen had also asked for a meeting, it should be convened in accordance with the rules of procedure of the UNSC, which were very clear on the subject. But the Americans and their partners were determined to prevent it, or at least delay it by a few weeks. They were being helped by Bagbeni Adeito Nzengeya, the president of the UNSC. I took the position that the rules of procedure must be respected.

Bush and other Americans began to caution the people that the war could go on for weeks, even months, that Iraq might spring surprises and score successes from time to time and that Iraq had got many more scuds than estimated and there might be casualties. The war could go on even until summer, in which case the hi-tech weaponry might become unusable because of heat and sand.

Iraq launched seven scuds against Israel on 25 January, all of which were claimed to have been shot down by the Patriots. But since the Patriots make contact with the scuds only a short while before they reach their target, the debris caused by crash in the air was big enough reason to cause damage. Ten people were reported to be injured. The Americans soon had over 500,000 troops in the Gulf, nearly the same strength as the peak reached in Vietnam. More than 25,000 sorties were flown in the 14 days since the war began.

Saddam Remains Confident

Peter Arnett of the CNN, the only Western journalist still in Baghdad, was taken for an interview with a 'senior official', who turned out to be seniormost of them, Saddam Hussain. He talked tough. He was adamant that Kuwait should remain as part of Iraq. God alone knew how long the war would last, he said, but he had no doubt Iraq would win. 'Lots of blood will be shed, lots of blood.' Iraq, he said, had nuclear, chemical and biological weapons. He wished the Americans well and prayed that none of their sons would die, but he suggested that if his losses became too great, he would be obliged to use unconventional forces at his disposal. About the oil spill, he said the US had used oil as a weapon by attacking Iraqi tankers and oil installations on land. If his commanders used oil in the framework of self defence, they would be justified in taking such measures.

A lot of attention was paid to the over 80 Iraqi aircraft that had landed in Iran. The US first took the view, perhaps as wishful thinking, that the pilots were defecting. But later it became clear that this was not the case. The US was worried that Iraq was sending the planes to Iran for safe haven, to be used later as necessary. Publicly, the administration gave credence to Iranian assurance that it would impound the planes until the end of the war. At the same time, Iran also said that if Israel attacked Iraq, it would take the side of a fellow Muslim country.

The Washington Post reported on 28 January that according to well–placed officials, important parts of Iraq's war machine had not been significantly hurt so far; about 65 per cent of Iraqi airfields were still operational. Nearly all of Iraq's air defence radar was claimed to have been taken out, but at least 20 per cent was now back in operation. Only eight of Iraq's 30 scud missile launchers had been damaged enough to disable them. Saddam had also been able to maintain communications with his forces. The Iraqis had shown great resourcefulness in repairing roads and runways. The command-and-control systems were largely operational.

Ground skirmishes started a few days later. American and other ground forces had been moving northwards and were now dug in the border with Iraq.

It was admitted that at least 19 allied aircraft, including 12 American and five British, were lost in the fortnight since the war started, while Iraq claimed a tally of close to 200.

An important development on 29 January was the resignation of Jean-Pierre Chevènement, the French defence minister. He was always opposed to the war. He said the war operations were way beyond the objectives set in the UN resolutions. He obviously knew what he was talking about. His resignation would have an impact on the controversy, not yet intense, regarding the 'hidden agenda' of the US and the UK.

One 'allied' prisoner of war, a human shield, was reported to have been killed in air raids on civilian targets. Saddam told Arnett that had he not listened to the Western leaders, and kept the 5,000 hostages, Bush would not have started the war.

The peace efforts in the UNSC were completely stymied. The US and the UK, with more than enthusiastic support from the Soviets, blocked all action. They did not permit a formal meeting of the UNSC, going against the rules that clearly laid down that the president shall convene a meeting when a member of the council requested it. Many delegates were feeling frustrated and impatient with the UNSC for doing nothing when the war was raging.

An 80-mile-long and eight-mile-wide oil spill was causing ecological havoc in the Gulf. The Americans alleged that Iraq had deliberately caused the leak, whereas Iraq held the US bombing responsible. The US admitted that the oil spill would affect, to some extent, the efficacy of the amphibious landings planned as part of the land operations. It was an environmental catastrophe that entered its third week on 31 January. More than 30,000 sorties had been flown. The television coverage was like Star Wars or a Nintendo game—pinpoint hits by smart bombs, tomahawk missiles, cruise missiles fired from submarines (the first one on 19 January being the first in history), visuals of bridges and highways being hit by cluster bombs. The allies achieved air superiority. Iraqi air forces, for all purposes, ceased to exist.

The first major ground encounter took place around Khafji, 10 km south of Kuwait in Saudi Arabia. On 29 January, Iraq started moving tanks and soldiers southwards. Khafji had been deserted several weeks earlier. Iraqi troops had come to occupy it; they repulsed several counter attacks by the Saudis and marines. The battle for Khafji had made a big impact. Saddam claimed it to be the beginning of the 'mother of all battles' and a big success. People were stunned at his audacity. Even Schwarzkopf had said that those attacks indicated that Iraqis had a lot of fight left in them.

The PLO had shelled Israel from across the Lebanese territory. Was this Saddam's second front opened by Arafat?

The Baker–Besmertnykh meeting in Washington on 29 January had issued a communiqué. It read,

> The ministers continue to believe that a cessation of hostilities would be possible if Iraq made an unequivocal commitment to withdraw from Kuwait. They also believe that such a commitment must be backed by immediate, concrete steps leading up to full compliance with the UN resolutions. Both ministers agreed that in the aftermath of the crisis in the Persian Gulf, mutual US–Soviet efforts to promote Arab–Israeli peace and regional stability […] make a substantial contribution to the achievement of a comprehensive settlement in the Middle East.

The statement had caused an uproar. The reference to 'cessation of hostilities' had been interpreted as a willingness to consider a pause, which Bush had categorically rejected. The suggestion of 'cessation' went beyond 'suspension', something India had suggested. The references to the Middle East were regarded as admission of 'linkage'. Israel was very upset as to how could the US commit Israel without even consulting them. Bush read the statement in his limousine on his way to the Capitol to deliver the State of the Union address. The White House had rejected the joint communiqué.

The Soviets were thrilled with the statement and their diplomatic success. They claimed that the US had changed its position. But from Baker's point of view, the communiqué was a small price to pay to keep the Soviets firmly in the coalition. Even this was significant because the Soviet commitment to the coalition would depend on the American attitude towards the Baltic problem. The US–Soviet summit had been postponed from February until an unspecified date. The official reason for the postponement was the Gulf War and the delay in the finalization of some of the details of the Strategic Arms Reduction Treaty. The real reason was that the US Congress would have reacted extremely negatively if Bush had intended to go ahead with the summit at a time when the Soviet army was cracking down on the pro-independence elements of the Baltic republics.

During the last 48 hours of January, there were reports to the effect that large columns of Iraqi armours and tanks were preparing to cross into Saudi territory. The 'allied' command had said it would welcome this kind of move because it would provide them an opportunity to destroy Iraq's tanks. Saddam must have heard them since the alleged south-bound movement stopped.

The battle for Khafji continued to be the subject of considerable attention. At first, the British had claimed that 330 Iraqis had been killed. The final figure, generally accepted, later came down to 30. More than 400 Iraqi soldiers were captured. The 11 marines, who were killed near Khafji, could have been unwitting victims of 'friendly fire'. One C-130 gunship had crashed behind enemy lines, with 14 on board. Two more US aircraft were shot down, bringing the total to 14. Allied spokesmen had admitted that the Iraqi activity was still continuing. According to some reports, the allied pilots were suffering from fatigue. The scud attacks on Israel and Saudi Arabia had become more sporadic than before.

On the diplomatic side, the US and its allies had successfully prevented the UNSC from holding a formal meeting. I suggested to Pickering that the UNSC could endorse the Baker–Bessmertynikh joint statement. He had said, 'Oh, no, please don't, we have had enough trouble with that statement already.'

Meanwhile in India, the Chandra Shekhar government

had given clearance to the US army transport aircraft to refuel in India on their way from the Philippines to the Gulf. The news had inevitably leaked out and caused uproar. Rajiv had protested. Other parties had protested against Rajiv's protest. The government was under pressure. But Chandra Shekhar had refused to cave in. He had spoken about the Iraqi withdrawal as the first inevitable step. But Saddam's popularity was increasing day by day. He had already done three times better than what Nasser had done in 1967. His posters had started selling in India, too.

As many as 15 NAM countries were scheduled to meet in Belgrade on 12 February. Tehran saw simultaneous but separate visits from senior officials of Iraq, France, Algeria and Yemen in the second week of February.

From Bad to Worse

Meanwhile, Iran was taking its peacemaking role seriously. On 4 February, Rafsanjani disclosed that he had sent a message to Saddam, with some ideas for a solution of the crisis. He expressed his readiness to talk to the Americans. Lord Palmerston's* dictum of no permanent friends or foes embodied eternal truth. Iran was having talks with the Saudis, too.

The public opinion in Morocco, Algeria and Tunisia was running very high. In Rabat, 300,000 people demonstrated. Iranians in New York denied that Iran would fight on Iraq's side in case Israel entered the war.

Divergences among the coalition partners about the extent of destruction inflicted on Iraq began to surface. *The New York Times* reported that the damage, in fact, had not been

---

*British PM in the nineteenth century.

as severe or crippling as expected and that bombings might have to continue for many weeks. The Pentagon's reaction was swift—they were angry. A French general said that 30 per cent of Iraq's ground forces' fighting ability had been destroyed; the British believed it was much more.

Iraq announced on 6 February that it was breaking off diplomatic relations with the US, the UK, France, Italy, Saudi Arabia and Egypt. It was obviously an anomalous situation in which countries fighting such fierce war should have retained diplomatic relations. King of Jordan lashed out against 'the savage and large-scale war' being waged against the 'brotherly Iraq' and called on Arabs and Muslims to force the US-led coalition to agree to a ceasefire. 'This is a war against all Arabs and all Muslims,' he said. 'The real purpose of the war is to rearrange the region in a manner far more dangerous to our nations' present and future than the Sykes-Picot Agreement.* This rearrangement would put the nation, its aspirations and its resources under direct foreign hegemony.'

Cheney and Gen. Powell left for Saudi Arabia on 7 February to assess the Iraqi morale and the effect of the non-stop pummeling of the Republican Guards units. They were to report and submit their recommendations to the President, following which the latter would take a call. He was still confident and kept repeating the mantra that 'we are on track'.

Iran was reported to have proposed a seven-point plan to Iraq through Sa'dun Hammadi, a senior Iraqi politician who became the PM. Iran's spiritual leader Ali Khamenei would appeal to Saddam to pull out of Kuwait. He or Rafsanjani, the president of Iran, together with leaders of some Muslim

*It was a secret treaty between France and Britain in January 1916 to define agreed spheres of influence after the end of the First World War.

countries, would thereafter go to Baghdad, from where they would appeal to the other side to withdraw their forces from the region. Troops from Muslim countries would be deployed. A committee of wise men from these countries would be constituted to assist Iraq and Kuwait in resolving their differences. A fund would be set up to cover expenses to rehabilitate the regions devastated by war. A non-aggression pact would be signed between Iraq, Iran, the countries of the GCC, which might include Turkey and Pakistan.

This emphasis on Islam was extremely worrying. Even Western countries were resorting to it. Douglas Hurd, the British foreign secretary, said in a speech that in the post-Gulf War scenario, countries of the region, together with some Islamic states, such as Egypt, Pakistan, Turkey and Syria, would have to forge close security cooperation. Vorontsov had told me some time ago that troops from Muslim countries would be deployed in the region after the war. More and more, the war was assuming the character of crusades, a war between Islam and Christianity. This might have suited Saddam but certainly did not suit India.

10

A COMICAL SURRENDER AND AN UNEASY PEACE

The war entered its fourth week on 7 February. As many as 52,000 sorties had been flown in the first three weeks and 85,000 tonnes of bombs had been dropped on Iraq and Kuwait. The US claimed that nearly 120 Iraqi planes had flown to Iran, whereas the latter claimed that the number was less than 20.

Cheney and Gen. Powell held a meeting with Schwarzkopf and field commanders for nine hours and returned to Washington on 10 February. After they reported to Bush, the latter informed the media that he was in no hurry to order the ground operations and that the air operations would continue and stepped up.

Schwarzkopf was reported to be of the view that the air operations ought to continue for another three or four weeks. While the enemy had been subjected to heavy bombing, it had not been heavy enough! Iraqi war machine was claimed to have been destroyed by 20 per cent. The next 15–20 days were expected to witness increased tempo of the bombings. There were 2,900 sorties on 12 February—more than two a minute—and was destroying Iraq's tanks at the rate of 2–3 per cent a day. Was Saddam right when he told Glaspie that the US did not have stomach for large number of casualties?

Hammadi returned to Tehran with Saddam's reply to Rafsanjani. The latter admitted that the reply was not of the expected level. Iraq announced that it would never agree to a ceasefire unless the other side sued for peace. Primakov was in Baghdad with a message from Gorbachev. He was taken on a sightseeing tour of the destruction caused by allied bombing. He seemed to have been kept waiting for his meeting with Saddam who probably was in some bunker somewhere.

Israel's side-show of pounding the PLO positions in Southern Lebanon continued undisturbed without any noise from the international community or the UNSC. According to *The Washington Post*, Syria had been quietly cooperating with Israel in the liquidation of the PLO.

On 14 February, the American F-117A stealth bombers bombed an air-raid shelter in Baghdad, killing hundreds of civilians. The CNN relayed graphic pictures of dead bodies of women and children being dug out of the debris. There was uproar in many countries. Iraq maintained that it was and had always been a civilian shelter. The US claimed that it was an important command and control centre in which Saddam had deliberately placed civilians. The Indian foreign minister lost no time in issuing a statement, deploring the loss of civilian lives and saying that the allied bombing clearly exceeded the mandate given in Resolution 678. Several persons in senior positions in Washington expressed concern that the adverse reaction generated by the attack on the shelter might compel Bush into ordering a ground offensive. Gorbachev had already expressed his concern that there was a severe risk of the allied offensive going beyond the mandates given by the UNSC.

On 15 February, I was woken up by the BBC calling directly from London with the 'good news' that Iraq had announced withdrawal from Kuwait.

On the same day, the Iraqi Revolutionary Command Council (RCC) announced on the radio a long communiqué, which became the subject of much discussion in the world and much activity in the UNSC. In the communiqué, Iraq expressed its readiness to deal on the basis of Resolution 660 'with the aim of reaching an honourable and acceptable political solution, including withdrawal'. But the statement went on to enumerate a long list of issues, which, it said, were linked to the pledge by Iraq regarding withdrawal, some of them already raised in the past, some new ones. Among the latter was a demand that the UNSC should abolish all the 11 resolutions passed after Resolution 660; Israel must be made to withdraw from the occupied territories; if it did not, sanctions should be imposed against it as in the case of Iraq; all the debts of Iraq should be waived and the countries that had joined in destroying Iraq should foot the entire bill of rebuilding Iraq and, by implication, Jordan.

One thing was clear. The entire statement did not amount to an unambiguous offer to withdraw. But at the same time, everyone, even Bush admitted that there was something new. For the first time, Iraq has talked of 'withdrawal', the magic word for which the US and the UK had been waiting.

Bush reacted within four hours of the announcement. He described the offer as a 'cruel joke' and went on to call upon the Iraqi armed forces and people to take the matter in their own hands and overthrow Saddam—an unprecedented step to take for the head of a superpower. Pickering, to whom I spoke later, felt quite embarrassed.

Most countries outside the coalition took the position that the opportunity offered by Iraq must be explored. It opened a window of opportunity for diplomacy to become active again. Several efforts were already underway. Aziz's visit to Moscow was arranged before the announcement. The centre of focus was on that visit. Incidentally, Vorontsov in New York took a position that was somewhat at variance from that in Moscow. The official reaction in Moscow was that the Soviet Union welcomed the statement with hope. But Vorontsov talked only of the conditions and contradictions. Whether this was an orchestrated divergence in nuance or whether he followed his own line was not clear. He was too seasoned a diplomat to follow an independent position. He acted more American than many Americans.

There was spontaneous celebration in the streets of Baghdad after the announcement. The people obviously interpreted the news as agreement to withdraw from Kuwait. It was this manifestation of popular mood that seemed to have encouraged Bush to so blatantly call for a popular revolt against Saddam.

The Soviets had reportedly asked the US to not start the ground offensive at least until after Aziz's visit to Moscow. The official American position was that they had no such plans anyway. But Roland Dumas, the French foreign minister, said that a definite date had been set for ground war, whereas Chevènement said no date had been set. The general expectation was that the ground operations would start within a matter of days. The US military had clear images, aired by the CNN, which showed massive armada of state-of-the-art tanks, tank-killing helicopters and other hardware. Since the Iraqi air force was rendered completely inoperative, the allied tanks could move with impunity. As of 15 February, the US estimate was that 1,300 of 4,280 tanks, 800 of 2,870 armoured personnel carriers and 1,100 of 3,110 artillery pieces had been destroyed in the Kuwaiti theatre. This roughly represented 30 per cent of Iraqi armour, 35 per cent of Iraqi artillery and 27 per cent of other armoured vehicles located in Kuwait since the war began.

Aziz was on his way back from Moscow via Tehran. He carried with him Soviet proposals for his leadership. The Moscow talks were regarded as absolutely the last opportunity for a peaceful solution before the ground operation. In a sense, the ground war might have begun because skirmishes along the border were reported for several days. Two American soldiers were killed on 18 February.

There was considerable speculation about Soviet moves. The most popular interpretation was that Gorbachev was positioning himself to play the role of a peace broker in the Middle East to ensure a crucial role for the Soviet Union in the post-war arrangements. The Americans would be unpopular because of their military presence and for humiliating Arab people, but the Soviet Union would be popular if it was perceived as a friend of the Arab people. The distrust of the Soviets was still intense among the Pentagon and the CIA. In this kind of game, each played for itself. But there was little doubt that the Soviets were working in close league with the US.

The Soviets insisted that they had not consulted the Americans for their peace plan given to Aziz, but conveyed its gist to Washington after giving it to Iraq. Bush, in effect, rejected the peace plan, saying, 'It falls well short of what needs to be done.' He added there would be no concessions to Saddam, but the Soviet foreign minister said it was for Iraq to accept or reject the plan.

The editorial of *The Washington Post* on 19 February reflected American concern behind the Soviet peace initiative. The Soviets had made absolutely no contribution to the allied war effort, but wanted to be the peacemaker and get enormous political advantage for themselves. This seemed to be the real worry for Bush. Having made so many preparations for so long, not launching ground operations would be a huge anti-climax. He was determined to humiliate Saddam if not to destroy him.

A Partial Withdrawal?

In Resolution 678, the UNSC had decided to remain seized of the matter. We had several rounds of informal consultations during which the US, the UK and France presented oral reports as required under the resolution, but they opposed demands for a formal meeting, with effective help from Vorontsov.

The president of the UNSC for January 1991 was Ambassador Simbarashe Mumbengegwi of Zimbabwe. He was very correct and firm. He declared that he would have to convene the meeting, and fixed 13 February as the date. The US and the UK then started lobbying for a private and closed meeting. They tried to browbeat the president into announcing that the meeting would start off as a private one, but the President said the UNSC would make the decision at its formal meeting. When the UNSC met on 13 February, the UK raised a move for a private meeting. The proposal received nine votes in favour, the required majority—the US, the UK, France, the USSR, Austria, Romania, Belgium, Ivory Coast and Zaire. Yemen and Cuba voted against. India, Ecuador, China and Zimbabwe abstained.

There were rapid development of events in the third week of February. Aziz returned from Moscow on 21 February, via Tehran as always. While he was on his way, a Baghdad radio channel broadcasted an address by Saddam. It was a hard-hitting speech talking about the 'mother of battles', taking the oil price up. While most people became gloomy, Bush probably welcomed it. Aziz arrived in Moscow late in the evening, around midnight, and was rushed to the Kremlin. He and Gorbachev held a meeting for two hours and 20 minutes. A little later on the same day, the Soviet spokesman announced to the waiting world that Aziz had received a 'positive response' from Saddam. He went on to elaborate the eight points that had been agreed upon:

1. Full and unconditional withdrawal from Kuwait
2. Withdrawal would begin the day after cessation of hostilities
3. Withdrawal would be completed within a fixed timeframe
4. Sanctions would be removed with the completion of two-thirds withdrawal
5. After full withdrawal, all other UN resolutions would lapse
6. Prisoners of war would be released immediately after ceasefire
7. The UN would monitor the withdrawal
8. Final details being worked out would be presented to the UNSC

This was a tremendously important development, putting Bush in a difficult situation. On the one hand, he was all set to launch a general offensive. He believed Iraqi forces had been 'softened' so effectively that the allied troops would meet with very little resistance. Thus, Bush could score a decisive military victory. On the other hand, here was Iraq, willing to pull out immediately, which really was the basic demand of the international community. This was obviously backed by Gorbachev. If Bush did not agree to Gorbachev's plan, would he be risking a split with his most important ally?

Bush did not keep the world waiting for long. He talked to Gorbachev on the phone for about 35 minutes. His spokesman told the media that night that the coalition had serious concerns about the proposal and would give a reply the following morning, i.e., on 22 February.

It was obvious that Moscow and Washington kept talking to each other the whole night. Aziz was having talks in the Kremlin, giving rise to a lot of speculation. Bush went on air at about 10.30 p.m. from the Rose Garden and delivered a brief and tough ultimatum for starting the withdrawal from Kuwait the following day. Soon after, the US released its list of demands: return of the legitimate government of Kuwait, 48 hours for the release of prisoners of war, leave Kuwait within 48 hours and complete allied control over Kuwaiti air space.

Shortly thereafter, the Soviet spokesman announced a six-point plan, officially described as the Gorbachev plan:

1. Full adherence to Resolution 660
2. Withdrawal to begin the day after ceasefire
3. Withdrawal from Kuwait to be completed within 21 days and within four days from Kuwait City
4. The UN resolutions to become null and void upon completion of the withdrawal
5. Prisoners of war to be released within 72 hours
6. Ceasefire and withdrawal to be monitored and supervised by peacekeeping forces of the UN

One conspicuous omission from all these plans was the complete omission of Palestine or a conference on Middle East post-conflict.

Bush and Gorbachev spoke again for 90 minutes before each side published its plan. They managed to avoid confrontation. While there were differences, they were not unbridgeable. Pickering phoned me to say that we might soon be close to resuming the process of consultations in the UNSC, but he would still like to wait for a complete understanding and agreement before going to the council. Iraq, too, would have to write to the council, accepting the plan.

In a brief statement on 22 February, Bush spoke of 'scorched earth policy' unleashed by Saddam in Kuwait, with 150 oil wells set on fire.

Israel's reaction, even before the US reacted, was that the Soviet plan was unacceptable, but they were very happy with Bush's ultimatum. Israel would rather have a weak Iraq with Saddam than a strong Iraq without Saddam.

Saddam did not react for some time. Bush undoubtedly wanted Saddam to react and reject the Soviet plan. I even advised Vorontsov to advise Saddam to not overreact or not react at all. On the same day, the RCC issued a statement that did not explicitly reply to Bush's ultimatum. It promised to work for the success of the Soviet proposal and described Bush as 'God's enemy and devil's friend'. Iraq also proposed, in answer to Bush's charges of 'scorched earth policy', that the UNSC should set up an ad hoc committee consisting of China, the USSR and others from the UNSC who were not participating in the fighting or not supporting the parties in the coalition to investigate who was responsible for civilian destruction in Iraq and Kuwait.

A Pitiful War

The ground war started on 23 February. The allied forces penetrated 40–50 miles inside Kuwait. They encountered practically no resistance. The Iraqi troops did not put up any fight and surrendered by the thousands. Within 22 hours since the ground operation started, at least 10,000 had surrendered or been captured. In fact, the allied military troops said that dealing with the large number of prisoners of war was proving to be one of the most difficult problems. Television channels showed footage of long lines of Iraqi soldiers surrendering, abandoned oil- filled tankers, overturned tanks and artillery guns. No actual engagement seemed to have taken place. The Iraqis had been 'softened' sufficiently and effectively. The Americans had put Saudi and Kuwaiti troops up front, for political reasons, but it was the US troops who were the mainstay of the operations.

Bush's ultimatum, described as 'Don Quixote' ultimatum by Baghdad, expired on the second half of 23 February. Soon thereafter, Bush authorized Schwarzkopf to start the ground offensive at any time of his choosing. The favourable weather conditions—no moon and high tides—were available only for two more days, so the Operation Desert Storm commander's choice was obvious. But we in New York came to know of the beginning of the ground offensive only at about 9.30 p.m. Bush went on air at 10.00 p.m. and announced that the final phase of the liberation of Kuwait had begun.

The UNSC met on the morning of 23 February at the request of the Soviet Union. Vorontsov had instructions to present Gorbachev's plan before the expiry of the ultimatum at high noon. The five permanent members first met at the US Mission. As told to me by Li Daoyu, Pickering tried hard to persuade Vorontsov not to insist on a formal meeting, and present the plan to an informal meeting. Vorontsov would not budge. Pickering even suggested that Vorontsov call Moscow right from his office, to ask for instructions. But Vorontsov knew the strength of his boss's instructions and refused to oblige (Li Daoyu told all of this to me).

The UNSC met just after 11.00 a.m. on 23 February. Vorontsov, taking the floor first, read out Gorbachev's plan and said that it had been accepted by Saddam, and added that it was the optimum plan they could achieve for the moment, and suggested that the council prepare an integrated plan on the basis of all the proposals. He then added a note, which intrigued everyone for a few hours, by informing the UNSC that Aziz had given a positive response to the American statement from the previous day. Even Pickering was caught off-balance. Immediately after the meeting, Vorontsov reconfirmed to me that Aziz, in Tehran, had categorically accepted the US plan. But this news turned out to be false. It was amazing, and still a mystery, how the Soviet Union could commit a blunder like that.

Pickering then read out Bush's ultimatum, with its accompanying demands. China, which spoke next, suggested that the council should prepare its own plan. Before the meeting, Li Daoyu, the permanent representative of China, had told me that his instructions were to support whatever draft the non-aligned caucus produced. I told him the non-aligned members were in no position to do any such thing and added that I would speak immediately after him, which I did. I strongly supported Li Daoyu and Vorontsov, and suggested that the council should be in continuous session and try to bridge the differences between the American and the Soviet plans, harmonize them and prepare a comprehensive text. I suggested that if the council as a whole was not prepared to do so, then at least the 10 non-permanent members ought to do something.

The formal meeting was followed by informal consultations, where I repeated my position that the UNSC should make efforts to harmonize the two plans. The Austrian ambassador suggested that the president of the UNSC should consult members individually in the matter. This was agreed to. I met the president at about 6.00 p.m. He told me that most of the members had till then favoured setting up a working group to prepare the draft, to which I fully agreed. He further said he would like India to play an active role in the working group, to which I again agreed. He and I worked out the composition of the working group as Austria, Ecuador and India.

But the president was going to meet the real hardliners later, in the alphabetical order. So, when the UNSC reassembled at about 10.30 p.m., he could not give a clear decision. He said that a distinct majority wanted to set up a working group, but a few delegations were not in favour and suggested, instead, that the matter should be left for the governments to decide in their respective capitals. This was the end of the attempt to forge a role for the council. Ricardo Alarcón, the brilliant Cuban permanent representative, suggested that the council should immediately adjourn, rather than continue and give the impression that it was engaged in some serious peacemaking effort. This was accepted by Pickering and Hannay. I said India would not be a party to a decision whereby the council would abdicate its responsibility.

Natwar, who spoke to me on 24 February from the Frankfurt airport, said that my bit about the council abdicating its responsibility had prominently figured in the morning news 'around the world', as he put it, and had been quoted by Rajiv in Moscow. Yes, Rajiv had decided it was time for him to offer his services in support of peace. So, he went to Moscow and met Gorbachev; from there, he was scheduled to go to Tehran. Besides Natwar, Bhandari and Mani Shankar Aiyar had accompanied Rajiv.

As we broke at about 11.30 p.m., Vorontsov told me, 'We tried.' But did we? Or, rather, did he? Not at all. Apart from a half-hearted statement in the formal meeting, he did not make the slightest effort to push for the council to prepare a compromise text in the informal meeting. It was obvious to everyone that the Soviets only wanted to go on record with their own peace plan, but would not do anything, anything at all, to incur American displeasure. We witnessed a charade in which there was a glimmer of hope for a while that the Soviets might be willing to pull their weight, whatever was left of it, but it was played out by Gorbachev with some help from Bush.

Gorbachev spoke to Bush umpteen times and assured him, repeatedly, that he was fully with him. He also telephoned British PM John Major, Mitterrand, Mubarak and Kaifu. Yoshio Hatano, the permanent representative of Japan, told me the following story about Gorbachev's talk with Kaifu.

Gorbachev said, 'Saddam Hussain is finished, he is already defeated, please ask Bush not to launch the ground offensive for the present.'

In response, Kaifu said, 'No.'

In India, people harbored the illusion that Soviet Union was still what it used to be, as if 'perestroika' was only a slogan. Natwar and Dubey had questions about the Soviet efforts. The former asked me, 'What about the Soviets?' and Dubey asked, 'Even the Soviets did not make much of an effort?'

So, as far as the council was concerned, we just had to wait when the Americans achieved the unconditional surrender of Saddam, preferably his elimination, political and, hopefully, physical. Pickering condescendingly said that the UNSC would have a role to play at the proper time.

At midnight, Indian ambassador Abid Hussain called from Washington. The Undersecretary of State had called him at 11.45 p.m. with a request from Baker to convey to PM Chandra Shekhar his deep appreciation to me! Everyone else was intrigued. What had I done to deserve this appreciation? I assured Dubey that it must have something to do with my non-offensive, non-combative style and my practice of not springing any surprises on the Americans. This was not a good time in India to get praise from the Americans!

The allied casualties were reported to be surprisingly less—less than a dozen killed and less than two dozen wounded. The generals and Cheney kept cautioning, increasingly unlikely, against unpleasant surprises. The so-called elite Republican Guards had not come into play so far, but I wondered if they too had been softened enough by now. Air war had been going on in full force. Perhaps, they were going in for all the places where Saddam could be sheltering.

Confusion, Rumours and Defeat

On 25 February, there was a report that the Republican Guards were moving southwards. In the latter half of the day, there was an announcement on Baghdad radio and it electrified the atmosphere in the UN. The announcement included the following points: political leadership had approved the withdrawal of the Iraqi troops from Kuwait in accordance with the Resolution 660 through the acceptance of the Soviet initiative; orders had been issued to the troops to return in an organized manner to the positions as on 1 August 1990; the

Iraqi foreign minister had informed the Soviet foreign minister of this decision; and Saddam had asked Gorbachev to bring about a ceasefire.

There was confusion. Which Soviet initiative was Iraq talking about? Because, on 25 February, the Soviets had come out with yet another initiative that Vorontsov had presented to the council at informal consultations in the afternoon. According to this proposal, the council would fix a time and date for the withdrawal. The withdrawal and the accompanying cessation of hostilities would be monitored and supervised by the UN observers. Vorontsov added that they had reason to believe that Iraq would respond constructively to this initiative.

Despite Iraqi announcement, the war continued. The official US position was that Iraq must officially and formally accept the UN resolutions before the war could stop. Some US officials were saying that if the Iraqis wanted to go back to safety, they must get out of the tanks and start walking!

Iraqis were not being smart. Instead of a radio announcement, which really amounted to surrender without any assurances of protection, they should have come to the UNSC with an undertaking to accept the resolutions. The council was convened for 10.00 p.m. on 26 February.

The war in the Gulf was nearly over on 27 February. Kuwait City and the whole country had been liberated. The Iraqis had put up a stiff fight at the Kuwait international airport, but that seemed to have been an exception to the general all-round collapse of the Iraqi army. As many as 50,000 Iraqi soldiers had surrendered. At his briefing on 27 February, Schwarzkopf first used the word 'destroyed' while describing the fate of 29 Iraqi divisions, but corrected himself immediately to say that they had been rendered 'ineffective'. 3,700 tanks,

1,856 artillery pieces and 2,140 armoured personnel carriers were claimed to have been destroyed.

What the Americans claimed could be the biggest tank battle since the Second World War was in the offing around Basra. The Republican Guards, deployed on the border with Kuwait, had nowhere to go. They obviously could not proceed southwards to Kuwait. Their retreat to Baghdad had been cut off by the US–French forces, a US contingent with very heavy armour and comparatively light French–American force further northwest near Nasiriyah.

'We shall cut it off, then we will kill it,' Gen. Powell had said a few days ago, with respect to the renowned Republican Guards. At one point, Schwarzkopf said the allied forces were only 150 miles from Baghdad. Meanwhile, the Iraqi diplomacy baffled everyone and greatly pleased the allies. It was always a case of too little, too late.

On 27 February, Aziz sent a letter to the president of the UNSC, saying that Iraq accepted Resolutions 662 and 674, provided the council cancelled the resolutions imposing sanctions. This was clearly unacceptable to the allies and gave them pretext to continue to 'take out' the Iraqi army. So, I proposed that the council president should tell Iraq that as soon as it conveyed acceptance of all the resolutions and committed itself to release all prisoners of war, the council would meet to arrange a ceasefire. Even Hannay could not object to my proposal. It was accepted by the council. The president was asked to convey this to the Iraqi permanent representative.

Al-Anbari was very frustrated with the way his government had been handling the situation, especially during the last few days. He had advised Aziz to accept all resolutions to stop the massacre of the army. I understood the drafting of the letter was done by the RCC as a whole and not by an expert.

The way these letters were drafted, the Iraqi leadership would appear to nurture the illusion that they were in a position to dictate terms.

Bush went on air at 9.00 p.m. on 27 February. He announced that at midnight, exactly 100 hours after the ground offensive started, the US and coalition forces would suspend all offensive combat operations. He laid down the terms for a formal ceasefire: acceptance by Iraq regarding the resolutions requiring rescinding of the annexation of Kuwait and responsibility for compensation for loss or damage, releasing prisoners of war and civilians, returning remains of those killed in action and furnishing information about the location of land and sea mines. He announced that the objectives of the war had been achieved; Baker would travel to the region to discuss with coalition partners about the questions relating to peace. A brilliant stroke indeed. The Americans kept the initiative with themselves. They denied to the UN the possibility, the opportunity to force the coalition to agree to a ceasefire. Was it possible that our activities in the council earlier in the day might have forced Bush's hand? Because, according to the CNN, the earlier idea was that Bush would deliver the speech on 28 February. No harm in thinking so!

The war lasted exactly six weeks. Schwarzkopf said Saddam's 'mother of all battles' became a 'mother of retreats'. Bush said that it was not the time for euphoria or to gloat. But he and his team were certainly entitled to become euphoric. The outcome of the war was never in doubt, but the speed and decisiveness were unexpected. Bush's biggest contribution was that he had finally destroyed the Vietnam syndrome; he had cleansed the American psyche of the Vietnam complex.

Ceasefire and Peace?

On the night of 27 February, Pickering and Al-Anbari met to discuss ceasefire arrangements. Pickering asked Al-Anbari to contact Baghdad to identify military commanders who would meet with allied commanders to work out the practical arrangements for a permanent ceasefire.

Al-Anbari transmitted a letter from Aziz, addressed to the president of the council, confirming Iraqi acceptance of all the UNSC resolutions. During the informal consultations on the next day, Pickering and Hannay found fault with the letter, and asked that the president seek clarification from Iraq as to why it had not conveyed acceptance of all 'relevant' resolutions. Several members, including myself, objected, saying that the letter was clear enough. The president clarified the situation. He said he had advised Iraq's permanent representative that it would be safer for Iraq to intimate acceptance of all resolutions, even including the irrelevant ones.

The attention was switched to diplomacy, to arrangements for peace and security, to economic reconstruction. At the council meeting, Pickering stated that the US would like the council to play an important role in finalizing ceasefire as well as other issues. But it became obvious, during discussions, that the US would determine the extent and pace of the council's involvement. I pressed hard for the Secretary General to immediately send a small team of observers or monitors to the area to help monitor the ceasefire and generally to register the UN presence. Only Cuba supported me vocally. The only decision the council was allowed to take was that the president would hold immediate bilateral consultations with members and the council would meet as early as possible.

During the meeting, the Belgian ambassador suggested that had he been Iraq's permanent representative, he would have felt embarrassed to face the council. Al-Anbari's response was, 'We had held out much longer than the Belgians did during the Second World War!'

The allied losses were miraculously low—28 killed in ground war, 28 killed in the scud attacks on Dhahran and 23 killed in the air war.

The truth about some stories on atrocities was coming out. *The New York Times,* on 28 February, wrote that the report about 300 infants being killed in the initial days of Kuwait occupation was not true. It was also being given out that Iraqis had taken with them tens of thousands of Kuwaiti males as hostages. If true, they would have met the same fate as the retreating Iraqi soldiers—carpet bombing by the B-52s.

An End to Ridiculousness

Baker was scheduled to set out the following week to visit some of the countries of the region to discuss arrangements. While the physical map of the region remained unchanged, the political alignments would not remain so. Iraq's military strength was greatly, greatly diminished, to the extent that it would not be able to defend itself even against Syria, let alone Israel or Iran. How would Saudi Arabia behave towards Israel, since they were on the same side during the entire crisis? Would Syria enter into negotiations with Israel and even establish diplomatic relations with it? Where would the Palestinians fit into all this? On the one hand, Egypt, Syria and Saudi Arabia could push the US into taking more active and forceful steps to satisfy Palestinians aspirations, and on the other, the US as well as the Arabs were deeply indebted to

Israel for keeping the coalition together by not retaliating to the scud attacks.

What about the Soviets? The crisis had brought to surface the fact that the Soviet–US relationship was still fragile, to use Gorbachev's phrase. The Soviets claimed a major role in the post-war arrangements. The Americans recognized the Soviet role in the Middle East in the Bush–Gorbachev communiqué. But in actual practice, the US was not too keen on that, first, because the Soviets made no contribution to the war effort, and, second, because Gorbachev tried to steal the thunder away from them at the last minute. Still, the Americans were grateful to the Soviets for not breaking the unity among the P-5 in the UNSC.

The Soviets were worried about the reputation of their weaponry. The Gulf War was a very hi-tech affair on the allied side—smart bombs with cameras in the nose cones, laser-guided precision munitions, fuel bombs, etc., were used. The Soviet spokesmen were quick to point out that the Soviet-made equipment in Iraq was not the latest type, and so on. Some of them also candidly admitted that the Gulf War had a lot of lessons for the Soviet military.

The war, of course, was an ideal opportunity for the US as well as for the UK and France to test their latest 'toys'. An Indian working in Raytheon, which made the Patriot missile, told me that the company had got enough orders to keep going for 30 years! There was a tremendous boost in US arms exports. The Soviets were about to lose their markets, as might even Sweden and others. The US, which fought the war with others' money, made enormous amount of money in the reconstruction of Kuwait (and eventually in Iraq) as well as in the sales of arms. More than 200 contracts had already been signed with Kuwait.

The Gulf War demonstrated that the UNSC could be a potent instrument to fight injustice and aggression when the five permanent members acted in unison, when at least their respective interests were not in serious conflict. The primary responsibility of the council is to maintain international peace and security, but it has not been possible for it to effectively live up to that responsibility. The blame for that does not rest with the council, but with member states of the UN. The veto power conferred by the UN Charter in Article 27(3) on the five permanent members is a fact of life; it is not possible to delete or even modify it because that would require amendment of the Charter. Any amendment needs the approval of the P-5. The responsibility for the council's inability to discharge its mandate also rests, at least partly, with the 10 non-permanent members. Collectively, they constitute a veto if they join hands in opposing a particular initiative of one or two permanent members. But they, too, follow Lord Palmerston's adage and look after their interests rather than uphold justice or any principle.

Article 27(3) does not contain the term 'veto'. It states that any non-procedural resolution must have 'concurring' votes of the permanent members. Over the years, 'concurring' has come to be interpreted as not-negative. In other words, if a permanent member does not cast a 'no' vote but merely abstains or is absent, the resolution is declared adopted, so long as it receives at least nine positive votes. This is what had happened at the time of the Korean War in the early 1950s when the Soviet Union had walked out of the council meeting in protest regarding China's membership of the UN; they were demanding the membership for the People's Republic of China.

In the case of the Gulf War, the Soviets not only did not

abstain, they voted affirmatively on all the resolutions since it was in their national interest to do so. It was too much to expect that the interests of the P-5 would always coincide.

INDEX